Table of Contents

Contributors

Dr. Bruce Buchanan, Professor of Computer Science Research at Stanford Univeristy, is exploring problems of scientific inference, theory formation, and knowledge acquisition by computer. He received his Ph.D. in Philosophy from Michigan State University in 1966. He was a major contributor to the heuristic search model of scientific inference in the DENDRAL program, and his present MYCIN research is being extended to intelligent computer-aided instruction. He is on the editorial boards of *Artificial Intelligence, Machine Learning*, and *The Journal of Automated Reasoning*.

Dr. Randall Davis, Associate Professor at MIT's Sloan School of Management and a member of the MIT Artificial Intelligence Laboratory, received his Ph.D. in Artificial Intelligence from Stanford University in 1976. His current research focuses on systems that are capable of reasoning from "first principles" to support a wider range of more robust problem-solving performance. He is co-author with Douglas Lenat of *Knowledge-Based Systems in AI*, McGraw-Hill, 1982 and has recently been selected as one of the 100 outstanding scientists under age 40 by *Science Digest* Magazine.

Dr. Edward Feigenbaum is Professor of Computer Science at Stanford University, where he is Principal Investigator of the Heuristic Programming Project, a leading laboratory for work in knowledge engineering and expert systems. He received his Ph.D. from Carnegie Institute of Technology in 1960. He has served on the NSF Computer Science Advisory Board, and on DARPA's Advisory Committee for the Strategic Computing Program. He has co-edited and co-authored several books, the latest with Pamela McCorduck, *The Fifth Generation: Artificial Intelligence and Japan's Computer Challenge to the World*, Addison-Wesley, 1983, New American Library, 1984.

Dr. Mark Fox heads the Intelligent Systems Laboratory of the Robotics Institute, and is an Assistant Professor of Industrial Administration at Carnegie-Mellon University. His primary interests are: artificial intelligence, and knowledge-based management and manufacturing systems. At present, his laboratory is extending artificial intelligence techniques to the design and construction of engineering, production control, and management systems for "flexible" factory organization. Dr. Fox received his Ph.D. in Artificial Intelligence from CMU in 1983.

Dr. Douglas B. Lenat received his Ph.D. in Computer Science from Stanford University in 1976. He began an inquiry into the fundamental nature of heuristic reasoning and in 1982 presented an AAAI award-winning paper on a new synthesis, the new field of Computational Heuretics. He was co-editor of *Building Expert Systems*, Addison-Wesley, 1984, and a co-author with Randall Davis of *Knowledge-Based Systems in AI*. He presently is Principal Scientist, Artificial Intelligence, at Microelectronics and Computer Technology Corporation (MCC), the U.S.A's research consortium in artificial intelligence and microelectronics.

Dr. David McDonald is Professor of Computer and Information Science at the University of Massachusetts. He is well known for his work on language generation. His primary research areas are natural language processing, knowledge representation, planning, high-performance programming environments, machine tutoring, description and explanation, presentations by intelligent interfaces, and data-directed control and planning. When he received his Ph.D. in 1980, he was a member of MIT's Artificial Intelligence Laboratory. He edited and contributed to The Brattle Reports.

CDR Ronald B. Ohlander, recently retired from the U.S. Navy and DARPA, is currently the Division Director for Intelligent Systems at the Information Sciences Institute of USC. He received his Ph.D. in Computer Science and Artificial Intelligence from CMU in 1975. After several years at NAVELEX, he transferred to DARPA where he managed the Intelligent Systems Program and became Assistant Director for Computer Science Research. He managed the DARPA AI program and played a major role in structuring the Strategic Computing Program.

Dr. Harry Tennant is currently developing a new symbolic processing research group for Texas Instruments. He received his Ph.D. in Computer Science from the University of Illinois in 1981. His research has centered on natural language understanding and he invented the concept of menu-based natural language understanding systems. He is the author of *Natural Language Processing: An Introduction to an Emerging Technology*, Petrocelli, 1981. He was recently selected as one of the 100 outstanding scientists under age 40 by *Science Digest* Magazine.

Foreword

The first era of computer applications has focused on numerical calculations. Now, we are making the transition to another era—one in which computers will be able to reason with knowledge. Artificial intelligence (AI), the part of computer science concerned with designing intelligent computer systems, is emerging from the laboratory and is beginning to take its place in human affairs. With AI, the role of the computer in our lives changes from something useful to something essential.

AI is creating a new computer revolution. *Business Week* featured it as "the second computer age," but it's not just the *second* computer revolution—it's the *important* one. The computer is the knowledge worker's most important tool. Knowledge is power, and the computer is an amplifier of that power. With the new knowledge systems, computers will be able to engage in intelligent activities such as conducting natural conversations with people and solving complex problems that heretofore have been the exclusive province of human experts. Knowledge itself is about to become the new wealth of nations.

There has been much activity and progress throughout the history of artificial intelligence research, and there is more activity now than ever. Increasing research support is coming from the private sector, where interest in using and marketing AI programs is on the rise. There are active, well-funded AI research groups in the United States and abroad.

In Japan, the Fifth Generation Project aims to overtake the American lead in this most important of all modern technologies by establishing a "knowledge industry" in which knowledge will be a salable commodity like food and oil. Towards this end, the Japanese have announced research and development with extremely ambitious goals. The stakes are high; the American response to the challenge of the Fifth Generation may determine our role in the post-industrial world, a world that will revolve around a new technology that will embody knowledge as its central feature.

It is impossible to exaggerate the impact that AI research and its resulting technologies will have on the world of the not-too-distant future. If this book serves to introduce you to this critically important technology, to increase your understanding of its implications for all of our lives, to pique your curiosity about the remarkable developments that are taking place—if this book in any way helps to familiarize you with the many faces of artificial intelligence, then it is serving a purpose that is both valuable and timely.

Edward A. Feigenbaum

Excerpts from the following are contained in the above:
Feigenbaum, E.A., and McCorduck, P. *The Fifth Generation*. Reading, MA: Addison-Wesley Publishing Company, 1983.

Barr, A., Cohen, P.R., and Feigenbaum, E.A., eds. *The Handbook of Artificial Intelligence*, Vol I, II and III, Los Altos, CA: William Kaufman, Inc., 1981, 1982.

Preface

Imagine—it is sometime in the future. You are a businessperson at your office in the middle of a busy day; or perhaps you are a student in the school library, gathering information for a research project. Fortunately, you have your computer close at hand. Unfortunately, you've never taken the time to learn how to use it.

With some trepidation, you type "Do you have any information about industrialization in the 19th Century?" Will the computer understand that, you wonder? Much to your relief, words form on the computer screen saying, "Sure—what do you need to know?"

"What I need to know," you ruminate aloud, "is how the invention of the Jacquard loom influenced subsequent automation trends." To your surprise, the computer talks back to you: "Do you want this information structured in the form of a formal report, or would you rather conduct an interactive conversation?"

You opt to conduct an interactive conversation, and the computer leads you through a question-and-answer session until you are satisfied that you have all the information you need. Finally, you explain to the computer why you need the data, and the computer offers its advice as to how you can use the information most effectively.

Reluctantly, it is time to return to the present. Of course, there is no computer currently in existence that offers the capabilities of the wondrous machine in the preceding fable. However, the seeds of those capabilities do indeed exist today in research laboratories, and some of the technologies are becoming commercial realities. The scientists and businesspeople who are investigating the potential of these new technologies are working in several different fields, but those fields often are grouped together under a common heading: *artificial intelligence.*

This book on artificial intelligence, or *AI* as it is commonly known, has been written to answer the questions, "What is AI?", "How is it used?", and "What impact will it have on our lives?" It begins by investigating the various definitions of AI; surveys past and present AI research; defines knowledge-based systems and discusses expert systems, both rule-based and model-based; explains natural language processing, speech recognition, computer vision, and robotics; and cites intelligent computer-assisted instruction, software development, planning and decision support, and factory and office automation as important AI application areas. After this overview of the fundamentals, details on symbolic processing, expert system development tools, LISP machines, and continuing research in AI complete the book.

As the book points out, researchers in all of the areas of artificial intelligence are involved in the development of "smarter" machines, computers that are more useful than the ones with which we are familiar—and which are, at the same time, much easier to use. AI techniques already are allowing computers to process English instead of "computerese," to recognize and understand speech, to offer expert advice, and to personalize their operation to your needs. And these are but a few of the areas in the world of AI.

In the last 40 years, computers have become invaluable resources to those who understand how to use them. This book is dedicated to the computers of the future, computers that—through developments in artificial intelligence technology—will be smart enough so that we won't *have* to understand how to use them. They will be smart enough to understand how we want them to be used.

H.M.

What Is Artificial Intelligence?

ABOUT THIS BOOK

Today, as artificial intelligence (AI) technology begins to emerge from the laboratory and to venture into the commercial marketplace, it is being greeted with a strange mixture of welcome and anxiety, an uneasy blend of anticipation and trepidation. Unfortunately, it is not being met by a great deal of *understanding*, a situation that this book may help to remedy.

Reading this book will not, of course, make you an "AI expert," any more than you could become an expert in physics by reading a single physics book. The aim of this book is to familiarize you with various aspects of artificial intelligence, including:

- The fundamental concepts of AI;
- Where AI has been, its current status, and where it is going;
- The different technologies that comprise AI; and
- The potential impact of AI on your life.

The book also is designed to whet your appetite for more knowledge about AI. Reading this book will provide you with a solid foundation if you wish to delve deeper into specific features of the exciting world of artificial intelligence.

ABOUT THIS CHAPTER

AI researchers do not agree on a single definition for artificial intelligence; therefore, several definitions are presented in this chapter.

It would be easier to impart a clear understanding of AI if a concise and generally-accepted definition were available; unfortunately, there is wide disagreement within the field itself as to exactly what constitutes artificial intelligence. It is not unusual to find scientists who consider themselves to be working in the field of AI who are not considered to be doing so by some of their colleagues. Conversely, there are scientists working in areas that are "traditionally" considered to be part of AI who refuse to apply that label to their work.

Nonetheless, it is helpful to examine some of the definitions of artificial intelligence that have been suggested. By considering what various people in the field have said about AI, it is possible to find similarities that can help you grasp the essence of what artificial intelligence is all about.

This chapter explores the implications of several useful definitions of artificial intelligence and discusses some of the current technologies which are generally considered to comprise AI.

A DEFINITION OF ARTIFICIAL INTELLIGENCE

The following definition of AI may seem vague at first glance:

> **"Artificial intelligence is the study of how to make computers do things at which, at the moment, people are better."**[1]

> Elaine Rich, *Artificial Intelligence*

However, a further exploration of Rich's definition shows it to be quite thought-provoking.

What Computers Can Do Better Than People

Some of the functions that computers do better than people are performing numerical calculations, storing information, and repeating operations.

Implicit in Rich's definition is the idea that there are indeed things that computers do better than people, which probably does not surprise you.

Here are discussions of some of the things that machines do better than people.

Numerical Computation

One small, special-purpose computer with which you're undoubtedly familiar is the hand-held calculator (*Figure 1-1*). If you were asked to multiply 6218 by 9337, would you rather perform the computation in your head or use a calculator? Which technique would be faster? More accurate?

**Figure 1-1.
TI-66 Programmable
Calculator**

[1] Elaine Rich, *Artificial Intelligence* (New York: McGraw Hill, 1983), p. 1.

Obviously, even a tiny calculator can outperform a human when it comes to mathematical computations. (Computers were, in fact, invented specifically for this purpose.) Larger computers are so fast and accurate that they can perform calculations that literally would be impossible for one person to complete in a lifetime using any other means.

Information Storage

It is likely that many of the bills you receive each month are processed by a computer. A typical business computer might contain, for example, the names and addresses of thousands of customers, accompanied by complete records of their financial transactions (*Figure 1-2*).

If you didn't have a computer, do you suppose that it would be possible for you to *remember* all of that data? Of course not. Yet a computer can "remember" voluminous amounts of information and recall any of it at your command.

Repetitive Operations

We frequently instruct computers to perform the same tasks, day in and day out, over and over again. Fortunately for us, computers don't get bored. If you use a computer to print 1000 copies of a customer report, for example, the quality of the last report is as good as that of the first. If you tried to copy those reports manually, the quality probably would start to diminish quickly after the first few copies.

Figure 1-2.
Sample Records Stored
in a Computer

NAME	ADDRESS	AMOUNT OWED
SANDY ADAMS	6682 FIELD AVE., ARNOLD, MD 21012	$ 12.53
JOE ALLEN	1225 CONNECTICUT AVE., AUSTIN, TX 78703	0.00
ELIZABETH BROWN	47 LIBERTY LANE, WASHINGTON, DC 20008	386.92
RICHARD COX	10362 MAPLE AVE., WICHITA, KS 67212	64.82
GEORGE DIXON	8123 PECAN LANE, DALLAS, TX 75230	211.15
DOROTHY EVANS	555 TRAILS END ST., AUSTIN TX 78703	0.00
GENE FRANKLIN	3 WESTGROVE DR., ROWLAND HTS., CA 91748	2.17
JENNIFER GREEN	7119 WAVERLY AVE., SAN ANTONIO, TX 78213	0.00

Computers Are "Just Machines"

The kinds of things that computers do better than people, such as those just discussed, are activities that we call *mechanical*—"mindless" activities that are obviously capable of being performed by machinery. Ever since the industrial revolution, humans have accepted the fact that machines are often superior in performing many purely mechanical *physical* activities.

Similarly, in the last 40 years, we've come to accept the fact that computers—computing machines—can outperform humans in purely mechanical *mental* activities. That fact has not damaged our collective self-image, however, because we remain secure in the belief that there are also many things that people can do better than computers.

What People Can Do Better Than Computers

People have traditionally outperformed computers in activities that involve *intelligence*.

We do much more than just *process* information; we *understand* it. We "make sense" out of what we see and hear; we come up with new ideas seemingly out of thin air; we use *common sense* to make our way through a world that sometimes seems highly illogical.

One definition of AI is based on the goal of making computers exhibit intelligent behavior.

If people are more intelligent than computers and if, as in Rich's definition, AI tries to improve the performance of computers in activities that people do better, then the goal of AI is to make computers more intelligent. This concept forms the basis of a second definition of AI:

> **"Artificial intelligence is the part of computer science concerned with designing intelligent computer systems, that is, systems that exhibit the characteristics we associate with intelligence in human behavior."**[2]

Avron Barr and Edward A. Feigenbaum, *The Handbook of Artificial Intelligence*

Intelligent Behavior

The goal of AI, according to Barr and Feigenbaum, is to develop intelligent computers. It is important to notice that they define an intelligent computer as one that emulates intelligent behavior in humans.

But exactly what *do* we consider to be intelligent behavior in humans? In other words, what is intelligence?

---

[2] Avron Barr and Edward A. Feigenbaum, *The Handbook of Artificial Intelligence*, 3 vols. (Los Altos, CA: William Kaufman, 1981-82), 1:3.

That question is not nearly as easy to answer as it might seem. Referring to his teaching experiences as director of the AI Laboratory at the Massachusetts Institute of Technology (MIT), Patrick Winston notes that "defining intelligence usually takes a semester-long struggle, and even after that I am not sure we ever get a definition really nailed down."[3]

However, to explain what an "intelligent" computer should be able to do, we need a better understanding of what we mean by intelligence.

WHAT IS INTELLIGENCE?

Knowing some of the characteristics of intelligence can help clarify what is required to make computers intelligent.

Why do we reserve the term *intelligence* for humans? Why don't we consider computers to be intelligent? What is it that people can do better than computers that makes people intelligent but not computers?

While an exact definition of intelligence has proven to be extremely elusive, the following characteristics are suggested by Douglas Hofstadter in a list of "essential abilities for intelligence" from his Pulitzer Prize-winning book *Gödel, Escher, Bach: An Eternal Golden Braid*.[4]

- "To respond to situations very flexibly"—You do not necessarily respond the same way each time you are confronted with an identical problem. If you did, you would be exhibiting mechanical, rather than intelligent, behavior.
- "To make sense out of ambiguous or contradictory messages"—You are able to understand many statements that appear to be ambiguous or contradictory largely because your knowledge and experience allow you to place them in context.
- "To recognize the relative importance of different elements of a situation"—Although you are bombarded with an overwhelming amount of information each day, you "make sense" of your world by assigning different levels of importance to different events.
- "To find similarities between situations despite differences which may separate them"—By recognizing similarities, you can base your future actions on what you have learned in the past. Two situations do not have to be identical for you to apply the lessons of your experience.
- "To draw distinctions between situations despite similarities which may link them"—Although two situations may appear to be similar on the surface, you are able to notice differences which may lead you to adjust your reactions accordingly.

[3] Patrick H. Winston, "Perspective," in *The AI Business*, eds. Patrick H. Winston and Karen A. Prendergast (Cambridge, MA: MIT Press, 1984), p. 1.

[4] Douglas R. Hofstadter, *Gödel, Escher, Bach: An Eternal Golden Braid* (New York: Vintage, 1980), p. 26.

These abilities share at least one attribute: they all come very easily to people. In fact, we often group these abilities under the heading of *common sense*. The implication is that there is nothing special about possessing these kinds of mental abilities; they are, in fact, *common*.

Cognitive Science

When human intelligence is being simulated, tasks that are difficult for humans to do may prove easy to program on a computer.

Oddly enough, the very abilities that come most naturally to people, such as those just mentioned, have proven to be among the most difficult to simulate on a computer. This surprised some of the early AI researchers, who assumed that skills that were easy for people also could be programmed easily into a computer. In many cases, the reverse turned out to be true.

The more difficult a task is for you to do, the more deliberate and conscious thought you have to devote to it. If you have to concentrate on the precise steps that are necessary to produce a certain result, it may not be difficult to program those steps into a computer.

Activities which are based on rules and skills are easy to program on a computer; while activities based on problem-solving and decision-making are difficult to program.

Mathematicians can describe in great detail the technique for multiplying two numbers together, for example, and accountants can describe accounting procedures with precision. Multiplication and accounting are just two examples of activities that are difficult for many people; but because they can be described in intricate detail, they are performed easily by computers.

On the other hand, if an activity comes so naturally to you that you don't have to think about it at all, you may have great difficulty in describing exactly how you did it. After all, it may seem so trivial that you may have never thought about the mental processes involved.

What did you have for dinner last night? Now, can you list the mental steps you went through to remember what you ate? How do you coordinate the intricately interconnected series of muscular contractions necessary to pick up a coffee cup? Can you describe the process of reading and understanding this book? Can you explain how black marks on pieces of paper are transformed to knowledge in your brain?

The field that investigates these details of the mechanics of human intelligence is known as *cognitive science*. The research conducted by cognitive scientists that helps to explain the workings of human intelligence is a great help to those in AI who are trying to simulate that intelligence on a computer.

Modeling Human Performance

How do you program a computer so that it exhibits intelligent behavior?

Researchers in AI have used many different techniques to make computers more intelligent; many of them are discussed throughout this book. One commonly used technique is to determine the process used by humans to produce a particular type of intelligent behavior, and then to simulate that process on a computer.

AI researchers help test cognitive science theories by trying to simulate models of human behavior on a computer.

As cognitive scientists determine the processes that produce human intelligence in a given situation, these processes may be programmed into a computer in an attempt to simulate that behavior. This AI technique is called *modeling* or *simulation*. In effect, you are creating a *model* of intelligent human behavior to try to *simulate* that behavior on a computer to determine if the computer will exhibit the same intelligent behavior as a human.

As shown in *Figure 1-3*, the link between cognitive science and computer modeling is bidirectional. Cognitive scientists develop theories of human intelligence that are programmed into computer models by AI researchers; the computer models are then used to test the validity of those theories. The feedback from the computer models allows the cognitive scientists to refine their theories, which can be used to implement better models, and so on.

How Important Is the Process?

How important is it to simulate the *processes* of human intelligence? Is it the goal of AI to simulate intelligent behavior with a computer by any means? Or is it truly artificial intelligence only if you simulate intelligence by using the same techniques as a human?

**Figure 1-3.
The "Feedback Loop" in
AI Computer Modeling**

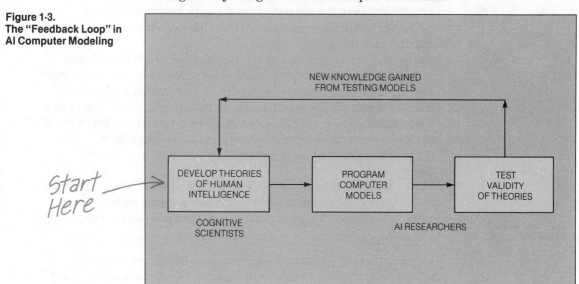

AI researchers disagree on whether or not intelligence must be simulated using the same procedures a human would use.

As with other aspects of the definition of artificial intelligence, there is disagreement in the AI community about this point. Some scientists believe that the goal of artificial intelligence is simply to simulate intelligent behavior on a computer, using any techniques that prove to be effective. (Some of these people prefer the term "machine intelligence" to "artificial intelligence.") Others claim that it is not AI if you simulate intelligence using procedures other than those that might be used by humans.

For example, suppose you wanted to program a computer to play a good game of chess. You could write the program to imitate the thought processes of a human chess expert, and most people would agree that your program demonstrated artificial intelligence. Alternatively, you might write the program to consider the relative merits of 10,000 different moves before making a move, although no human would ever evaluate that many possibilities.

Even if both programs played championship chess, there still would be some disagreement as to whether the second program should be categorized as AI. Some scientists would say that the second program was exhibiting intelligent human behavior, so it is AI; others would say that the program is not AI because it uses techniques that are not representative of intelligent human thought processes.

People and Computers

Developing a computer that can think may depend not only on the definition of intelligence but also on the definition of the brain.

Some researchers propose an ultimate goal for AI that is even more ambitious than having the computer simulate human processes or exhibit intelligent human behavior. These people claim that AI eventually will produce computers that "think"—machines that actually *are* intelligent.

Will computers ever be as intelligent as people? That's an extremely difficult question to answer for several reasons. As we have seen, an examination of our concept of human intelligence reveals that, while we may possess an instinctive understanding of the nature of intelligence, it is a difficult concept to define with great precision. If we cannot even agree on what constitutes *human* intelligence, how will we know when we have successfully achieved *artificial* intelligence?

Whether or not you believe that a computer will ever possess the intelligence of a human brain may hinge not only on how you define *intelligence*, it may depend also on how you define *brain*.

Meat Machines

Our notions of ourselves as living, conscious beings are intimately linked to our notions of brains and thought. "Cogito, ergo sum," said Descartes—"I think, therefore I am"—basing the proof of his very existence on his awareness of his own mental processes.

But what is the nature of the brain? Can thought, feelings, and emotions be represented by a set of rules that can be reproduced in a machine? Is the brain nothing more than an incredibly sophisticated computer?

Based on ideas dating back to Plato and Aristotle, some people think that the human brain works like a machine. Thus, the brain could be called a "meat machine."

The debate over the essence of human rationality is literally thousands of years old. Plato and Aristotle were among the first to divide human capabilities into two distinct areas: the physical body and the rational mind. If the mind is considered to be separate from our physical, "animal" nature, it is not a large step to believe that the mind operates as a useful machine.

The *mechanistic* view is the belief that the workings of the mind can be described in terms of the electro-chemical functioning of the brain. Containing about 100 billion cells with complex interrelations that are still only dimly understood, the brain would have to be considered an extraordinarily intricate machine and certainly an unusual one in that it is composed of living material—a "meat machine."

Although some scientists say that some day a computer will be intelligent, many people feel that a computer will never think like they do.

Is the development of intelligent machines just a matter of achieving a more complete understanding of the workings of this meat machine and programming a computing machine accordingly? Will a computer so programmed not just *simulate* intelligence—not just *appear* to be intelligent—but actually *be* intelligent in the same sense that people are intelligent? Will a computer someday be able to say "Computo, ergo sum"? (See *Figure 1-4* for comments about thinking machines from Doug Lenat, head of AI at MCC, the Microelectronics and Computer Technology Corporation).

No matter what the scientists may say, many of us instinctively feel that the workings of our minds can never be programmed into a machine and that no computer ever will have a mind of its own. While conceding that someday it may be possible to program a computer so that it *appears* to be intelligent, it is difficult to accept the proposition that a machine actually can be made to think in the sense that people think, to understand information rather than just to process data.

Philosopher Hubert Dreyfus, a persistent critic of AI, refuses to subscribe to the mechanistic view of the human mind. "If one thinks of the importance of the sensory-motor skills in the development of our ability to recognize and cope with objects, or of the role of needs and desires in structuring all social situations, or finally of the whole cultural background of human self-interpretation," he maintains, "the idea that we can simply ignore this know-how while formalizing our understanding as a complex system of fact and rules is highly implausible."[5]

[5] Hubert Dreyfus, *What Computers Can't Do: The Limits of Artificial Intelligence* (New York: Harper & Row, 1972).

Figure 1-4.
An Interview with Doug Lenat on "People vs. Computers"

Q: Is the question "Can a machine think?" a meaningful question?
LENAT: It's a fair question, I suppose. I think the answer is: sure, it's possible.

If you claim that it's not a fair question, you'll have to explain to me why you believe that other *people* think. You'll get to the fact that you can say things to them, and they *act* as if they were thinking; the responses they give are (at least on occasion) thoughtful responses; and the behavior they exhibit over time shows that they are occasionally thinking, and learning from what they've seen, and reacting intelligently, and so forth.

To the extent that I could build machines that more or less acted as appropriately in various situations, it would be hard to say that they think any more or less than you would say that other *people* think.

Q: So you think that machines will some day be able to think, just as people think?
LENAT: That's right. Remember, down deep we're just machines of a sort, too. We're really just meat machines instead of metal machines. Although that sounds extremely callous and antihumanistic, I don't think it needs to be.

It's very much like automobiles. I took a course on automotive repair a couple of years ago, and I came away with a profound sense of awe and respect for automobiles. I never dreamed they were nearly as complicated as I found them to be.

I think the same thing is true with people. It doesn't matter whether they are "just machines." The more you find out about them—for instance, by trying to simulate their behavior—the more respect you actually gain for people. You end up believing that people are actually much more sophisticated than you believed when you started. In that sense, it is a humbling experience rather than a "shallowing" experience, in terms of your respect for human beings.

OTHER DEFINITIONS OF AI

Other definitions of AI are concerned with symbolic processing, heuristics, and pattern matching.

The two definitions of AI presented previously concentrated on the comparison between the abilities of humans and the abilities of computers. The following definitions of artificial intelligence focus on the difference between programming techniques used in AI and more conventional methods of programming.

Symbolic Processing

A third definition mentions that AI solves problems by symbolic and nonalgorithmic methods, instead of numeric and algorithmic methods.

According to Bruce Buchanan and Edward Shortliffe, *symbolic processing* is an essential characteristic of artificial intelligence:

> **"Artificial intelligence is that branch of computer science dealing with symbolic, nonalgorithmic methods of problem solving."[6]**
>
> Bruce G. Buchanan and Edward H. Shortliffe, *Rule-Based Expert Systems*

[6] Bruce G. Buchanan and Edward H. Shortliffe, *Rule-Based Expert Systems* (Reading, MA: Addison-Wesley, 1984), p. 3.

This definition focuses on two characteristics of computer programs:

- Numeric vs. Symbolic—As has been noted, computers originally were designed specifically to process numbers. People, however, tend to think *symbolically* rather than numerically; our intelligence seems to be based, in part, on our mental ability to manipulate *symbols*, rather than just numbers. (Symbolic processing is explored further in Chapter 7.)
- Algorithmic vs. Nonalgorithmic—An algorithm is a step-by-step procedure with well-defined starting and ending points, which is guaranteed to reach a solution to a specific problem. Computer architecture readily lends itself to this step-by-step approach; computer programs traditionally have been based on algorithms. Many human reasoning processes, however, tend to be *nonalgorithmic*; in other words, our mental activities consist of more than just following logical, step-by-step procedures.

Much AI research continues to be devoted to symbolic and nonalgorithmic processing techniques in an attempt to emulate more closely human reasoning processes with a computer.

Heuristics

AI researchers rely on heuristics (rules of thumb) to solve problems.

In an encyclopedia article, Bruce Buchanan includes *heuristics* as a key element of artificial intelligence:

> **"Artificial intelligence is the branch of computer science that deals with ways of representing knowledge using symbols rather than numbers and with rules-of-thumb, or heuristic, methods for processing information."**[7]

Bruce G. Buchanan, *Encyclopedia Britannica*

Like the previous definition, this definition notes that symbolic processing is an important AI concept. It also introduces a concept that we have not yet discussed: heuristic processing.

A *heuristic* is a "rule of thumb" that helps you to determine how to proceed. While you may not be familiar with the term, you frequently use heuristics, consciously or otherwise, to help you decide what you are going to do, as illustrated in *Figure 1-5*.

By using a heuristic, you do not have to rethink completely every problem with which you are faced. If you have a handy rule of thumb that applies to your situation, it may suggest to you exactly how to proceed.

---

[7] *Encyclopedia Britannica*, 1985 Yearbook of Science and the Future, s.v. "Artificial Intelligence: Toward Machines that Think," by Bruce G. Buchanan.

**Figure 1-5.
Samples of
Subconscious and
Conscious Heuristics**

SUBCONSCIOUS HEURISTIC   CONSCIOUS HEURISTIC

Heuristic programming incorporates this same rule-of-thumb approach into the process of using AI to solve problems with computers.

Pattern Matching

A fifth definition of AI focuses on the use of pattern-matching techniques in an attempt to discover relationships between activities just as humans do.

Another definition of artificial intelligence focuses on *pattern-matching* techniques:

> **"In simplified terms, artificial intelligence works with pattern-matching methods which attempt to describe objects, events, or processes in terms of their qualitative features and logical and computational relationships."[8]**

Brattle Research Corporation, *Artificial Intelligence and Fifth Generation Computer Technologies*

Computers can be used to collect information about objects, events, or processes; and, of course, computers can organize large amounts of information more efficiently than people can. People, however,

[8] Brattle Research Corporation, *Artificial Intelligence and Fifth Generation Computer Technologies* (Boston), p. 5.

instinctively do something that has been very difficult to program into a computer: we discover relationships between things; we sense qualities and spot patterns that explain how various items relate to each other.

Newspaper photographs are nothing more than collections of minute dots (*Figure 1-6*); yet without any conscious effort, we discover the patterns that reveal faces and other objects in those photos. Similarly, one of the ways that we make sense of the world is by recognizing the relationships and patterns that help give meaning to the objects and events that we encounter.

If computers are to become more intelligent, they must be able to make the same kinds of associations between the qualities of objects, events, and processes that come so naturally to people.

AI TECHNOLOGIES

The debate about the essence of artificial intelligence is not one that will be resolved quickly.

**Figure 1-6.
The Texas Instruments
Professional Computer
Pictured as a Collection
of Dots**

*We easily
sense the
pattern*

As a relatively new science, AI continues to experience rapid changes in focus and scope. Its primary tool, the computer, has continually and dramatically increased in power, and decreased in cost, throughout the history of AI. These advances in computer technology often are accompanied by correspondingly dramatic advances in AI research.

"At the Moment . . ."

AI researchers tend to explore new frontiers in computer science. Therefore, some of these researchers move on to new problems as soon as current problems essentially are solved.

One seemingly insignificant phrase in Elaine Rich's definition of artificial intelligence presented at the beginning of this chapter is the notion that AI studies what people do better than computers "at the moment."

With this definition, Rich has identified yet another area of contention among those who would define artificial intelligence: when an AI technology is developed to the extent that humans no longer outperform computers, some AI researchers no longer consider that technology to be part of AI. After all, if AI studies only what people do better than computers "at the moment," then AI ceases to study a problem when computer performance reaches or exceeds the level of human performance.

AI research has traditionally been at the cutting edge of computer science. AI continually redefines what computers can do and pushes existing computer technology to its limits. When a particular AI problem is substantially solved, AI researchers typically move on to newer, more challenging problems. The former problem is "no longer interesting," they may say, or it has become "simply a matter of engineering."

This results in a very fluid definition of artificial intelligence as the scope of the field continually shifts in new directions. One difficulty with the "at the moment" concept is that it renders it impossible to ever develop an "AI product." If a technology advances sufficiently to allow for product development, that technology can no longer be classified as artificial intelligence.

The AI Evolution

Thus far, areas of AI research have been evolving continually. However, as more people identify research taking place in a particular area as AI, that area will tend to remain a part of AI. This could result in a more static definition of artificial intelligence.

With all the factors that contribute to imprecision in the definition of AI, one useful way to understand AI has been to inspect what it is that AI researchers do. In other words, it has been useful to define AI not by using a formal definition, but by identifying the areas of research that are being conducted by people who consider themselves (and/or who are considered by others) to be working with artificial intelligence. Because so many people in AI continually seek new directions in search of more challenging problems, defining the field by examining the research has contributed to a continually evolving definition of AI.

Roger Schank, head of the AI Lab at Yale University, stresses that to understand AI, you must understand that it is in a constant state of change. "AI tends to be an elusive subject," he notes. "Artificial intelligence is best understood as an *evolution* rather than a revolution."[9]

Although the boundaries of AI will certainly continue to expand, it is reasonable to assume that the definition of AI may be in the process of becoming more static. Awareness of AI among the general public is increasing dramatically. As fields of research become firmly identified with AI in the public perception, it is likely that those fields will continue to be classified as AI even after the focus of AI research moves on to greener pastures.

Areas of AI Research

There are identifiable areas of research that generally, if not universally, are included in discussions of artificial intelligence. Here are brief introductions to several of the AI technologies that are explored in this book.

Expert Systems

Currently, the most well-known area of AI research is expert systems, where programs include expert-level knowledge of a particular field in order to assist experts in that field.

An *expert system* is a computer program designed to act as an expert in a particular domain (area of expertise). Also known as a *knowledge-based system*, an expert system typically includes a sizable knowledge base, consisting of facts about the domain and heuristics (rules) for applying those facts (*Figure 1-7*).

**Figure 1-7.
The Components of the
Knowledge Base of an
Expert System**

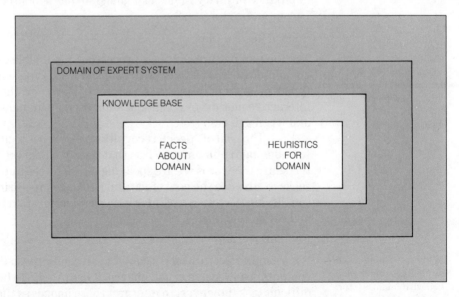

DOMAIN OF EXPERT SYSTEM

KNOWLEDGE BASE

FACTS
ABOUT
DOMAIN

HEURISTICS
FOR
DOMAIN

[9] Roger C. Schank and Peter G. Childers, *The Cognitive Computer* (Reading, MA: Addison Wesley, 1984), p. 26.

Expert systems currently are designed to assist experts, not to replace them. They have proven to be useful in diverse areas such as medical diagnosis, chemical analysis, geological exploration, and computer system configuration.

Since the expert systems field promises a great deal of practical application and commercial potential in the near future, it has begun to attract an enormous amount of attention. Expert systems technology is poised to become the first AI technology to have a widespread impact on business and industry.

Natural Language Processing

The two areas of natural language processing, understanding and generation, are intended to simplify our communication with a computer.

The utility of computers is often limited by communication difficulties. The effective use of a computer traditionally has involved the use of a programming language or a set of commands that you must use to communicate with the computer. The goal of natural language processing is to enable people and computers to communicate in a "natural" (human) language, such as English, rather than in a computer language.

The field of natural language processing is divided into the two sub-fields of:

- Natural language *understanding*, which investigates methods of allowing the computer to comprehend instructions given in ordinary English so that computers can understand people more easily; and
- Natural language *generation*, which strives to have computers produce ordinary English language so that people can understand computers more easily.

Speech Recognition

Through speech recognition research, we someday may be able to communicate with a computer by speaking naturally instead of typing.

The focus of natural language processing is to enable computers to communicate interactively with English words and sentences that are typed on paper or displayed on a screen. However, the primary interactive method of communication used by humans is not reading and writing; it is speech.

The goal of speech recognition research is to allow computers to understand human speech so that they can hear our voices and recognize the words we are speaking. Speech recognition research seeks to advance the goal of natural language processing by simplifying the process of interactive communication between people and computers.

Computer Vision

Providing computers with the ability to understand their surroundings is the goal of computer vision research.

It is a simple task to attach a camera to a computer so that the computer can receive visual images. It has proven to be a far more difficult task, however, to interpret those images so that the computer can *understand* exactly what it is seeing.

People generally use vision as their primary means of sensing their environment; we generally see more than we hear, feel, smell, or taste. The goal of computer vision research is to give computers this same powerful facility for understanding their surroundings. Currently, one of the primary uses of computer vision is in the area of robotics (*Figure 1-8*).

Robotics

Although we currently have robots that can perform pre-programmed activities, AI robotics researchers want to design robots that can change their actions based on their environment.

A *robot* is an electro-mechanical device that can be programmed to perform manual tasks (*Figure 1-8*). The Robotic Industries Association formally defines a robot as "a reprogrammable multi-functional manipulator designed to move material, parts, tools, or specialized devices through variable programmed motions for the performance of a variety of tasks."[10]

**Figure 1-8.
An Inspection Robot That Combines a Robot Arm and a Computer Vision System to Inspect Parts and Assemblies**

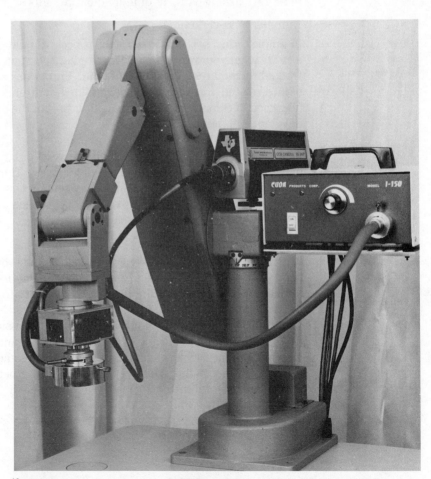

[10] William B. Gevarter, *Intelligent Machines* (Englewood Cliffs, NJ: Prentice-Hall, 1985), p. 159.

Not all of robotics is considered to be part of AI. A robot that performs only the actions that it has been pre-programmed to perform is considered to be a "dumb" robot, possessing no more intelligence than, say, a dishwasher. An "intelligent" robot includes some kind of sensory apparatus, such as a camera, that allows it to respond to changes in its environment, rather than just to follow instructions "mindlessly."

Intelligent Computer-Assisted Instruction

Intelligent computer-assisted instruction programs customize instruction by using learning techniques that are appropriate for a particular student.

Computer-assisted instruction (CAI) has been in use for many years, bringing the power of the computer to bear on the educational process. Now AI methods are being applied to the development of intelligent computer-assisted instruction (ICAI) systems in an attempt to create computerized "tutors" that shape their teaching techniques to fit the learning patterns of individual students.

Automatic Programming

To simplify and shorten the programming process, tools are being developed to write computer programs automatically.

In simple terms, *programming* is the process of telling the computer exactly what you want it to do. Developing a computer program frequently requires a great deal of time. A program or system (a group of interrelated programs) must be designed, written, tested, debugged (cleansed of errors), and evaluated, all as part of the program development process.

The goal of automatic programming is to create special programs that act as intelligent "tools" to assist programmers and expedite each phase of the programming process. The ultimate aim of automatic programming is a computer system that could develop programs by itself, in response to and in accordance with the specifications of a program developer.

Planning and Decision Support

Making a computer capable of aiding in business planning is one of the goals of planning and decision support research.

When you have a goal, either you rely on luck and providence to achieve that goal or you design and implement a *plan*. The realization of a complex goal may require the construction of a formal and detailed plan.

The development of plans in business, for example, may necessitate the collection and evaluation of significant amounts of information. Intelligent planning programs are designed to provide active assistance in the planning process and are expected to be particularly helpful to managers with decision-making responsibilities.

DOES IT MATTER?

Is the goal of artificial intelligence to create machines that actually *are* intelligent or to create machines that *simulate* intelligence? Must the techniques of AI programming be modeled after human cognition, or are the means of creating intelligent machines irrelevant? Which areas of research can be labeled AI, and which ones cannot be so labeled?

The presence of questions like these is a direct result of the lack of an accepted definition of artificial intelligence. This raises another question: how important is it to develop a concise, generally-accepted definition of artificial intelligence?

While it may be awkward to discuss something that we have not defined precisely, our human intelligence allows us to overcome the ambiguity and grasp the essential concepts that underlie AI. In fact, some people in the field downplay the importance of arriving at a precise definition of AI.

When the editors of the journal *Artificial Intelligence* asked a series of questions to several AI luminaries, they included questions such as "Is AI a single discipline?" and "What distinguishes it from other fields?" None of the respondents mention any discomfort with the lack of precision in the definition of AI, and several stress its lack of importance.

Saul Amarel of Rutgers University, for example, says that he "would not be overly concerned at present with the 'nature of AI' and definitions of the discipline."[11] Jerome Feldman of the University of Rochester is even more direct; he does not "think it matters at all whether AI is a discipline or where its boundaries might lie."[12] In *Figure 1-9*, Randy Davis expresses his opinion on the importance of developing a definitive definition of artificial intelligence.

WHAT HAVE WE LEARNED?

1. There is not universal agreement among AI researchers about exactly what constitutes artificial intelligence.
2. Various definitions of AI focus on different aspects of this branch of computer science, including intelligent behavior, symbolic processing, heuristics, and pattern matching.
3. Cognitive science investigates the mechanics of human behavior and provides valuable insights to AI researchers.
4. One common way of programming a computer to exhibit intelligent behavior is to model, or simulate, human behavior.
5. Areas of AI research include expert systems, natural language processing, speech recognition, computer vision, robotics, intelligent computer-assisted instruction (ICAI), automatic programming, and planning and decision support.

[11] Daniel G. Bobrow and Patrick J. Hayes, eds., "Artificial Intelligence—Where Are We?", *Artificial Intelligence* 25 (March 1985): 375-415.
[12] Ibid.

**Figure 1-9.
An Interview with Randy
Davis on "The
Importance of Defining
Artificial Intelligence"**

Q: For a program to be considered AI, must it solve problems using the same technique that a person would use?

DAVIS: No. There are at least two different agendas you could have. One is closer to what cognitive scientists are trying to do, which is to understand how people solve problems. The other is more oriented toward what we call *machine intelligence*, which is that you want to solve the problem in any reasonable fashion, and you are not concerned about whether it models people exactly.

People fall at all points of the spectrum. It's not an "either-or" issue—it's "and." *Yes*, you can understand how people work; and *yes*, you can develop ideas and techniques which solve difficult problems in ways that are less like people; and *yes*, all of the above.

In fact, I get a little impatient with a question like "Do you want to do X or Y?" The answer is not "or." The answer is "*Yes*, all of the above."

Q: Some AI people seem to be quick to point at someone else's work and say, "That's not AI." Are you suggesting a more inclusive policy—saying that AI covers many different things?

DAVIS: There are many legitimate concerns; one need not choose one or the other.

The map is populated by all sorts of approaches which have all sorts of goals. Where you want to draw the line and call one "AI" and another "not AI"—that is also a question that I will admit to some impatience on. Because I don't know what you get out of it.

Suppose I draw the line somewhere. So? Other than name calling, what have I accomplished?

Q: So it is not an important question?

DAVIS: I don't think it is particularly important. The only time it starts to get important is when it starts to have pragmatic consequences.

The most obvious example of that is in marketing—because, of course, AI has become a hot, new "buzzword." Somebody says "This is an AI product," and the only reason I will enter into an argument and say "No, it isn't" is when I think somebody is being lied to. Somebody is trying to sell something uninteresting that is probably an old idea wrapped up in a reprogram and given a new label so somebody will buy it again.

The only reason to be concerned about the label is if somebody is trying to take unfair advantage of the label.

WHAT'S NEXT?

This chapter has discussed the general concepts of artificial intelligence and introduced you to several areas of AI technology. The next chapter explores the history of AI and introduces you to some of the key people in the field.

Quiz for Chapter 1

1. Which of the following have computers traditionally done better than people?
   a. Storing information
   b. Responding flexibly
   c. Computing numerically
   d. All of the above
   e. a and c above

2. Which of the following have people traditionally done better than computers?
   a. Recognizing relative importance
   b. Finding similarities
   c. Resolving ambiguity
   d. All of the above
   e. a and c above

3. The field that investigates the mechanics of human intelligence is:
   a. artificial science.
   b. cognitive science.
   c. psychology.
   d. sociology.

4. One method of programming a computer to exhibit human intelligence is called modeling or:
   a. simulation.
   b. cognitization.
   c. psychic amelioration.
   d. duplication.

5. A bidirectional feedback loop links computer modeling with:
   a. pattern matching.
   b. heuristic processing.
   c. human intelligence.
   d. cognitive science.

6. Comparing the human mind to a "meat machine" is a _____ view of the workings of the mind.
   a. cognitive
   b. behaviorist
   c. mechanistic
   d. relativistic

7. The brain contains about _____ cells.
   a. one thousand
   b. one million
   c. one billion
   d. 100 billion

8. One definition of AI focuses on problem-solving methods that process:
   a. numbers.
   b. symbols.
   c. actions.
   d. algorithms.

9. A key element of AI is a/an _____, which is a "rule of thumb."
   a. heuristic
   b. cognition
   c. algorithm
   d. digiton

10. An AI technique that allows computers to understand associations and relationships between objects and events is called:
    a. cognitive science.
    b. heuristic processing.
    c. relative symbolism.
    d. pattern matching.

11. A computer program that contains expertise in a particular domain is called an:
    a. automatic processor.
    b. intelligent planner.
    c. expert system.
    d. operational symbolizer.

12. The knowledge base of an expert system includes both facts and:
    a. theories.
    b. heuristics.
    c. algorithms.
    d. analyses.

13. The area of AI that investigates methods of facilitating communication between people and computers is:
    a. natural language processing.
    b. decision support.
    c. symbolic processing.
    d. robotics.

14. Natural language processing is divided into the two subfields of:
    a. time and motion.
    b. algorithmic and heuristic.
    c. symbolic and numeric.
    d. understanding and generation.

15. The primary interactive method of communication used by humans is:
    a. reading.
    b. writing.
    c. speaking.
    d. seeing.

16. The primary method that people use to sense their environment is:
    a. reading.
    b. writing.
    c. speaking.
    d. seeing.

17. An intelligent robot:
    a. responds to changes in its environment.
    b. follows instructions mindlessly.
    c. possesses no more intelligence than a dishwasher.
    d. does all of the above.

18. Shaping teaching techniques to fit the learning patterns of individual students is the goal of:
    a. automatic programming.
    b. decision support.
    c. intelligent computer-assisted instruction.
    d. expert systems.

19. Special programs that assist programmers are called:
    a. symbolic programmers.
    b. heuristic processors.
    c. intelligent programming tools.
    d. program recognizers.

20. Intelligent planning programs may be of special value to managers with _____ responsibilities.
    a. programming
    b. customer service
    c. personnel administration
    d. decision-making

The History of Artificial Intelligence

ABOUT THIS CHAPTER

To gain a better understanding of where you are, it is often helpful to examine where you've been.

This chapter traces the development of artificial intelligence, from its early days to the present. Several of the personalities that have figured prominently in the growth of AI are introduced, and trends in computer technology that are currently contributing to advances in AI are discussed.

Because artificial intelligence is a relatively new science, exploring its history might not seem to be especially worthwhile. However, the history of AI is a rich and fascinating story. Some of the most advanced scientific thinkers of the last 40 years have given much thought to the workings of human minds and electronic computers and have invested a great deal of time and effort investigating ways to make computers work more like minds.

Since much fundamental work in artificial intelligence remains to be done, many of the "historic" projects discussed in this chapter are still very much in progress. While a knowledge of the history of AI may not be essential to a basic understanding of the subject, the historical perspective offered by this chapter provides a context in which you can interpret current developments and further your appreciation of artificial intelligence.

THE "PRE-HISTORY" OF ARTIFICIAL INTELLIGENCE

The "pre-history" of artificial intelligence dates as far back as Greek mythology.

Long before there was a field called artificial intelligence—long before there were computers, or even a knowledge of electronics—people were irresistibly drawn to the idea of creating intelligence outside the human body.

Several examples date back all the way to Greek mythology. Hephaestus, son of Hera, seems to have fashioned human-like creations regularly in his forge; and Talos, one of Hephaestus' bronze men, guarded and defended Crete. Disenchanted with human women, Pygmalion made his own woman out of ivory (*Figure 2-1*); and Aphrodite brought Galatea, this man-made woman, to life. Daedalus, most famous for his artificial wings, also created artificial people.

**Figure 2-1.
Pygmalion and his
Statue, Galatea**
(Source: From Mythology *by
Edith Hamilton. Copyright 1942
by Edith Hamilton, Copyright
Renewed © 1969 by Dorian
Fielding Reid, Copyright
Renewed © 1969 by Doris
Fielding Reid, Executrix of the
Will of Edith Hamilton. Reprinted
by Permission of Little, Brown
and Company (Inc.).)*

Examples of people attempting to create intelligent beings also can be found in medieval Europe and the sixteenth century.

In medieval Europe, Pope Sylvester II is credited with building a talking head with a limited vocabulary and a knack for prognostication—Sylvester would ask it a simple question about the future, and the artificial head would answer yes or no. Arab astrologers are said to have constructed a thinking machine called the *zairja*; the missionary Ramon Lull answered with a Christian adaptation, the *Ars Magna*.

In the early sixteenth century, Paracelsus, a prominent physician, claimed to have invented a *homunculus*, a little man. "We shall be like gods," he wrote enthusiastically. "We shall duplicate God's greatest miracle—the creation of man."[1] If he was successful, he must not have been much of a businessman—Paracelsus died a pauper.

Later in the sixteenth century, the Czech rabbi Judah ben Loew is reported to have sculpted a living clay man, Jospeh Golem, to spy on the gentiles of Prague (*golem* has become a synonym for an artificial human). Unfortunately, this particular golem grew overly aggressive and had to be dismantled.

[1] Pamela McCorduck, *Machines Who Think* (New York: Freeman, 1979), p. 12.

Fictional examples of artificially intelligent creations can be found in *Frankenstein*, *2001*, and *Star Wars*, to name a few.

In Mary Shelley's *Frankenstein*, perhaps the classic horror story, Dr. Victor Frankenstein created a humanoid who turned into the archetypical monster and became a murderer. The moral of *Frankenstein*, like that of Golem, is clearly that humans should not dabble in the province of the gods: the creation of intelligent beings.

HAL, the lethal computer in Arthur Clarke's *2001*, was endowed with somewhat over-developed instincts for self-preservation. Interestingly, HAL exhibited features that are currently the subjects of AI research: he performed speech recognition and natural language processing, he was capable of making intelligent decisions, and he was designed to assist humans in the operation of a space vehicle. Unfortunately, his computer vision also was exceptionally well developed; it allowed him to read the lips of the crew and learn that they were planning to disconnect him. HAL was eventually turned off, but not before he killed one of the crew in an attempt to remain "alive."

(Did you notice the use of the words "he" and "him" in reference to the computer, HAL, in the preceding paragraph? As machines exhibit increasing numbers of intelligent characteristics, there is a natural tendency to refer to them in human terms—"he" or "she" instead of "it." This assigning of human attributes to non-human entities is called *anthropomorphism*.)

Of course, not all of the smart machines in modern fiction are villains. Two of the lead characters in the *Star Wars*® movie trilogy were machines, and quite intelligent machines at that. One of them, C-3PO®, was a humanoid robot; his faithful companion, R2-D2®, while not humanoid in form, possessed an unmistakable human-like intelligence.

As you see, the concept of artificial intelligence is hardly new. It seems that for as long as people have been able to build machinery, they have speculated about building intelligent machines. And ever since the first computers were built, scientists have been trying to make them think.

CAN A MACHINE THINK?

After using computers initially for numerical calculations, scientists eventually began to wonder how intelligent computers could become.

Computers were used first by the Americans and the British during World War II to expedite complex tasks such as numerical computations and codebreaking, activities that previously had been assumed to require human intelligence. (Notice the shift in the frontier of "intelligence" in the last 40 years. We have become so accustomed to calculating machines that we now consider that kind of activity to be "mechanical.") It was probably inevitable that the scientists working with the first computers would speculate about how intelligent these new electronic marvels could become.

Alan Turing, a brilliant and innovative mathematician, was an integral part of Project Ultra, the successful British effort to break the German "Enigma" code during World War II. As part of his role in that project, Turing helped design one of the first computers ever built.

Turing also wrote several papers about various theoretical aspects of mathematics and computing that are still considered classics in their fields. In his 1937 paper, "On Computable Numbers," for example, he described how a hypothetical machine (now appropriately known as a "Turing Machine") could use a system of binary codes to perform any algorithmic operation.

In 1950, Turing wrote a provocative article entitled "Computing Machinery and Intelligence," which secured for him the distinction of being generally recognized as the "father" of artificial intelligence. Not being one to waste words, Turing began the article with a proposition that continues to be debated after more than 35 years (although Turing himself concluded that the question was "meaningless"). "I propose to consider the question," he began succinctly, " 'Can machines think?' "[2]

Turing foresaw that there would be many objections to the proposition that machinery could produce thought. In fact, he considered and responded to several possible objections in the article. Recognizing that semantic difficulties alone could render it impossible ever to answer the question satisfactorily (remember the difficulty of defining "intelligence" in Chapter 1), Turing suggested a test, in the form of game, that could help to decide the issue. He called it the "imitation game"; but in his honor, it has since generally become known as the "Turing Test."

The Turing Test

Picture yourself in a room that is empty except for you and a computer terminal. In a similar room, hidden from your view, are a man and a woman with a terminal similar to yours. You communicate with them by typing questions on the keyboard of your computer. As you type, your questions appear on the screen of their computer. They respond to you by typing on their keyboard, and you see their responses on your screen.

You are the "interrogator"; you can direct questions to either Person A or Person B, but you do not know which is the man and which is the woman. The object of the game is to try to guess which person is male and which is female—solely by analyzing their responses.

[2] Alan M. Turing, "Computing Machinery and Intelligence," *Mind* LIX.

If both people were obliged to tell you the truth, you could just ask, "Person A: Are you male or female?", and the game would jerk to a screeching halt. But in Turing's game, only one of the people is obligated to reply truthfully; the other person is actively engaged in attempting to fool and confuse you, using any deceitful tactics that will make you guess incorrectly.

How would you fare as the interrogator in the imitation game? How often would your incisive questions enable you to sort out the genders of Persons A and B correctly? How often would you be fooled?

In the next part of the Turing Test, you try to determine whether your respondent is a person or a computer. Depending on how well you do, the conclusion could be that the computer is thinking.

Next—and this is the critical part of the Turing Test— substitute a *computer* for one of the people. Now the human is obligated to give you truthful, human-like responses; but the computer is trying to fool you into thinking that it is human!

Look at the sample Turing Test presented in *Figure 2-2*. How would you fare in this version of the imitation game? Could you tell when you were addressing a human and when your respondent was a machine? How often would you be fooled?

Turing's point is that if your success rate in the computer/human version of the imitation game is no better than your success rate in the male/female version, then you might as well say that the machine is thinking. That is, the machine is at least as intelligent as a human.

**Figure 2-2.
A Sample of the Imitation Game**
(Source: Alan M. Turing, "Computing Machinery and Intelligence," in Mind *LIX)*

Interrogator: In the first line of the sonnet which reads "Shall I compare thee to a summer's day," would not "a spring day" do as well or better?
Witness: It wouldn't scan.
Interrogator: How about "a winter's day"? That would scan all right.
Witness: Yes, but nobody wants to be compared to a winter's day.
Interrogator: Would you say Mr. Pickwick reminded you of Christmas?
Witness: In a way.
Interrogator: Yet Christmas is a winter's day, and I do not think Mr. Pickwick would mind the comparison.
Witness: I don't think you're serious. By a winter's day one means a typical winter's day, rather than a special one like Christmas.

The "Revised" Turing Test

Currently, a Turing Test need only consist of trying to determine which respondent is a person and which is a computer by participating in a thoughtful conversation.

The Turing Test in its original form is somewhat complex, involving a three-way interrogator/male/female exchange prior to the interrogator/human/computer conversation. The general concept of a Turing Test has evolved with the passage of time; currently, a Turing Test is considered to be any situation in which a human converses with an unseen respondent and attempts to determine if the dialogue is being conducted with a human or a computer. If a computer can fool you into believing that you are talking to a human, one school of thought holds that the computer can be said to be intelligent.

It is important to remember that the dialogue must be clearly "thoughtful," as in *Figure 2-2*, if the computer is to be called intelligent. It is currently possible to program computers to carry on shallow conversations in limited areas, and it is not difficult to fool unsuspecting humans into believing that they are addressing other humans.

Some programs have been developed that can carry on conversations in a specific area; however, not all of these programs pass the Turing Test. ELIZA, developed at MIT, is an example.

One well-known example of this phenomenon is a program called ELIZA developed by Joseph Weizenbaum at the Massachusetts Institute of Technology (MIT). ELIZA simulates a Rogerian therapist; you can conduct a dialogue with ELIZA just as if you were on a psychiatrist's couch. However, ELIZA certainly cannot be said to "think"; instead, it uses several clever programming techniques to ask predetermined questions and parrot segments of your responses back to you.

For example, if you were to tell ELIZA that you missed your children, ELIZA might respond with "Why do you miss your children?" or "Tell me more about your family." Either response might lead you to believe that ELIZA *understands* what you are saying, when actually it is using some programming tricks to construct responses from your statements. Although it has fooled many people into thinking that they were conversing with an "intelligent" program, ELIZA generally is not considered to have passed the Turing Test.

Clever conversational programs, such as ELIZA, indicate that the Turing Test may not be such a good judge of machine intelligence after all; it seems to be all too easy to convince people that a cleverly-programmed machine is intelligent.

While the letter of the Turing Test may have fallen from favor, its spirit endures. Many people in AI continue to maintain that when we can simulate intelligent behavior so closely that it is impossible for even the most discerning individuals to tell the difference between a human and a computer, it will be fair to say that we have created a machine that thinks.

Other Theorists

Other people besides Turing began studying the possibility of intelligent machines at the same time.

While Turing was certainly a brilliant and original theorist, he did not work in a vacuum. At the same time that he was developing his theories, other mathematicians and logicians, mostly in the United States and Great Britain, also were considering similar questions of minds and machines.

Warren McCulloch

Warren McCulloch found similarities between the human brain and a computer.

Warren McCulloch did not approach the study of the mind from a background of mathematics or computers. As a neurophysiologist and a graduate of the Columbia University medical school, he was especially interested in developing a greater understanding of the functioning of the human brain.

In 1943, McCulloch coauthored an article entitled "A Logical Calculus of the Ideas Immanent in Nervous Activity" in the *Bulletin of Mathematical Biophysics*. At the time, McCulloch was the Director of the Laboratory for Basic Research in the Psychiatry Department of the University of Illinois (he subsequently joined the Electronics Laboratory at MIT). The article proposed that a network of neurons (a "neural net") in the brain worked much like the hypothetical Turing Machine—in other words, it might be useful to think of the brain as a computer.

McCulloch admitted that his analogy between brains and computers suffered from an incomplete understanding of the functioning of neurons in the brain. As we have learned more about the brain, the precise correspondence between minds and machines suggested by McCulloch seems increasingly unlikely. However, his persuasive descriptions of the similarity between minds and machines contributed a great deal to the development of a field called *information science* and eventually to artificial intelligence.

Claude Shannon

Claude Shannon's research contributed to the binary number system being used in digital computers.

In 1854, the British mathematician George Boole proposed a system for describing logic—the "laws of thought"—in mathematical terms; Boole's approach came to be known as *Boolean algebra*. In 1937, Claude Shannon, a graduate student at MIT, used Boolean algebra to describe the operation of electrical switching circuits. Shannon's ideas contributed to the developing field of information science and led directly to the binary system of information storage (*Figure 2-3*) used in the digital computer.

**Figure 2-3.
Examples of Binary
Numbers**

DECIMAL (BASE 10)	BINARY (BASE 2)
0	00000
1	00001
2	00010
3	00011
4	00100 ← *5-bit code*
5	00101
6	00110
7	00111
8	01000
9	01001
10	01010
15	01111
20	10100
25	11001
30	11110

"The problem of how the brain works and how machines may be designed to simulate its activity," Shannon wrote at Bell Labs in 1953, "is surely one of the most important and difficult questions facing current science."[3] He suspected that if Boolean algebra, a representation of human thought, could be used to describe electrical circuits, then perhaps circuits could be used to describe thought.

Shannon also wrote articles about using computers to play chess, an early area of AI research.

Shannon is remembered also for an article that appeared in *Scientific American* in 1950 in which he discussed the possibility of using computers to play chess. Shannon may have been the first to point out that having a computer consider every possible combination of moves was not a practical chess-playing strategy. He estimated that even if it could evaluate one million moves per second, a computer would take 10^{95} years (that's a 1 followed by 95 zeros) to select a move! Interestingly, although Shannon did not continue to pursue AI after its early days, chess-playing computers continued to be popular in early AI research.

Norbert Wiener

Norbert Wiener's father, Leo Wiener, taught linguistics at Harvard University. "I am a machine," Leo once mused. "How should a machine ever come to think?"[4] Leo put his son through an intense regimen of intellectual training at an early age, as if attempting to program Norbert as a thinking machine. Although the rigors of his

[3] Claude E. Shannon, "Computers and Automata," *Proceedings of the IRE* (1953).
[4] David Ritchie, *The Binary Brain* (Boston: Little, Brown, 1984), p. 98.

early training inflicted deep emotional wounds, Norbert indeed became an intellectual prodigy. He was graduated from Tufts University in 1908 at the tender age of 14 and received a Ph.D. from Harvard four years later. He spent much of the remainder of his life in MIT's mathematics department.

Norbert Wiener is best known for developing a new approach to understanding the workings of the universe. Since the time of Newton, scientists had concentrated on an *energy* model, explaining events and processes in terms of the transfer of energy. Wiener suggested a model that has proven to be extremely valuable in understanding computers as well as people—he suggested that the transfer of *information*, rather than energy, is the best way to model many different kinds of scientific phenomena.

Cybernetics was the name Wiener used both to describe his informational approach and to entitle his 1948 book on the subject. By describing interrelated systems in terms of the exchange of information, cybernetics points out the functional similarities between humans and machines, similarities which troubled Wiener but which proved to be invaluable in early artificial intelligence research.

THE DARTMOUTH CONFERENCE

In the summer of 1956, at a conference in the small college town of Hanover, New Hampshire, the home of Dartmouth College, the AI revolution was launched.

The handful of unlikely "revolutionaries" who participated in the Dartmouth Conference were about a dozen scientists representing several different disciplines: mathematics, neurology, psychology, and electrical engineering, among others. The common thread that connected the interests of this diverse group was that they all used the same powerful tool to conduct their research: the computer.

More than just the fact that they *used* computers, it was the *way* in which they used computers that distinguished their work from that of their contemporaries. They all, in their various fields, were using computers to try to simulate various aspects of human intelligence.

A new branch of computer science crystallized at the conference, combining elements of several different avenues of research into a unified field. There was no universal agreement about what to call the new science; however, *artificial intelligence*, the name suggested by John McCarthy, one of the conference organizers, has come to be associated firmly and irrevocably with the field.

Norbert Wiener proposed that some phenomena could be modeled best by describing the transfer of information between interrelated systems.

At the Dartmouth Conference, researchers who were trying to simulate human intelligence on a computer met to discuss their research.

The conference, funded by a $7500 Rockefeller Foundation grant, was organized by four scientists, two from academia and two from industry. According to their proposal, the conference was intended to explore the conjecture "that every aspect of learning or any other feature of intelligence can in principle be so precisely described that a machine can be made to simulate it."[5] That conjecture, of course, continues to be a focus of AI research.

The Dartmouth Conference is noteworthy not so much for what transpired at the conference as for the people that it brought together. There were no spectacular scientific developments at the conference, no startling insights that would shake the foundations of the scientific community. But the new field did come away with a name and with an "elite"—the major pioneers of AI research in the United States were all participants in the conference. Even today, the leadership of the American artificial intelligence community is composed largely of the conference participants, their students, and their students' students.

The Conference Organizers

The Dartmouth Conference was organized by John McCarthy, Marvin Minsky, Nathaniel Rochester, and Claude Shannon.

The four scientists who organized the Dartmouth Conference were:

- John McCarthy, an assistant mathematics professor at Dartmouth. McCarthy was the primary moving force behind the conference.
- Marvin Minsky, a junior fellow in mathematics and neurology at Harvard University. Minsky had been a graduate student with McCarthy at Princeton University; both had subsequently worked briefly with Claude Shannon at Bell Labs.
- Nathaniel Rochester, Manager of Information Research for IBM™. Rochester had a keen interest in intelligent machines, especially in getting machines to exhibit original behavior in problem solving.
- Claude Shannon of Bell Labs. Shannon had established his reputation firmly in the field of information science, as discussed earlier.

Of these four "founding fathers" of AI, McCarthy and Minsky continue to be leaders of the AI community; Rochester and Shannon, however, did not devote themselves to AI after the Dartmouth Conference.

John McCarthy

**Figure 2-4.
John McCarthy**
(Photo © 1985 Roger Ressmeyer)

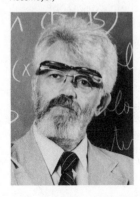

Currently a professor of computer science at Stanford University, John McCarthy, pictured in *Figure 2-4*, has been responsible for several major developments in artificial intelligence and in computer science in general. In 1958 he invented LISP (LISt Processor), the most commonly used AI programming language, which is especially popular in the United States. McCarthy has received the Turing Award,

[5] Frank Rose, *Into the Heart of the Mind* (New York: Harper & Row, 1984), p. 22.

John McCarthy's many accomplishments include inventing the LISP programming language and time sharing on computers.

bestowed yearly by the Association for Computing Machinery (ACM) for significant contributions to computer science.

McCarthy's most significant contribution to the world of computers is perhaps a process called *time-sharing*. This process, which enables many people to use a single computer at one time, has become an essential ingredient of modern computing. McCarthy initiated the robotics research at Stanford. He also has worked extensively on the formalization of common sense knowledge and reasoning.

Marvin Minsky

Marvin Minsky has contributed to AI research through his work in the organization and representation of knowledge structures.

Figure 2-5.
Marvin Minsky
(Photo Courtesy of MIT)

With John McCarthy, Marvin Minsky (*Figure 2-5*) founded the Artificial Intelligence Laboratory at MIT, one of the most prestigious centers of artificial intelligence research in the world. Minsky served as the MIT AI lab's director for a few years; his current title at MIT is "Donner Professor of Science in the Department of Electrical Engineering and Computer Science." Minsky is a past-president of the American Association for Artificial Intelligence (AAAI); and like McCarthy, Minsky is a recipient of the Turing Award.

Minsky is perhaps best known for his work in the organization and representation of knowledge structures, an area with important implications throughout the various AI technologies. He has been a prolific writer in both technical and general publications, and remains one of the more outspoken proponents of AI. His optimistic candor leads him to make bold predictions that occasionally seem foolish in retrospect; in 1967, for example, he confidently asserted that "within a generation the problem of creating *artificial intelligence* will be substantially solved."[6]

Other Conference Participants

The Dartmouth Conference proposal suggested a meeting of 10 people for two months. There were seldom, however, exactly 10 attendees present at the conference; the number varied according to the schedules of the participants.

Other researchers at the Dartmouth Conference included Allen Newell, Herbert Simon, Arthur Samuel, Alex Bernstein, and Oliver Selfridge.

In addition to the organizers, those who attended the conference included:

■ Allen Newell and Herbert Simon, sometimes referred to as "the Carnegie-RAND group." Newell and Simon were both on the faculty of the Carnegie Institute of Technology (now Carnegie-Mellon University or CMU) and on the staff of the RAND (Research ANd Development) Corporation, a Santa Monica "think tank."

■ Arthur Samuel and Alex Bernstein of IBM. Independently, Samuel and Bernstein were programming computers to play games, one of the first areas of AI research.

[6] Marvin Minsky, *Computation: Finite and Infinite Machines* (Englewood Cliffs, NJ: Prentice-Hall, 1967), p. 2.

- Oliver Selfridge of MIT. Selfridge had served as Norbert Wiener's assistant during the preparation of *Cybernetics*. A Selfridge presentation at RAND of a pattern-recognition program first interested Allen Newell in the field that was to become known as artificial intelligence.

Newell and Simon may have been invited to the Dartmouth Conference as an afterthought because the conference organizers were only casually familiar with their work. As it has turned out, Newell and Simon are now considered to be, along with McCarthy and Minsky, the leading American AI pioneers.

Newell and Simon

Prior to the Conference, Newell and Simon had worked with J.C. Shaw and had developed the Logic Theorist, a program which used heuristic (rule-of-thumb) reasoning to generate proofs of mathematical theorems.

Allen Newell and Herbert Simon came to the Dartmouth Conference with something that no one else at the conference had: a working AI program. Of course, Newell and Simon did not call it an *artificial intelligence* program; that term was not in general use before the Dartmouth Conference. Instead, they preferred to call their program, the Logic Theorist, an *information processing* program.

In collaboration with J. C. Shaw, a RAND computer scientist, Newell and Simon had developed the Logic Theorist to generate proofs of mathematical theorems. Specifically, the theorems that the Logic Theorist was designed to prove were those of *Principia Mathematica*, the early 20th-century propositional calculus (logical inference) system of Bertrand Russell and Alfred North Whitehead.

The Logic Theorist successfully developed proofs of many theorems; it even discovered a proof that Russell and Whitehead had overlooked. It may have been the first program to use heuristic, rather than algorithmic, reasoning. Algorithms are certain to arrive at a result; while heuristics (rules of thumb) "may solve a given problem, but offer no guarantee of doing so."[7]

The multitalented Herbert Simon has strong credentials in such diverse fields as political science, economics, business administration, and psychology, in addition to computer science. He was a founder of CMU's Graduate School for Industrial Research; his 1947 work *Administrative Behavior* has been credited with changing modern techniques of business economics and administrative research; and he even was awarded the 1978 Nobel Prize in Economics.

Allen Newell, the junior partner of the Newell and Simon team, left the graduate program in mathematics at Princeton in order to join the RAND staff. His work at RAND brought him into contact with logistical organizations in the Department of Defense, where he

---

[7] Avron Barr and Edward A. Feigenbaum, *The Handbook of Artificial Intelligence*, 3 vols. (Los Altos, CA: William Kaufman, 1981-82), 1:109.

became interested in studying the way people behaved in organizations. It occurred to Newell that the study of organizational behavior could be approached scientifically by modeling human behavior on a computer, and he became interested in the relationship between the computer and the brain.

Newell and Simon also worked with Shaw on other projects, including the development of the IPL programming language.

In addition to the Logic Theorist, Newell and Simon also collaborated with J. C. Shaw on the development of IPL (Information Processing Language), a precursor of LISP. They also created the General Problem Solver, an early AI program that solved problems by choosing an appropriate path to a specified goal ("means-ends analysis").

Like Marvin Minsky, Allen Newell has served as president of the AAAI (in fact, Newell was the first president of the organization). Like John McCarthy and Marvin Minsky, both Allen Newell and Herbert Simon are recipients of the ACM's Turing Award.

Arthur Samuel

Arthur Samuel wrote a checker-playing program that was probably the first program to learn from its mistakes.

The name of Arthur Samuel has become linked inextricably in AI literature with one program: the program that has come to be known as Samuel's Checker Player.

In 1947, one year after leaving Bell Labs, Samuel first proposed that a checker-playing machine be built. The purpose of the machine was to generate publicity in an effort to raise funds to build a computer at the University of Illinois. He assumed that it would be a trivial task to build a small machine that could play championship-level checkers; he hardly suspected that he was embarking on a 20-year project.

When Samuel left Illinois for IBM, he continued to think about a checker-playing machine. As he became involved in the design of IBM's first general-purpose computers, he began to write—and continually rewrite—the checkers program he had conceptualized at Illinois.

The feature of Samuel's Checker Player that has earned him a place in AI history is that it actually learned from its mistakes, and it may have been the first program ever to do so. By 1961, the program played at the level of a checkers master; and it could beat Samuel, who ironically was never very good at checkers, with ease. Samuel had disproved the pervasive notion that a computer only can do exactly what it is programmed to do and thus can never exhibit original behavior.

Alex Bernstein

Unlike Arthur Samuel, who did not even enjoy playing checkers, Alex Bernstein was a competent enthusiast of the game he programmed: chess (*Figure 2-6*).

**Figure 2-6.
Alex Bernstein Watching
Chess Expert Ed Lasker
Try to Beat Bernstein's
Chess Program**
*(Photo Courtesy of Andreas
Feininger,* Life Magazine, ©
Time Inc.)

Alex Bernstein developed
a chess-playing program
which used heuristic
techniques, an important
concept in AI research.

While working at IBM, Bernstein used sophisticated heuristics
to improve the level of play of his program. By the time the program
was complete, it was able to play what was considered to be a fair
game of chess—for a novice. Bernstein's chess program never reached
the master's level as did Samuel's Checker Player; however, chess is a
significantly more complex game than checkers.

Bernstein's chess program is important in AI history because
of the heuristic techniques it employed to search for the best moves.
The complexity of chess required Bernstein to explore, in great detail,
various methods of eliminating possibilities, a concept central to AI
research.

AI RESEARCH CONTINUES

Artificial intelligence has come a long way since the Dartmouth
Conference.

Currently, AI research is being conducted in universities, high-technology corporations, and AI companies.

For several years, AI research was confined largely to a few institutions, mostly university research centers. As the field began to develop in the 1970's, AI research centers were formed at increasing numbers of educational institutions; AI courses are presently among the most popular courses offered by many computer science departments.

Successes in AI research have been slow to be translated into products, but an enormous commercial development effort is now underway at many corporations. Most major American high-technology companies have their own AI research departments and are racing to develop AI products for what is seen as a massive potential market. Many specialized AI companies also debuted in the early 1980's. Although AI products have yet to become proven commercial successes, *artificial intelligence* is the newest high-tech "buzzword" sweeping the country.

Developments in AI are not confined to the United States. Major AI research efforts are underway in Great Britain and France, and the Japanese are conducting one of the world's largest AI research efforts—the 10-year $450 million Fifth Generation Project (see Chapter 10).

AI in the University

The universities leading in AI research are Carnegie-Mellon University, Massachusetts Institute of Technology, and Stanford University.

Although many schools have joined the quest for artificial intelligence, the three universities that conducted much of the early AI research are still the undisputed leaders in the field. These schools are:

- Carnegie-Mellon University (CMU),
- The Massachusetts Institute of Technology (MIT), and
- Stanford University.

See *Figure 2-7* for a discussion of the groups of "hackers" that emerged at these three prominent schools.

Carnegie-Mellon University (CMU)

Among the AI researchers who have been or are associated with CMU are Ed Feigenbaum, Doug Lenat, John McDermott, and Raj Reddy.

The early information-processing work by Newell and Simon at CMU (then Carnegie Tech) quickly established the school's reputation as a leading center for AI research.

The following is a list of several of the prominent names in AI that have been associated with CMU.

- Ed Feigenbaum, currently a computer science professor at Stanford, was an undergradute student at Carnegie's Graduate School of Industrial Administration when Newell and Simon were developing the Logic Theorist. He developed the Elementary Perceiver and Memorizer (EPAM), a verbal learning system, in conjunction with Herbert Simon in the early 1960's.

**Figure 2-7.
An Explanation of the
Term "Hackers"**

Because artificial intelligence research continually explores new frontiers of
computer science, AI labs are often very exciting places to be. The early
university AI labs attracted many students who became so hooked on the thrill of
pushing a computer to its limits that they tended to divorce themselves from
other university activities. Members of this subculture of AI "addicts" came to
be known as *hackers*.

Currently, the term hacker has acquired a negative connotation, often
referring to someone who uses a computer for mischievous—and often
illegal—purposes. But in its original usage, a hacker was simply someone who
was filled with the sheer joy of computing; who breathed, ate, and slept
computers; who lived only to see what miraculous and unexpected feats the
computer could be coaxed to perform.

While there has always been some communication between the groups,
separate hacker traditions developed at MIT, CMU, and Stanford. Even their
vocabularies were different; each school developed its own hacker slang that
differed in some respects from the jargon in vogue at the other schools. With the
passage of time, and with the accelerating mobility of students and faculty
among the three schools, the distinct hacker traditions are fading.

Feigenbaum was a developer of DENDRAL, a knowledge-based
heuristic program created in the late 1960's to help chemists
analyze mass spectrograph data. With DENDRAL, Feigenbaum
pioneered the rule-based approach that is currently popular in the
development of expert systems. Feigenbaum co-authored the
three-volume classic *Handbook of Artificial Intelligence* and is one
of the authors of the popular book about the Japanese AI effort,
The Fifth Generation.

- Doug Lenat, a former student of Feigenbaum's, has been on the
faculty of both CMU and Stanford. At CMU in 1975 Lenat developed
AM, a heuristic program that formulates concepts of mathematics
and set theory; at Stanford in 1977 he created an extension of AM
called EURISKO, which discovers new heuristics. Lenat currently
directs AI research for Microelectronics and Computer Technology
Corporation (MCC).

- John McDermott developed R1, perhaps the first commercially
viable expert system, as part of a joint project between CMU and
Digital Equipment Corporation (DEC™). R1, which is still in use at
DEC, has helped configure orders for DEC VAX™ computers since
1980, maintaining an accuracy rate of over 95 per cent (*Figure 2-8*).

**Figure 2-8.
A Sample of R1, an Expert
System from Carnegie-
Mellon University and
Digitial Equipment
Corporation**
*(Source: Mark Stefik et al., "The
Architecture of Expert
Systems," in Building Expert
Systems, Addison-Wesley,
Copyright © 1984)*

If	the most current active context is assigning a power supply, and a UNIBUS adapter has been put in a cabinet, and the position it occupies in the cabinet (its nexus) is known, and there is space available in the cabinet for a power supply for that nexus, and there is an available power supply, and there is no H7101 regulator available,
then	add an H7101 regulator to the order.

- Raj Reddy was one of the developers of HEARSAY, a speech-understanding system that has been described as "one of the most influential of all AI programs."[8] HEARSAY, developed in 1976, was an early component of the five-year Speech Understanding Research (SUR) program sponsored by the Defense Advanced Research Projects Agency (DARPA). Reddy now directs CMU's Robotics Institute.

  Recently, the CMU Robotics Institute has become one of the leading American robotics research centers. Research at CMU also continues in many AI areas, especially factory automation, speech recognition, computer vision, AI programming, and planning technology.

The Massachusetts Institute of Technology (MIT)

Many of the AI theorists discussed previously in this chapter have worked at MIT.

As we have discussed, research about the nature of minds and machines has had a long and rich tradition at MIT. For example:
- John McCarthy helped create the MIT AI lab shortly after the Dartmouth Conference.
- Warren McCulloch settled at the MIT Electronics Laboratory in 1952 and remained there until his death 17 years later.
- Claude Shannon was, at various times, a member of both the student body and faculty at MIT.
- Norbert Weiner wrote *Cybernetics* at MIT in 1948, after over 25 years in the mathematics department.

In addition, Marvin Minsky, cofounder and former director of the MIT AI lab, has affected significantly the direction of AI research at MIT. The following is a list of some of the AI luminaries who have passed through MIT, often as Minsky's students.

[8] Ibid., 1:343.

Other AI researchers who have been or are at MIT include Daniel Bobrow, Joel Moses, Seymour Papert, Bert Raphael, and Terry Winograd.

- Daniel Bobrow developed a natural language program called STUDENT for his doctoral dissertation in 1968. STUDENT reads algebraic problems in "story" form, converts them to algebraic equations, and solves them. Bobrow, the editor of the journal *Artificial Intelligence*, is currently with the Xerox™ Palo Alto Research Center (PARC).
- Joel Moses helped to develop MACSYMA in the late 1960's. MACSYMA, a knowledge-based AI program that serves as a mathematician's assistant, uses heuristics to manipulate algebraic expressions with considerably more speed and accuracy than humans can.
- Seymour Papert has been a co-director of the AI lab. Papert, who studied with the renowned Swiss child psychologist Jean Piaget, created LOGO, a programming environment for children, in 1976 (*Figure 2-9*).
- Bert Raphael wrote an understanding program in 1968 called SIR (Semantic Information Retrieval), which accumulated facts and made deductions. SIR was able to ask questions in an effort to obtain more information and resolve ambiguities. Raphael later helped to develop Shakey, a pioneering mobile robot, at Stanford Research Institute (SRI).
- Terry Winograd created a well-known program called SHRDLU in 1972 to operate in the "blocks world," a hypothetical environment consisting of blocks of various shapes, sizes, and colors. SHRDLU could conduct English conversations about the blocks world and manipulate blocks according to English instructions. Winograd is currently on the faculty of Stanford University.

**Figure 2-9.
A LOGO Procedure to
Draw a Box**

```
TELL TURTLE
FORWARD 10
RIGHT 90
FORWARD 10
RIGHT 90
FORWARD 10
RIGHT 90
FORWARD 10
RIGHT 90
```

Some of the areas in which
AI research is being con-
ducted at MIT are know-
ledge representation,
model-based expert
systems, and robotics.

Under Minsky's leadership, MIT has been the leader in
researching knowledge representation, a critical AI topic. MIT is
currently the center of research on *model-based* expert systems, a
promising technique being explored by Randy Davis and others that
differs markedly from the currently popular *rule-based* expert
systems (see Chapter 3).

Recently, MIT has launched a major effort in robotics
research, assembling a highly qualified staff from all over the world. A
project called the Programmer's Apprentice, under Charles Rich and
Richard Waters, plans to develop intelligent programming tools (AI
programs designed to assist programmers). Research also continues at
MIT in other areas of AI such as computer vision, problem solving, and
speech recognition.

Stanford University

Stanford University's AI
research includes rule-
based expert systems and
robotics.

Although it is physically thousands of miles from MIT and CMU,
Stanford has a close "spiritual" bond to those schools: some of the top
names in AI have migrated from MIT and CMU to Stanford. John
McCarthy, Michael Genesereth (part of the MACSYMA team), and
Terry Winograd moved to Stanford from MIT; Ed Feigenbaum and
Doug Lenat moved to Stanford from CMU.

Stanford's Heuristic Programming Project has attracted
national attention as the leading center of research on rule-based
expert systems, perhaps the most popular topic in AI today. The best-
known product of the Heuristic Programming Project is an expert
system called MYCIN, developed in the early 1970's as a joint project
of Bruce Buchanan of the Stanford Department of Computer Science
and Edward Shortliffe of the Stanford Medical Center.

MYCIN is designed to work as a physician's assistant in the
diagnosis of bacteriological blood infections. Although it clearly
incorporates concepts explored in earlier programs such as MACSYMA
and DENDRAL, MYCIN is often considered to be the prototype for the
current crop of rule-based expert systems. "This is not just any old
expert system," says Allen Newell, speaking of MYCIN, "but the
grandaddy of them all—the one that launched the field."[9]

Stanford is also heavily into robotics research, dating back to a
project initiated by John McCarthy in the mid-1960's. Work continues
at Stanford on a wide range of AI projects, including research in
computer vision, automatic programming, problem solving, and
planning systems.

---

[9] Allen Newell, Foreword to *Rule-Based Expert Systems*, by Bruce G. Buchanan and
Edward H. Shortliffe (Reading, MA: Addison-Wesley, 1984), p. xi.

Other University AI Research Centers

AI research also is being conducted at numerous other universities in the United States and other countries.

AI research is, of course, no longer confined to three universities. Most schools with computer science departments offer AI courses. The following is just a sample of AI activities at American universities.

- Medical expert systems are being developed under Saul Amarel at Rutgers University and Harry Pople at the University of Pittsburgh. The AI group at the University of Rochester has strong ties to expert system development at Stanford.
- Yale University, under the direction of Roger Schank, has become one of the leading centers of natural language research; and the natural language effort at the University of California at Berkeley was initiated by Robert Wilensky, one of Schank's former students. The University of Massachusetts, where David McDonald explores natural language generation, also has become a major center of AI research, as has the University of Pennsylvania.
- Robotics research at Purdue University features substantial industrial involvement. Other schools involved in robotics include the University of Rhode Island, the University of Michigan, Ohio State University, and the University of Illinois.
- AI groups investigate software development technology at Harvard University, theorem proving at the University of Texas, problem solving at the University of Maryland and the University of California at Los Angeles (UCLA), computer vision at Rensselaer Polytechnic Institute (RPI), and speech recognition at Virginia Polytechnic Institute (VPI).

AI research is certainly not confined to schools in the United States. The University of Edinburgh in Scotland, for example, has a tradition of AI research that dates as far back as that of any American university. Expert systems are being developed at the University of Toronto and at Tokyo University. There are AI groups at Imperial College and the University of Sussex in Great Britain and at the University of Marseilles in France.

Stanford Research Institute (SRI)

The Stanford Research Institute is a private research organization involved in projects that combine various AI technologies.

Several private research organizations, or "think tanks," such as the RAND Corporation, are involved in AI research programs. The most notable of these is the Stanford Research Institute (SRI); SRI was affiliated with Stanford University at one time but is now a separate organization. SRI is the only research organization with a tradition of AI research as rich as those of CMU, MIT, and Stanford University.

Nils Nilsson, author of the classic AI text *Principles of Artificial Intelligence*, directs the AI Center at SRI. In 1969, Nilsson headed the team that built Shakey, an ambulatory robot that featured sophisticated computer vision and problem-solving techniques (*Figure 2-10*).

**Figure 2-10.
Shakey, a Robot
Developed at the
Stanford Research
Institute**
*(Photo Courtesy of SRI
International)*

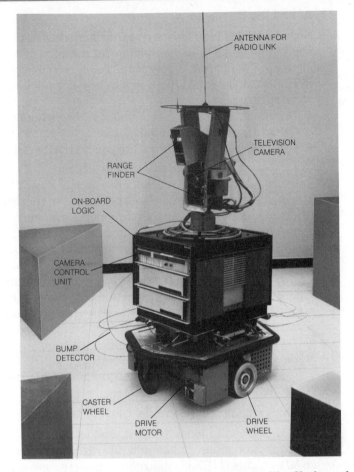

ANTENNA FOR
RADIO LINK

TELEVISION
CAMERA

RANGE
FINDER

ON-BOARD
LOGIC

CAMERA
CONTROL
UNIT

BUMP
DETECTOR

CASTER
WHEEL

DRIVE
MOTOR

DRIVE
WHEEL

Shakey and the Computer-
Based Consultant are two
of SRI's projects.

One focus at SRI has been projects, like Shakey, that combine various AI technologies. For example, the Computer-Based Consultant (CBC), designed at SRI in the early 1970's, was a knowledge-based system intended to assist in the repair of electromechanical equipment. CBC included speech recognition and synthesis so that it could communicate with its user in spoken English; it also featured a computer vision system to enable visual inspection of the device being repaired.

SRI's many contributions to AI include:

- DEDALUS—An automatic programming system,
- LIFER—An intelligent "tool" designed to simplify the development of natural language systems,
- NOAH—A planning system for robots,
- PROSPECTOR—An expert system that acts as a geologist's assistant in mineral exploration, and
- The SRI Vision Module—A self-contained computer vision system.

AI and Big Business

Many high-technology companies are involved in AI research to develop techniques which can improve their productivity and products that can be sold commercially.

Not all artificial intelligence research is conducted in university labs and "think tanks." As the commercial potential of AI has become increasingly apparent, many of the major technology companies have instituted their own AI R&D (research and development) programs with two primary goals:

- To stimulate the use of AI techniques throughout the company in order to increase productivity, and
- To develop AI products that are commercially viable.

Corporate AI activity is more difficult to evaluate than university AI activity. University research is generally not conducted in secret. In fact, it is usually well publicized so that the free exchange of ideas can stimulate research throughout academia. Corporate research, of course, tends to be more covert; protecting "trade secrets" and "proprietary information" is often considered to be an essential ingredient of maintaining a competitive edge.

In the area of AI research, however, corporations have been slightly more open about the direction and scope of their research activities. "High-tech" companies always want to project the image that they are continually exploring the "leading edge" of technology; and currently, of course, the leading edge of computer technology is artificial intelligence.

The following are brief descriptions of AI activities at several major high-technology companies.

Digital Equipment Corporation (DEC)

Digital Equipment Corporation has developed minicomputers which are used in AI labs, as well as expert system computer programs.

DEC, the nation's first and largest producer of minicomputers, has a lengthy history of involvement with artificial intelligence. Founded by an MIT engineer, DEC's minicomputers were especially welcomed in research labs where, at under $20,000, they offered a low-cost and convenient alternative to IBM's million-dollar mainframes.

DEC inaugurated the minicomputer revolution in 1965 with its PDP-8, followed four years later by the best-selling minicomputer ever, the PDP-11 (*Figure 2-11*). In 1977, DEC unveiled the VAX 11/780, a "supermini" with computing power rivaling that of a mainframe. The VAX quickly became the standard in AI labs across the country; and although its popularity has been eroded by the advent of single-user LISP machines, the VAX is still a long way from obsolescence.

**Figure 2-11.
The PDP-11, a
Minicomputer Developed
by Digital Equipment
Corporation**
*(Photo Courtesy of Digital
Equipment Corporation)*

In addition to manufacturing the hardware for AI research, DEC assisted in the development of some of the earliest commercial expert systems:

- XCON™ (the eXpert CONfigurer) was developed as a joint project of DEC and CMU's John McDermott (XCON is more popularly known at CMU as R1). Advertised in a DEC brochure as "the world's first expert system used routinely in an industrial environment," XCON has helped configure VAX orders since 1980.
- XSEL (the eXpert SELling assistant), a follow-up project to XCON, is designed to assist DEC's sales force with configuration and customer site preparation.

Currently, DEC is developing its own expert systems in Hudson, Massachusetts, the headquarters of its Intelligent Systems Technologies Group.

Schlumberger

Schlumberger is involved in several areas of AI research, including computer vision, knowledge representation, and expert systems.

With two separate American AI centers, Schlumberger maintains one of the largest industrial commitments to AI research, estimated at more than $5 million a year.

At its Fairchild AI Laboratory in the Silicon Valley area of California, Schlumberger conducts basic AI research in several areas, including computer vision and knowledge representation.

Schlumberger develops expert systems at its corporate research center in Ridgefield, Connecticut. Their best-known expert system, the Dipmeter Advisor, interprets geological data to assist in Schlumberger's oil exploration activities.

Texas Instruments (TI)

The Texas Instruments AI research effort has resulted in the development of both a LISP machine and AI programs. Other programs are being designed for internal use to improve the company's productivity.

A diversified high-technology company with a strong commitment to AI, TI uses artificial intelligence both internally in productivity programs and in the commercial products it develops. Examples of the TI AI products include:

- The Explorer™—A low-cost LISP machine introduced in 1985 (*Figure 2-12*),
- NaturalLink™—A natural language interface system created in 1983 that lets you communicate in English sentences with many popular programs for the Texas Instruments Professional Computer (TI PC),
- The Personal Consultant™—A 1984 program designed to help knowledge engineers develop rule-based expert systems on the TI PC, and
- Speech Command—A speech recognition peripheral developed in 1983 that allows you to train a TI PC or any IBM-compatible personal computer to respond to spoken commands.

As a major defense contractor, TI is involved in projects to develop AI devices that perform a range of tasks, from assisting in equipment maintenance to helping pilots fly airplanes and helicopters. TI is also under contract to the Department of Defense to develop a custom LISP microprocessor—a single chip with 10 times the power of current commercial processors that contain hundreds of chips.

**Figure 2-12.
The Explorer, a LISP
Machine Developed by
Texas Instruments**

Currently in the midst of an ambitious AI research program, TI also uses AI to increase productivity in various areas of its business. Expert systems, for example, are being designed for several internal applications, such as assisting in circuit design, raising production yields, and increasing the efficiency of TI's geological instrumentation business.

Xerox Palo Alto Research Center (PARC)

The Xerox Palo Alto Research Center has developed programming languages, development tools, and computers for AI.

Located in California's high-tech "Silicon Valley," in close proximity to the resources of Stanford University and SRI, Xerox PARC has had a long history of innovative AI research. Xerox has developed several significant products based on PARC research, including the following.

- InterLISP-D is PARC's popular extension of InterLISP™, a version of LISP developed at Bolt, Beranek and Newman (BBN). InterLISP-D, developed in the early 1970's, is sometimes called "West Coast" LISP, in contrast to the MacLISP™ variations of "East Coast" LISP that are descended from research at MIT.
- KRL, a "Knowledge Representation Language" developed in 1977, is a software development tool designed to expedite AI programming.
- Smalltalk™, a sophisticated and easy-to-use programming language that is especially conducive to AI programming, was developed in 1977.
- The Xerox 1100 series of computers, including the Dorado and the Dandelion, were introduced in 1982 and are among the lowest-cost LISP machines currently on the market.

AI Companies

Some of the companies that specialize in AI research are Artificial Intelligence Corporation; Bolt, Beranek and Newman; Carnegie Group; Cognitive Systems; LISP Machine Inc.; Symbolics; and Teknowledge. Some of these companies have developed AI programs, and others have developed LISP machines.

The major high-technology companies are not alone in investigating the commercial aspects of artificial intelligence. Encouraged by the recent financial successes of some of the new computer-related enterprises, many AI researchers are starting their own companies and becoming entrepreneurs in the AI business (*Figure 2-13*). "If someone is going to get rich out of the technology developed here," says Raj Reddy, Director of the Robotics Institute at CMU and a founder of the Carnegie Group, "it ought to be the people who developed it."[10]

The following are brief descriptions of just a few of the companies that specialize in artificial intelligence.

[10] "The Academics Cashing In at Carnegie Group," *Business Week*, 9 July 1984, p. 58.

**Figure 2-13.
An Explanation of "The
Entrepreneurial
University"**

As AI moves into the corporate world, there is frequently a fundamental change in research goals. Corporations are not as much interested in "pure" research—research for the sake of research—as are the university labs; companies look at AI *research* as a prelude to the development of AI *products*.

Some people in AI bemoan the "brain drain" that occurs when researchers are enticed away from the universities by lucrative offers from the business world. They fear that progress in AI research will be endangered if the best minds are lured away from research to develop commercial products.

Not all AI researchers share this view. Roger Schank, for one, promotes the concept of the "entrepreneurial university," in which professors would be encouraged both to remain on the faculty and to develop outside commercial interests. Schank practices what he preaches—he is both chairman of the computer science department at Yale University and chairman of the board of Cognitive Systems, a small AI company.

Artificial Intelligence Corporation (AI Corp.)

Larry Harris, president and founder of AI Corp., conducted extensive research on natural language processing as a professor in the Computer Science Department of Dartmouth College. His primary product at AI Corp. is Intellect, a natural language system designed in 1979 to "interface" between computers and computer users and to allow communication in English.

Bolt, Beranek and Newman (BBN)

A pioneer in the commercial exploitation of AI, BBN has made significant contributions in natural language processing, knowledge representation, intelligent computer-assisted instruction (ICAI), and speech recognition. With Xerox PARC, BBN is considered to be one of the oldest currently active commercial AI enterprises.

Carnegie Group

Drawing on the extensive AI talent available at CMU, the Carnegie Group was founded in 1983 to specialize in the application of artificial intelligence to manufacturing. The group also offers a wide range of courses and seminars covering various aspects of AI.

Cognitive Systems

Like AI Corp., Cognitive Systems develops and sells natural language "front ends." Cognitive Systems was founded in 1979 by Roger Schank, head of AI at Yale University and author of *The Cognitive Computer*, a popular book about the fundamentals of AI and natural language processing.

LISP Machine Inc. (LMI)

Founded by consummate AI "hacker" Richard Greenblatt in 1980, LMI™ makes computers that are based on MIT research and are especially designed for artificial intelligence. The Lambda™, the company's primary product, features an MIT-developed computer architecture called the NuBus™. LMI is partially owned by Texas Instruments, which also uses the NuBus in its Explorer system.

Symbolics

Founded in 1980 by alumni of the AI lab at MIT, Symbolics™ offers the 3600™, a "LISP machine" (a computer designed specifically for developing AI programs in LISP) that competes with the less expensive LMI Lambda. Like the Lambda, the 3600 is based on designs developed in the MIT AI lab. The Symbolics 3600 is the most popular LISP machine in use today.

Teknowledge

Advertising itself as "the single source for knowledge engineering technology," Teknowledge was the first company to develop and market expert systems as a commercial enterprise. Headed by expert systems pioneer Edward Feigenbaum, Teknowledge aims "to build knowledge systems that have exceptionally high value and that solve problems that other technologies cannot cope with."[11]

Defense Advanced Research Projects Agency (DARPA)

The Defense Advanced Research Projects Agency, a part of the Department of Defense, finances many AI research projects that could have military application.

No single organization has assumed greater financial responsibility for artificial intelligence research in the United States than the Department of Defense. Through the Defense Advanced Research Projects Agency (DARPA), organized in 1958 to fund long-term scientific "high-tech" research projects, the Defense Department has financed much of the AI research that has been conducted at American universities, research organizations, and private corporations.

Several DARPA-sponsored projects have been discussed in this chapter, including Shakey, SRI's mobile robot, and SUR, the Speech Understanding Research project conducted by several organizations including CMU, BBN, and SRI. DARPA also is responsible for a computer telecommunication network, called ARPANET, that allows AI researchers to exchange ideas quickly and efficiently. The five-year Strategic Computing Program (SCP), discussed in Chapter 10, was announced by DARPA in 1983.

---

[11] Patrick H. Winston and Karen A. Prendergast, *The AI Business*, (Cambridge, MA: MIT Press, 1984), pp. 295-6.

Of course, as part of the Department of Defense, DARPA is hardly interested in conducting research just for the sake of research. Instead, DARPA is looking for technology that has potential military application. Nonetheless, DARPA has allowed AI researchers a great deal of freedom within the boundaries of specific projects; as a group, AI researchers have not felt that DARPA has been unreasonably demanding and have welcomed DARPA support wholeheartedly.

WHAT HAVE WE LEARNED?

1. People have been drawn to the idea of artificial intelligence since ancient times, centuries before the term was coined.
2. In 1950, British mathematician Alan Turing suggested an imitation game (now known as the Turing Test) as a means of ascertaining whether a machine can think.
3. The AI revolution was launched "officially" in 1956 at the Dartmouth Conference, which was organized by John McCarthy of Dartmouth, Marvin Minsky of Harvard, Nathaniel Rochester of IBM, and Claude Shannon of Bell Labs.
4. Other notable participants in the Dartmouth Conference included Allen Newell and Herbert Simon of the Carnegie Institute of Technology and RAND Corporation, Arthur Samuel and Alex Bernstein of IBM, and Oliver Selfridge of MIT.
5. Although AI research is conducted at many colleges and universities, the primary academic centers of AI research are the three schools that were early leaders in the field: Carnegie-Mellon University (CMU), the Massachusetts Institute of Technology (MIT), and Stanford University.
6. The commercial potential of AI is being explored by major corporations, including Digital Equipment Corporation (DEC), Schlumberger, Texas Instruments (TI), and Xerox.
7. Many new companies have been formed specifically to bring AI technology into the commercial marketplace.

WHAT'S NEXT?

This chapter has explored the events that led to the formation of the field of artificial intelligence and mentioned some of the leading academic and corporate centers of AI activity. The next chapter discusses expert systems, a popular AI technology that captures human expertise in a computer program.

Quiz for Chapter 2

1. In the 16th century, a Czech rabbi reportedly created a living clay man whose name has become a synonym for an artificial human. The clay man's name was:
   a. Frankenstein.
   b. Golem.
   c. Hal.
   d. Paracelsus.

2. Who is considered to be the "father" of artificial intelligence?
   a. George Boole
   b. John McCarthy
   c. Allen Newell
   d. Alan Turing

3. What was originally called the "imitation game" by its creator?
   a. The Turing Test
   b. LISP
   c. Cybernetics
   d. The Logic Theorist

4. Warren McCulloch and Claude Shannon contributed to a field called _____, a precursor of artificial intelligence.
   a. information science
   b. cognitive science
   c. digital science
   d. cybernetics

5. Claude Shannon described the operation of electronic switching circuits with a system of mathematical logic called:
   a. mathematical biophysics.
   b. cybernetics.
   c. Boolean algebra.
   d. neural networking.

6. In his landmark book *Cybernetics*, Norbert Wiener suggested a way of modeling scientific phenomena using not energy, but:
   a. mathematics.
   b. intelligence.
   c. information.
   d. matter.

7. The conference that launched the AI revolution in 1956 was held at:
   a. Dartmouth.
   b. Harvard.
   c. MIT.
   d. Stanford.

8. The term "artificial intelligence" was coined by which of the conference organizers?
   a. John McCarthy
   b. Marvin Minsky
   c. Nathaniel Rochester
   d. Claude Shannon

9. The "Carnegie-RAND" group at the conference consisted of:
   a. John McCarthy and Marvin Minsky.
   b. Allen Newell and Herbert Simon.
   c. Arthur Samuel and Alex Bernstein.
   d. Oliver Selfridge and Warren McCulloch.

10. The Newell and Simon program that proved theorems of *Principia Mathematica* was:
    a. Elementary Perceiver.
    b. General Problem Solver.
    c. Logic Theorist.
    d. MACSYMA.

11. Arthur Samuel is linked inextricably with a program that played:
    a. checkers.
    b. chess.
    c. poker.
    d. backgammon.

12. Which of these schools was *not* among the early leaders in AI research?
    a. Carnegie-Mellon University
    b. Harvard University
    c. Massachusetts Institute of Technology
    d. Stanford University

13. The AI researcher who co-authored both the *Handbook of Artificial Intelligence* and *The Fifth Generation* is:
    a. Bruce Buchanan.
    b. Randy Davis.
    c. Ed Feigenbaum.
    d. Mark Fox.

14. One of the leading American robotics centers is the Robotics Institute located at:
    a. CMU.
    b. MIT.
    c. RAND.
    d. SRI.

15. Seymour Papert of the MIT AI lab
created a programming
environment for children called:
   a. BASIC.
   b. LOGO.
   c. MYCIN.
   d. SHRDLU.

16. Nils Nilsson headed a team at SRI
that created a mobile robot named:
   a. Adam.
   b. Dedalus.
   c. Shakey.
   d. Vax.

17. DEC advertises that it helped to
create "the world's first expert
system routinely used in an
industrial environment," called
XCON or:
   a. PDP-11.
   b. R1.
   c. VAX.
   d. XSEL.

18. Texas Instruments Incorporated
produces a low-cost LISP machine
called:
   a. The Computer-Based
      Consultant.
   b. The Explorer.
   c. The Personal Consultant.
   d. Smalltalk.

19. The company that grew out of
research at the MIT AI lab is:
   a. AI Corp.
   b. LMI.
   c. Symbolics.
   d. b and c above.
   e. all of the above.

20. DARPA, the agency that has
funded a great deal of American AI
research, is part of the Department
of:
   a. Defense.
   b. Education.
   c. Energy.
   d. Justice.

Expert Systems

ABOUT THIS CHAPTER

Throughout the 30-year history of artificial intelligence, many significant advances have been made that have never emerged from research labs. However, now that the impact of AI technology is starting to be felt in the "real world" outside the laboratory walls, there are unmistakable signs that interest in AI is increasing steadily: university AI classes routinely are filled to capacity, computer-related product advertisements boast that the products they tout feature AI, and magazine articles about AI appear regularly even in non-technical publications.

One area of AI that can claim a large measure of responsibilty for the current heightened AI awareness is *expert systems*, computer programs that embody human expertise. As one of the first AI technologies to help people solve important problems, the expert systems field has become imbued with a certain mystique, a high-tech aura that both illuminates the field and, at the same time, discourages closer examination. Expert systems hold much promise, but they also have been subjected to a great deal of "hype" as they have moved into the commercial marketplace.

This chapter attempts to demystify expert systems by examining, in detail, what they are and how they are developed. Also, examples of early and current expert systems are provided to increase your familiarity with these remarkable programs.

WHAT IS AN EXPERT SYSTEM?

An expert system contains knowledge about a particular field to assist human experts or provide information to people who do not have access to an expert in the particular field.

Human experts in any field are frequently in great demand and are, therefore, usually in short supply. For example, a general practitioner in a small rural town may be perfectly competent, but may be stymied when confronted by a patient with unfamiliar symptoms of an unusual blood infection. If a specialist is not accessible, the patient may have to settle for treatment that may be less than ideal.

The scarcity of expertise is hardly limited to medicine. Whether you're repairing automobiles, drilling for oil, managing a stock portfolio, filling computer orders, or analyzing chemicals, there are times when access to the knowledge, experience, and judgment of an expert in the field would be an invaluable asset. Unfortunately, in most fields there are more problems than experts.

One solution to this dilemma is the *expert system*, an AI computer program specially designed to represent human expertise in a particular *domain* (area of expertise). According to Paul Harmon and David King,[1] expert systems can help meet the following needs:

- New approaches to business organization and productivity,
- Expertise,
- Knowledge,
- Competence, and
- Smart automated equipment.

Expert systems act as intelligent assistants to human experts, as well as assisting people who otherwise might not have access to expertise.

A database program retrieves facts that are stored; while an expert system uses reasoning to draw conclusions from stored facts.

Although both expert systems and "database" programs feature the retrieval of stored information, the two types of programs differ greatly. In medicine, for example, a database program might be useful for enumerating the symptoms of various illnesses; while an expert system might help to diagnose an illness, determine its causes, and suggest programs of treatment. Database programs contain *knowledge* about their particular domains, but that knowledge is only declarative (factual) knowledge.

Since a database program cannot draw conclusions by reasoning about the facts in its domain, users of a database program are expected to draw their own conclusions. In contrast, expert systems contain *expertise*, consisting of both declarative and procedural knowledge, which allows them to emulate the reasoning processes of human experts (*Figure 3-1*).

**Figure 3-1.
Database Programs vs.
Expert Systems**

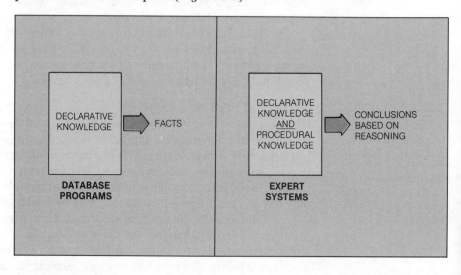

DECLARATIVE
KNOWLEDGE → FACTS

**DATABASE
PROGRAMS**

DECLARATIVE
KNOWLEDGE
AND
PROCEDURAL
KNOWLEDGE → CONCLUSIONS
BASED ON
REASONING

**EXPERT
SYSTEMS**

[1] Paul Harmon and David King, *Expert Systems* (New York: Wiley Press, 1985), p. 211.

Components of an Expert System

Although they vary in their design, most expert systems have a knowledge base, an inference engine, and a user interface.

There is currently no such thing as a "standard" expert system. Because a variety of techniques are used to create expert systems, they differ as widely as the programmers who develop them and the problems they are designed to solve. However, the principal components of most expert systems are a knowledge base, an inference engine, and a user interface, as illustrated in *Figure 3-2*.

Knowledge Base

Early in the history of artificial intelligence, many scientists believed that by emulating the process of human reasoning, computers could solve problems without having access to large amounts of specific knowledge. Although early attempts to solve problems with pure reason seemed promising, they ultimately proved to be unsuccessful.

The current approach taken by AI scientists who are developing expert systems is the opposite of the initial approach. It is now considered vital that, if an expert system is to give intelligent advice about a particular domain, it must have access to as much domain knowledge as possible. The component of an expert system that contains the system's knowledge is called its *knowledge base*. This element of the system is so critical to the way most expert systems are constructed that they are also popularly known as *knowledge-based systems*.

**Figure 3-2.
Expert System
Components**

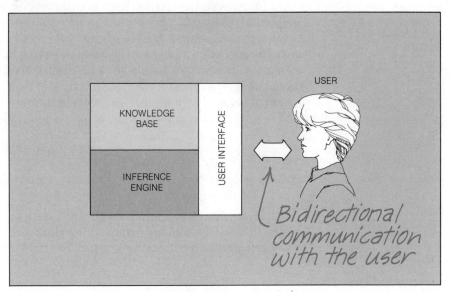

The knowledge base of an expert system contains both declarative and procedural knowledge. Presently, the procedural knowledge often is rule based.

A knowledge base contains both declarative knowledge (facts about objects, events, and situations) and procedural knowledge (information about courses of action). Depending on the form of knowledge representation chosen, the two types of knowledge may be separate or integrated. Although many knowledge representation techniques have been used in expert systems, the most prevalent form of knowledge representation currently used in expert systems is the *rule-based production system* approach discussed here and in Chapter 7.

In a rule-based system, the procedural knowledge, in the form of heuristic "if-then" *production rules*, is completely integrated with the declarative knowledge. For example, the following production rule is taken from the knowledge base of DEC's R1 (XCON™) expert system.[2]

```
If    the most current active context is assigning a power
          supply, and
      a UNIBUS adaptor has been put in a cabinet, and
      the position it occupies in the cabinet (its nexus) is
          known, and
      there is space available in the cabinet for a power
          supply for that nexus, and
      there is an available power supply, and
      there is no H7101 regulator available,
then  add an H7101 regulator to the order.
```

Some production rules provide guidelines that specify when other rules should be used.

However, not all rules pertain to the system's domain; some production rules, called *meta-rules*, pertain to other production rules (or even to themselves). A meta-rule (a "rule about a rule") helps guide the execution of an expert system by determining under what conditions certain rules should be considered instead of other rules. For example, the following meta-rule is from MYCIN, a medical expert system developed at Stanford University in the early 1970's.[3]

```
IF    1) there are rules which do not mention the current goal
         in their premise
      2) there are rules which mention the current goal in
         their premise
THEN  it is definite that the former should be done before
         the latter.
```

Note that although this meta-rule does not contain knowledge related to MYCIN's domain, it does contain knowledge that will help the system determine the order in which the rules should be executed.

---

[2] Mark Stefik et al., "The Architecture of Expert Systems," in *Building Expert Systems*, eds. Frederick Hayes-Roth, Donald A. Waterman, and Douglas B. Lenat (Reading, MA: Addison-Wesley, 1983), p. 103.

[3] Randall Davis and Bruce G. Buchanan, "Meta-Level Language," in *Rule-Based Expert Systems*, eds. Bruce G. Buchanan and Edward H. Shortliffe (Reading, MA: Addison-Wesley, 1984), p. 523.

Inference Engine

Simply having access to a great deal of knowledge does not make you an expert; you also must know how and when to apply the appropriate knowledge. Similarly, just having a knowledge base does not make an expert system intelligent. The system must have another component that directs the implementation of the knowledge. That element of the system is known variously as the *control structure*, the *rule interpreter*, or the *inference engine*.

The inference engine component of an expert system controls how and when the information in the knowledge base is applied.

The inference engine "decides" which heuristic *search techniques* are used to determine how the rules in the knowledge base are to be applied to the problem. (See Chapter 7 for a discussion of search techniques.) In effect, an inference engine "runs" an expert system, determining which rules are to be invoked, accessing the appropriate rules in the knowledge base, executing the rules, and determining when an acceptable solution has been found.

Since the knowledge is not "intertwined" with the control structure, an inference engine that works well in one expert system may work just as well with a different knowledge base, thus reducing expert system development time. For example, the inference engine of MYCIN is available separately as EMYCIN (Essential MYCIN). EMYCIN can be used with a different knowledge base to create a new expert system, eliminating the need to develop a new inference engine.

User Interface

The user interface component enables you to communicate with an expert system.

Even the most sophisticated expert system is worthless if the intended user cannot communicate with it. The component of an expert system that communicates with the user is known as the *user interface*.

The communication performed by a user interface is bidirectional. At the simplest level, you must be able to describe your problem to the expert system, and the system must be able to respond with its recommendations. In practice, a user interface generally is expected to perform additional functions. You may want to ask the system to explain its "reasoning," for example, or the system may request additional information about the problem from you. (The user interface of MYCIN is illustrated later in this chapter.)

Although the *designers* of expert systems generally have a great deal of experience with computers, the intended *users* of expert systems are frequently computer novices. It is, therefore, critically important to ensure that an expert system is especially easy to use.

Most user interfaces make heavy use of techniques developed in another AI discipline: natural language processing. Natural language techniques allow you to communicate with an expert system in ordinary English and enable the computer to respond to you in the same language. This type of user interface is sometimes called a *natural language front end*. (Natural language processing is discussed further in Chapter 4.)

Features of an Expert System

Although each system is unique, certain features are desirable for any expert system.

What are the features of a good expert system? Although each expert system has its own particular characteristics, there are several features common to many systems. The following list from *Rule-Based Expert Systems*[4] suggests seven criteria that the authors of that book feel are important prerequisites for the acceptance of an expert system by its intended users. These criteria form a useful list of features that are desirable in any expert system.

- "The program should be *useful*." An expert system should be developed to meet a specific need, one for which it is recognized that assistance is needed.
- "The program should be *usable*." An expert system should be designed so that even a novice computer user finds it easy to use.
- "The program should be *educational when appropriate*." An expert system may be used by non-experts, who should be able to increase their own expertise by using the system.
- "The program should be able to *explain its advice*." An expert system should be able to explain the "reasoning" process that led it to its conclusions, to allow you to decide whether to accept the system's recommendations.
- "The program should be able to *respond to simple questions*." Because people with different levels of knowledge may use the system, an expert system should be able to answer questions about points that may not be clear to all users.
- "The program should be able to *learn new knowledge*." Not only should an expert system be able to respond to your questions, it also should be able to ask questions to gain additional information.
- "The program's knowledge should be *easily modified*." It is important that you be able to revise the knowledge base of an expert system easily to correct errors or add new information.

---

[4] Bruce G. Buchanan and Edward H. Shortliffe, eds., *Rule-Based Expert Systems* (Reading, MA: Addison-Wesley, 1984), p. 59.

EXPERT SYSTEM CATEGORIES

The applications for which expert systems are designed can be divided into 10 categories.

We have said that expert systems may be applied to any situation that normally requires human expertise. The following table, adapted from information presented in *Building Expert Systems*,[5] divides typical expert system applications into 10 functional categories shown in *Table 3-1*.

Table 3-1.
Functional Categories
for Expert System
Applications

Category	Problem Addressed	Types of Systems
Interpretation	Infers situation descriptions from sensor data	Speech understanding, image analysis, surveillance
Prediction	Infers likely consequences of given situations	Weather forecasting, crop estimation
Diagnosis	Infers system malfunctions from observations	Medical, electronic
Design	Configures objects under constraints	Circuit layout, budgeting
Planning	Designs actions	Automatic programming, military planning
Monitoring	Compares observations in order to plan vulnerabilities	Nuclear power plant regulation, fiscal management
Debugging	Prescribes remedies for malfunctions	Computer software
Repair	Executes a plan to administer a prescribed remedy	Automobile, computer
Instruction	Diagnoses, debugs, and corrects student behavior	Tutorial, remedial
Control	Interprets, predicts, repairs, and monitors system behaviors	Air traffic control, battle management

DEVELOPING AN EXPERT SYSTEM

Although great strides have been made in expediting the process of developing an expert system, it often remains an extremely time-consuming task. It may be possible for one or two people to develop a small expert system in a few months; however, the development of a sophisticated system may require a team of several people working together for more than a year.

Knowledge engineers and domain experts work together to design an expert system.

There are two categories of people who are integral parts of the expert system development effort: knowledge engineers and domain experts.

[5] Frederick Hayes-Roth, Donald A. Waterman, and Douglas B. Lenat, eds., *Building Expert Systems* (Reading, MA: Addison-Wesley, 1983), pp. 13-16.

The knowledge engineer develops the expert system, and the domain expert provides the information for the knowledge base.

A *knowledge engineer* is an AI specialist, perhaps a computer scientist or programmer, who is skilled in the "art" of developing expert systems. Unlike other engineering disciplines, there are no generally accepted criteria to determine exactly who is a knowledge engineer; the field is much too new. You don't need a degree in "knowledge engineering" to call yourself a knowledge engineer; in fact, nearly everyone who has ever contributed to the technical side of the expert system development process could be considered a knowledge engineer.

A *domain expert* is an individual who has significant expertise in the domain of the expert system being developed. It is not critical that the domain expert understand AI or expert systems; that is one of the functions of the knowledge engineer.

The knowledge engineer and the domain expert usually work very closely together for long periods of time throughout the several stages of the development process.

An expert system typically is developed and refined over a period of several years. *Figure 3-3*, adapted from *Building Expert Systems*, divides the process of expert system development into five distinct stages. In practice, it may not be possible to break down the expert system development cycle precisely. However, an examination of these five stages may serve to provide you with some insight into the ways in which expert systems are developed.

Identification

Figure 3-3.
The Five Stages of Expert System Development
(Source: Frederick Hayes-Roth, Donald A. Waterman, and Douglas B. Lenat, Building Expert Systems, *Copyright © Addison-Wesley, 1983)*

Before you can begin to develop an expert system, it is important that you describe, with as much precision as possible, the problem that the system is intended to solve. It is not enough simply to feel that an expert system would be helpful in a certain situation; you must determine the exact nature of the problem and state the precise goals that indicate exactly how you expect the expert system to contribute to the solution.

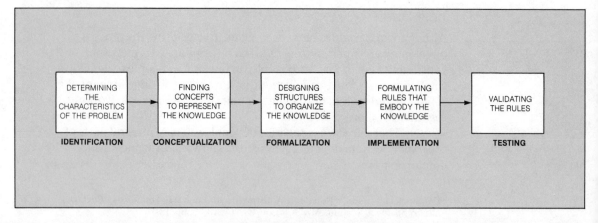

DETERMINING THE CHARACTERISTICS OF THE PROBLEM	FINDING CONCEPTS TO REPRESENT THE KNOWLEDGE	DESIGNING STRUCTURES TO ORGANIZE THE KNOWLEDGE	FORMULATING RULES THAT EMBODY THE KNOWLEDGE	VALIDATING THE RULES
IDENTIFICATION	**CONCEPTUALIZATION**	**FORMALIZATION**	**IMPLEMENTATION**	**TESTING**

In the identification stage of the development process, the knowledge engineer and domain expert work together closely to describe the problem that the expert system is intended to solve. The description may be revised several times before both of them are satisfied with it.

To begin, the knowledge engineer, who may be unfamiliar with this particular domain, consults manuals and training guides to gain some familiarity with the subject. Then the domain expert describes several typical problem situations. The knowledge engineer attempts to extract fundamental concepts from the cases presented in order to develop a more general idea of the purpose of the expert system.

After the domain expert describes several cases, the knowledge engineer develops a "first-pass" problem description. Typically, the domain expert may feel that the description does not entirely represent the problem. The domain expert then suggests changes to the description and provides the knowledge engineer with additional examples to illustrate further the problem's fine points.

Next, the knowledge engineer revises the description, and the domain expert suggests further changes. This process is repeated until the domain expert is satisfied that the knowledge engineer understands the problem and until both are satisfied that the description adequately portrays the problem that the expert system is expected to solve.

This "iterative" procedure (*Figure 3-4*) is typical of the entire expert system development process. The results are evaluated at each stage of the process and compared to the expectations. If the results do not meet the expectations, adjustments are made to that stage of the process, and the new results are evaluated. The process continues until satisfactory results are achieved.

Also in the identification stage, additional resources, such as other experts, other knowledge engineers, and reference materials, are identified.

The *problem* is not all that is identified at this preliminary stage; it is also important to identify your *resources*. Who is to participate in the development process? Does a single domain expert possess all the necessary expertise, or is the domain knowledge distributed over several people in an organization? Can a single knowledge engineer develop the system in a timely fashion, or is it necessary to provide additional technical assistance?

People are not the only resources that must be identified. It is unusual for all domain knowledge to be embodied in human experts; therefore, more tangible sources of information, such as reference books and procedure manuals, are usually identified and located.

Conceptualization

In the second stage of the development process, conceptualization, the iterative process between the knowledge engineer and domain expert continues. Diagrams often are used to clarify the problem.

Once you have formally identified the problem that an expert system is to solve, the next stage involves analyzing the problem further to ensure that its specifics, as well as its generalities, are understood.

In the conceptualization stage, the knowledge engineer frequently creates a diagram of the problem to depict graphically the relationships between the objects and processes in the problem domain. It is often helpful at this stage to divide the problem into a

Figure 3-4.
The Circular ("Iterative")
Process of Identifying the
Problem That the Expert
System Is To Solve

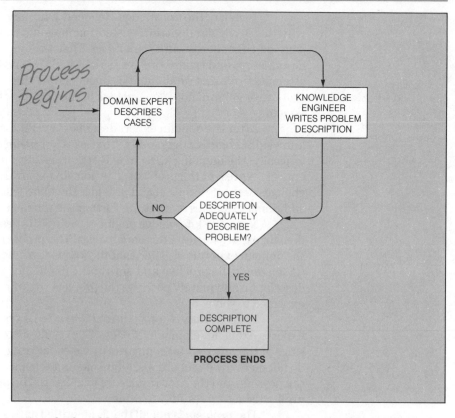

series of subproblems and to diagram both the relationships among the pieces of each subproblem and the relationships among the various subproblems.

As in the identification stage, the conceptualization stage involves a circular procedure of iteration and reiteration between the knowledge engineer and the domain expert. When both agree that the key concepts—and the relationships among them—have been adequately conceptualized, this stage is complete.

Not only is each *stage* in the expert system development process circular, the relationships among the stages may be circular as well. Since each stage of the development process adds a level of detail to the previous stage, any stage may expose a weakness in a previous stage.

During conceptualization, it is sometimes necessary to revise the description generated in the identification stage.

For example, a problem with the description generated in the identification stage may be discovered during conceptualization. A key element of the description may have been omitted, for example, or perhaps a goal was stated incorrectly. If this occurs, a brief return to the identification stage is required to increase the accuracy of the description (*Figure 3-5*). A similar process can occur in any stage of development.

Figure 3-5.
The Iterative Relationship
Between the
Identification and
Conceptualization
Stages of Expert System
Development

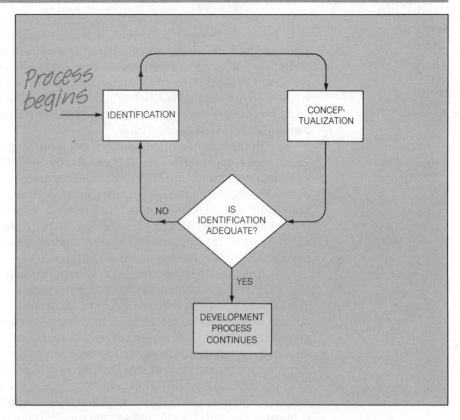

Formalization

In the formalization stage, the knowledge engineer selects the development techniques to be used for the expert system.

In the preceding stages, no effort has been made to relate the domain problem to the artificial intelligence technology that may solve it. During the identification and conceptualization stages, the focus is entirely on understanding the problem. Now, during the formalization stage, the problem is connected to its proposed solution, an expert system, by analyzing the relationships depicted in the conceptualization stage. The knowledge engineer begins to select the development techniques that are appropriate for this particular expert system.

During formalization, it is important that the knowledge engineer be familiar with the following:

- The various techniques of knowledge representation and heuristic search used in expert systems (described in Chapter 7),
- The expert system "tools" that can greatly expedite the development process (described in Chapter 8), and
- Other expert systems that may solve similar problems and thus may be adaptable to the problem at hand.

Often it is desirable to select a single development technique or tool that can be used throughout all segments of the expert system. However, the knowledge engineer may determine that no particular technique is appropriate for the entire expert system, making it necessary to use different techniques for different subproblems. Once it has been determined which techniques will be used, the knowledge engineer starts to develop a formal specification that can be used to develop a prototype expert system.

If a rule-based system is being developed, the knowledge engineer develops a set of rules for the domain expert to review. The rules are revised until everyone agrees on them.

In the case of a rule-based system, for example, the knowledge engineer develops a set of rules designed to represent the knowledge communicated by the domain expert. This is a critical part of the development process, requiring great skill on the part of the knowledge engineer. Many domain experts can explain *what* they do but not *why*; therefore, one of the knowledge engineer's primary responsibilities is to analyze example situations and distill from those examples a set of rules that describe the domain expert's knowledge.

The formalization process is often the most interactive stage of expert system development, as well as the most time consuming. The knowledge engineer must develop a set of rules and ask the domain expert if those rules adequately represent the expert's knowledge. The domain expert reviews the rules proposed by the knowledge engineer and suggests changes, which are then incorporated into the knowledge base by the knowledge engineer.

As in the other development stages, this process also is iterative: the rule review is repeated and the rules are refined continually until the results are satisfactory. It is not unusual for the formalization process of a complex expert system involving intricately related knowledge and a series of complex subproblems to last for several years. Bruce Buchanan, co-developer of MYCIN, discusses the iterative process of expert system development and the relationship between the knowledge engineer and the domain expert in *Figure 3-6*.

Automating the Creation of the Knowledge Base

To facilitate the formalization stage, AI researchers are looking for ways to reduce the amount of time required to enter the information into the knowledge base.

Because the process of transferring a domain expert's knowledge into the knowledge base of an expert system is so time consuming, AI researchers are experimenting with various methods of expediting the process. Much of the research is being conducted in the following directions.

- Simpler Tools—There are currently a wide variety of expert system development tools, which are special programs designed to simplify the process of constructing a knowledge base (see Chapter 8). However, the use of these tools is still relatively complex.

Figure 3-6.
An Interview with Bruce
Buchanan on
"Developing An Expert
System"

Q: Could you describe the "iterative approach" to developing expert systems?

BUCHANAN: You start by building a small prototype, running it on a set of sample test cases, and picking out the exceptions. Then you collect the exceptions to see if you can find some unifying rule that covers them. You fill in *that* rule and run the system on some more cases and iterate *that*.

That is a very important idea. That is one of the powerful ideas in the development of system-building tools: they encourage you to sit down and build a five-rule system just to see if you've got any idea about what the goal is and what some of the data are. You start with a five-rule system—and then expand it to 10 and 20. By the time you have 20 rules, you may begin to see that you don't have the goal quite right, so you scratch the whole thing and start over. It is very inexpensive because you've invested hardly any time at all in it.

Q: How does a knowledge engineer interact with a domain expert?

BUCHANAN: Case analysis is the key. If you ask an expert, "What do you know about heart disease?" he'll say, "Oh, not much." That is the end of the interview. But if you say "I've got this patient with a history of rheumatic fever whose EKG looks like this, and the guy is diabetic—what would you do?", he'll launch into a long scenario and the expertise comes out.

We emphasize the need for a case library. More than one example. That's the way we first come to understand a problem that the system is trying to solve. We understand the relevant features of that problem or situation; we understand the inferences among those features. We get an idea of the strengths of this emerging system by continually trying it out on cases.

Q: If I'm a domain expert, how much are you, as a knowledge engineer, going to ask me to figure out how I make my decisions?

BUCHANAN: I'm not going to ask you that. You're going to tell me what the answer is for *this* case; and then we are going to step through it, so I can understand how you got that answer. But you are not going to do the introspection. You are going to tell me, "In this case, the existence of A and B clearly indicate C; and C, in this kind of situation where you have D, E, and F, is an indicator of G." Now *that* is the story you tell.

Q: What if I say, "At this point in time, I decided to run *this* test," and you, as knowledge engineer, say "Why?" and I say "I really don't know. It just felt like the right test to run." How do you pursue it?

BUCHANAN: I drop it for now, but I'd better write down in my notebook that there is some inference that you made that the system is going to have to make that we don't understand yet.

What happens is that the expert will go home and will start to think about that, and he'll come back with reasons for why he made that decision. Even though he may say at first, "I don't know exactly why I do that—maybe intuition or experience," he really has set up some model in his own mind of a situation that occurs so that when certain conditions are like *that*, then *this* becomes his intuition.

Therefore, although it is much easier to construct an expert system using the appropriate tools than it would be otherwise, it nonetheless requires a good deal of AI experience to be able to use the tools effectively.

The goal of simpler development tools is to enable the domain expert to create the knowledge base.

Currently, the use of expert system development tools requires the expertise of a knowledge engineer. One aim of current research is to simplify the use of development tools to such an extent that a domain expert, with no prior computer experience, would be able to construct a knowledge base simply by interacting with the development tools, eliminating the need for a knowledge engineer.

- Automatic Knowledge Acquisition—Although the domain knowledge contained in a book cannot replace the knowledge of a domain expert, it can provide either a valuable supplement to that expertise or a foundation on which to build a knowledge base. AI researchers are investigating expert system development tools that could read books without human intervention and automatically incorporate the knowledge from those books into a knowledge base.

With automatic knowledge acquisition, the computer could include information from books in the knowledge base automatically.

Current computer vision technology enables a computer to "read" printed material in the sense of recognizing letters and words. However, natural language technology has not progressed far enough to allow a computer to "understand" everything that it has read, or even to extract the essential information. Although much work remains to be done, promising experiments have been conducted by scientists including Roger Schank at Yale University, who has developed natural language systems that show a limited degree of understanding in severely limited domains.

- Discovery of New Concepts—In spite of the widely-held misconception that a computer can never know anything but what it has been programmed to know, artificial intelligence research has clearly demonstrated that programs can "learn." This was illustrated early in the history of AI when game-playing programs like Samuel's Checker Player showed how well they had learned by becoming much better game players than their creators.

With computer learning, a computer could discover and add new facts to its knowledge base.

Most expert systems reach their conclusions by reasoning from known concepts, but methods of allowing them to learn new concepts are being investigated. Doug Lenat's AM program, for example, discovers new concepts, evaluates them, and adds them to its knowledge base. EURISKO, Lenat's extension of AM, actually discovers new heuristics in specific domains.

Implementation

During the implementation stage, the formalized concepts are programmed into the computer that has been chosen for system development, using the predetermined techniques and tools to implement a "first-pass" prototype of the expert system.

In the implementation stage, a prototype of the expert system is developed to help the knowledge engineer determine if the correct techniques were chosen.

Theoretically, if the methods of the previous stages have been followed with diligence and care, the implementation of the prototype should proceed smoothly. In practice, the development of an expert system may be as much an art as it is a science, because following all the rules does not guarantee that the system will work the first time it is implemented. In fact, experience suggests the opposite. Many scientists actually consider the first prototype to be a "throw-away" system, useful for evaluating progress but hardly a usable expert system.

If the prototype works at all, the knowledge engineer may be able to determine if the techniques chosen to implement the expert system were the appropriate ones. On the other hand, the knowledge engineer may discover that the chosen techniques simply cannot be implemented. It may not be possible, for example, to integrate the knowledge representation techniques selected for different subproblems. At that point, the concepts may have to be reformalized, or it even may be necessary to create new development tools to implement the system efficiently. The implementation stage is illustrated in *Figure 3-7*.

Figure 3-7.
The Implementation
Stage of Expert System
Development

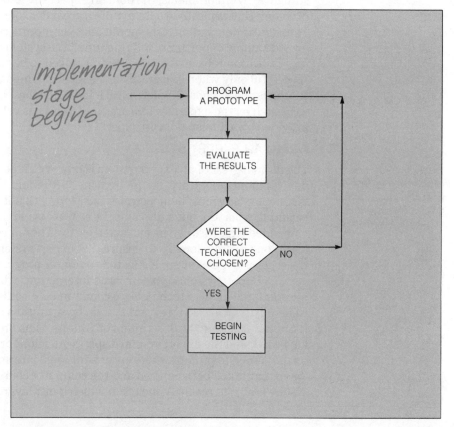

Once the prototype system has been refined sufficiently to allow it to be executed, the expert system is ready to be tested thoroughly to ensure that it executes *correctly*.

Testing

In testing, the last stage of the development process, the knowledge engineer revises the structure and implementation of the expert system until the system provides solutions as valid as those of a human expert.

The chances of a prototype expert system executing flawlessly the first time it is tested are so slim as to be virtually nonexistent. A knowledge engineer does not expect the testing process to verify that the system has been constructed entirely correctly. Rather, testing provides an opportunity to identify the weaknesses in the structure and implementation of the system and to make the appropriate corrections.

Depending on the types of problems encountered, the testing procedure may indicate that the system was implemented incorrectly, or perhaps that the rules were implemented correctly but were poorly or incompletely formulated. Results from the tests are used as "feedback" to return to a previous stage and adjust the performance of the system.

Once the system has proven to be capable of correctly solving straightforward problems, the domain expert suggests complex problems that typically would require a great deal of human expertise. These more demanding tests should uncover more serious flaws and provide ample opportunity to "fine tune" the system even further.

Ultimately, an expert system is judged to be entirely successful only when it operates at the level of a human expert. The testing process is not complete until it indicates that the solutions suggested by the expert system are consistently as valid as those provided by a human domain expert.

USING AN EXPERT SYSTEM

Typically, you communicate with an expert system in a question-and-answer format, which makes the system easy to use.

The ultimate test of an expert system is how well it performs, not in a development laboratory, but in "real life" situations. A completed system not only must demonstrate consistently that it can deliver the required expertise, but it also must be easy to use so that the embedded expertise can be extracted easily. Therefore, developers have gone to great lengths to ensure that expert systems are among the easiest to use of all sophisticated computer programs.

Expert systems typically are "interactive"; that is, you use a question-and-answer technique to communicate with them. Generally, you access an expert system by sitting at a computer terminal. You type the description of your problem on the computer keyboard, and the expert system displays questions or selection lists on the screen to prompt you to enter additional information. The "give-and-take" between you and the computer continues until the system is able to reach a conclusion which it displays on the screen.

A Session with MYCIN

MYCIN is an expert system that helps diagnose bacteriological blood infections. Excerpts from it are used as a demonstration.

The following excerpts of an actual session with MYCIN, an expert system designed to help diagnose bacteriological blood infections, are taken from *Rule-Based Expert Systems* by Bruce G. Buchanan and Edward W. Shortliffe.[6] Buchanan and Shortliffe developed MYCIN in the early 1970's as part of the Heuristic Programming Project at Stanford University.

Throughout this section, the questions and responses from the MYCIN session are presented as screen diagrams. The text produced by MYCIN appears as uppercase and lowercase letters; the information typed by the user of the system is indented and appears as uppercase letters only.

Patient Information

MYCIN initially asks general questions about the patient.

MYCIN begins by requesting some basic information about the patient, as follows.

```
1)  Patient's name:
        PT538
2)  Age:
        34 YEARS
3)  Sex:
        MALE
```

Notice that you use MYCIN with a question-and-answer technique similar to the way you might interact with a physician. You are not expected to know anything about expert systems or even about computers; all you have to do is type responses to the questions that MYCIN displays on the screen. Also note that MYCIN numbers its questions sequentially; this allows the program to refer to previous questions by number. (The numbers in this section are not sequential because the MYCIN session is not reproduced here in its entirety.)

Diagnosis

MYCIN also asks questions that help it diagnose the patient's problem.

Next, MYCIN begins to collect medical information by asking questions such as the following about test results, current treatment, and symptoms.

```
6)  Please enter the results of pending cultures in the
    following table.
                  culture          date          stain
        site      number           collected     examined
        CSF       1234             30-JAN-77      YES
```

[6] Bruce G. Buchanan and Edward H. Shortliffe, eds., *Rule-Based Expert Systems* (Reading, MA: Addison-Wesley, 1984), pp. 705-716.

> 10) Do you suspect PT538 may have an infection at a site from
>   which you have not obtained culture specimens?
>   **NO**
> 11) Please enter information on current antimicrobials.
>   drug   route of   date
>   name   administration   started
>   **CEPHALOTHIN   IV   23-JAN-77**
> 15) Has PT538 recently had objective evidence of abnormal
>   neurologic signs (nuchal rigidity, coma, seizures, etc.)
>   documented by physician observation or examination?
>   **YES**
> The CSF cultures will be considered to be associated with
> MENINGITIS.

After asking 15 questions (not all of which have been reproduced here), MYCIN has made a diagnosis of meningitis. To a physician familiar with the symptoms, the conclusion might seem to be obvious. (In fact, if the diagnosis is known before the start of the session, MYCIN can be used to verify the diagnosis, determine causes, and suggest treatments.) However, to a doctor who has not previously treated meningitis, MYCIN has provided expertise that might be available only through research—or perhaps not available at all.

The questions asked by MYCIN vary according to your responses to previous questions. MYCIN does not pursue lines of questioning that it considers to be unproductive in light of information that you have already given it.

Causes

After diagnosing the problem, MYCIN tries to determine the cause of the infection.

Next, MYCIN attempts to determine the causes of the infection that it has diagnosed.

> 17) Does PT538 have an abnormal chest X-ray?
>   **NO**
> 26) Has PT538 been exposed to any contagious disease recently
>   (e.g. meningococcal disease, mumps)?
>   **NO**
> 27) Please enter CSF findings in the following table.
>   CSF   Percent   CSF   Peripheral
>   WBC   PMN   Protein   Glucose   Glucose
>   **100   99   280   5   UNKNOWN**

Notice that one of the answers to question 27 indicates that not all of the information sought by MYCIN is available. One of the most important features of an expert system is that it be able to deal with incomplete information.

```
35) Is meningitis a hospital-acquired infection?
      YES
39) Is PT538 a burn patient?
      YES
I have found evidence (RULE545 RULE557) that treatment should
     cover for E.coli causing meningitis.
I have found evidence (RULE545 RULE557 RULE578) that treatment
     should cover for Pseudomonas-aeruginosa causing meningitis.
I have found evidence (RULE545 RULE557) that treatment should
     cover for Klebsiella-pneumoniae causing meningitis.
I have found evidence (RULE507) that treatment should cover for
     Diplococcus-pneumoniae causing meningitis.
```

Although MYCIN does not have enough information to offer a single, definitive determination of the cause of the infection, it states that it has "found evidence" of four possible causes. Notice that MYCIN indicates which rules led it to each of its conclusions, helping you to understand the process that led MYCIN to its conclusions.

Treatment

MYCIN also can suggest a treatment.

Now that MYCIN has diagnosed the infection and determined its causes, it describes its treatment criteria and asks additional questions to help it determine a suggested treatment.

```
My therapy recommendations will be designed to treat for
organisms that either are very likely or, although less likely,
would have a significant effect on therapy selection if they
were present. It is important to cover for the following
possible infection(s) and associated organism(s):
INFECTION-1 is MENINGITIS
+ <ITEM-1> E.COLI
+ <ITEM-2> PSEUDOMONAS-AERUGINOSA
+ <ITEM-3> KLEBSIELLA-PNEUMONIAE
+ <ITEM-4> DIPLOCOCCUS-PNEUMONIAE
41) Does PT538 have a clinically significant allergic reaction
      to any antimicrobial agent?
         NO
43) PT538's weight in kilograms:
         70
RECOMMENDATION-1
My preferred therapy is as follows:
In order to cover for items <1 2 3 4>:
     Give the following in combination:
     1) AMPICILLIN
     Dose: 3.5g q4h IV
```

```
2) GENTAMICIN
Dose: 119 mg q8h IV plus consider giving 5mg q24h
Intrathecal
Comments: Monitor serum concentrations
Since high concentrations of penicillins can inactivate
aminoglycosides, do not mix these two antibiotics in the
same IV bottle.
```

MYCIN has suggested a treatment, naming two specific antibiotics and their recommended dosages. Notice that MYCIN has enough pharmacological knowledge to recognize a potential problem in its recommendation and includes a warning to avert the problem.

MYCIN also can provide alternate treatment suggestions and detailed comparisons of its recommendations, as follows.

```
Looking at the coverage of the "most likely" items, we see
that:
    RECOMMENDATION-1 consists of 1 first choice drug
    (AMPICILLIN for ITEM-1 and ITEM-4) and 1 third choice drug
    (GENTAMICIN for ITEM-1, ITEM-2, and ITEM-3).
    RECOMMENDATION-2 consists of 1 first choice drug
    (PENICILLIN for ITEM-4) and 1 third choice drug
    (GENTAMICIN for ITEM-2, ITEM-1, and ITEM-3).
```

ORGANISMS	RECOMMENDATION-1	RECOMMENDATION-2
ITEM-1	AMPICILLIN-AND-GENTAMICIN-1st	GENTAMICIN-3rd
ITEM-2	GENTAMICIN-2nd	GENTAMICIN-2nd
ITEM-3	GENTAMICIN-3rd	GENTAMICIN-3rd
ITEM-4	AMPICILLIN-1st	PENICILLIN-1st

Explanation Facility

MYCIN includes an explanation facility, which allows you to ask it to explain its questions and conclusions.

In the last example, MYCIN explained why it made certain recommendations. The *explanation facility* (the ability to explain the reasoning process) is an important component of any expert system. The user of an expert system is unlikely to accept the system's advice if the system can offer no clue as to how it arrived at its conclusions. For an expert system to be truly useful, its user interface must include an explanation facility that can provide some insight into its inner workings.

An explanation facility can be as important to the developers of an expert system as it is to its users. Since testing is an integral part of the process of developing an expert system, the explanation facility can expedite the "debugging" (error-correcting) process when tests indicate that a problem exists in the execution of an expert system. Being able to trace the "reasoning" process of the system can help detect the exact location of faulty system logic.

MYCIN not only can explain why it reached a conclusion but also how it reached it.

The explanation facility of MYCIN is capable of providing various types of explanations. MYCIN can explain both *why* it asked a particular question and *how* it reached a particular conclusion.

For example, in the previous session, MYCIN asked if the infection had been acquired in the hospital (question 35). If you ask MYCIN to explain the relevance of that information, the explanation facility presents its reasoning as follows.

```
35) Is meningitis a hospital-acquired infection?
    WHY
(2.0) This will aid in determining the organisms (other than
      those seen on cultures or smears) which might be causing
      the infection. It has already been established that
      (2.1) the infection which requires therapy is meningitis,
      and
      (2.2) organisms were not seen on the stain of this pending
      CSF culture, and
      (2.3) the type of the infection is bacterial, and
      (2.4) neurosurgery is not one of the relevant items from
      the history of PT358, and (2.5) the age of PT538 is
      greater than 10 days
Therefore, if
      (2.6) the infection was acquired while the patient was
      hospitalized
then
      there is evidence that the organisms (other than those seen
      on cultures or smears) which might be causing the
      infection is e.coli (.75) staphylococcus-coag-pos (.3)
      pseudomonas-aeruginosa (.3) klebsiella-pneumoniae (.5).
```

Probabilities of correctness are attached to each conclusion.

Notice that each of the possible conclusions is given a "certainty factor" in parentheses, indicating the probability that the conclusion is correct. In this example, MYCIN explains that if "clauses" 2.1 through 2.6 are correct, there is a 75% probability that the infection is caused by e.coli, but only a 30% probability that it is caused by staphylococcus-coag-pos or pseudomonas-aeruginosa.

Each clause of the explanation is preceded by a number in parentheses to enable you to refer to an individual clause. For example, MYCIN could explain to you how it knows that the infection is bacterial if you type "HOW 2.3."

When you ask MYCIN "how" it reached a conclusion, it lists the production rules that it used and the certainty factors that emerged from the successive application of the rules. At any time, you can ask MYCIN to display any of its rules in order to gain a better understanding of how it reached its conclusions.

MODEL-BASED EXPERT SYSTEMS

Another approach to expert systems is to use a model-based system instead of a rule-based system. A model-based expert system typically is used to model the behavior of a device in order to diagnose problems.

MYCIN is a *rule-based* expert system; that is, knowledge in MYCIN is represented as a series of production rules. Because the technology of rule-based systems is relatively well developed, most expert systems currently being produced are rule-based. However, other approaches to expert systems are being investigated, and one of the most promising is the *model-based* expert system.

Model-based expert systems are especially useful in diagnosing equipment problems or "troubleshooting." Unlike rule-based expert systems, which are based on human expertise, model-based systems are based on knowledge of the structure and behavior of the devices they are designed to "understand" (*Figure 3-8*). In effect, a model-based expert system includes a "model" of a device that can be used to identify the causes of the device's failure. Because they draw conclusions directly from knowledge of a device's structure and behavior, model-based expert systems are said to reason from "first principles."

Rule-Based vs. Model-Based

The Hardware Troubleshooting Group in MIT's AI lab explores the use of model-based expert systems to diagnose malfunctioning computers. The group uses a computer-repair scenario to contrast the rule-based and model-based approaches. First, the rule-based approach:

> **"Consider the likely behavior of an engineer with a great deal of repair experience. He simply stares briefly at the console, noting the pattern of lights and error message, then goes over to one of the cabinets, opens it, raps sharply on one of the circuit boards inside and restarts the machine."[7]**

**Figure 3-8.
Two Approaches to
Expert Systems**

Type	Approach
Rule-based	A series of production rules based on human expertise.
Model-based	A model of a device based on knowledge of the structure and behavior of the device.

[7] Randall Davis et al., *The Hardware Troubleshooting Group* (Cambridge, MA: Artificial Intelligence Laboratory, Massachusetts Institute of Technology).

The diagnostic process used in this instance represents the approach that is incorporated into a rule-based expert system. A knowledge engineer formalizes the reasoning process that an expert uses to discover the source of the problem and encodes that procedure in a series of production rules.

A model-based approach, on the other hand, is represented by a scenario such as the following.

> **"Consider the new engineer fresh from training. He carefully notes the symptoms, gets out a thick book of schematics and spends the next half hour poring over them. At last he looks up, goes over to one of the cabinets, opens it, raps sharply on one of the circuit boards inside and restarts the machine."**[8]

In a rule-based expert system, conclusions are reached from the production rules; while a model-based expert system uses a model of a device to draw its conclusions.

Although in this example the rule-based and model-based approaches resulted in the same actions, the procedures used to arrive at the conclusions were very different. Since the novice engineer in the latter scenario could not rely on his expertise to diagnose and repair the computer, he had to refer to documentation that explained how the computer worked. Similarly, a model-based system depends on knowledge of the structure and behavior of a device, rather than relying on production rules that represent expertise. Although it remains largely experimental, the model-based approach looks very promising for expert systems designed for diagnosis and repair.

One especially attractive feature of model-based expert systems is their "transportability." A rule-based expert system that incorporates an expert's knowledge of troubleshooting problems with a particular computer might be of no value for repairing a different computer. On the other hand, if a model-based expert system could be developed that included a thorough working knowledge of digital electronic computer circuits, it theoretically could be used to diagnose problems with *any* computer.

OTHER EXPERT SYSTEMS

Expert systems have been developed in a variety of domains, such as teaching arithmetic, analyzing chemicals, and producing job-shop schedules for factories.

In this chapter we have used MYCIN, the archetypal rule-based system, as an example to help us explore various characteristics of expert systems. This section briefly describes other expert systems that have historical or practical significance.

BUGGY—Developed in the late 1970's at Bolt, Beranek and Newman (BBN) by John Seely Brown, Richard Burton, and Kathy Larkin, BUGGY is an ICAI (Intelligent Computer-Assisted Instruction) system that diagnoses a student's problems with arithmetic. (A brief discussion of BUGGY appears in the ICAI section of Chapter 6.)

[8] Ibid.

DENDRAL—Developed in the late 1960's by a team at Stanford University (including Bruce Buchanan, Edward Feigenbaum, and Joshua Lederberg) that became Stanford's Knowledge Systems Laboratory, DENDRAL analyzes unidentified chemical compounds. After interpreting data from mass spectrometers and nuclear magnetic resonance (NMR) spectrometers, DENDRAL produces topological models of the molecular structure of the compounds. Meta-DENDRAL, one of DENDRAL's subprograms, is a learning program that modifies existing analysis rules and discovers new ones. DENDRAL is currently in widespread use.

Dipmeter Advisor™—The first expert system developed by Schlumberger, the Dipmeter Advisor is a rule-based system that helps the company identify the most likely places to discover subterranean oil deposits. Designed to be used by experts and non-experts alike, the Dipmeter Advisor analyzes geological formations by interpreting data gathered from sensors dropped into bore holes.

Internist—Developed in the early 1970's by Jack Myers and Harry Pople at the University of Pittsburgh, Internist is a medical expert system that can diagnose about 500 diseases. Caduceus, an extension of Internist, is a model-based expert system designed to correct several of the deficiencies of Internist, including its inability to develop a general overview in cases involving complex interrelations of symptoms.

ISIS—Developed in the early 1980's by the Intelligent Systems Laboratory (including Mark Fox and Stephen Smith) of the Robotics Institute at Carnegie-Mellon University (CMU), ISIS is a factory automation system designed to produce job-shop schedules. ISIS considers variables such as productivity goals, resource requirements, and machine preferences in order to construct schedules, monitor performance, and avoid production bottlenecks.

MACSYMA—Developed in the late 1960's at MIT by Carl Engleman, William Martin, and Joel Moses, MACSYMA helps solve both numeric and symbolic mathematical problems. MACSYMA uses heuristic pattern matching techniques to solve many types of mathematical problems, including differentiation, integration, polynomial equations, and matrices. Currently, MACSYMA is used extensively by mathematicians and scientists.

MOLGEN—Developed in 1979 by Mark Stefik of Stanford University's Heuristic Programming Project, MOLGEN helps to plan experiments in molecular genetics. In addition to containing much knowledge about its specific domain, MOLGEN pioneered several heuristic planning techniques that are applicable to any domain. MOLGEN currently is being used to plan experiments concerning the synthesis of DNA and structural molecular analysis.

Prospector—Developed in the late 1970's at Stanford Research Institute (SRI), Prospector is an intelligent assistant in the search for mineral deposits. Having successfully predicted the discovery of a molybdenum deposit worth $100 million, Prospector's performance is considered to be comparable to that of an expert geologist.

TEIRESIAS—Developed in the late 1970's by Randy Davis at Stanford University, TEIRESIAS expedites the collection of knowledge for rule-based expert systems. Using an interactive question-and-answer technique to create a body of "meta-knowledge" (knowledge about knowledge), TEIRESIAS enables a rule-based system to have a "model" of its knowledge base—to "know what it knows."

WHAT HAVE WE LEARNED?

1. Expert systems represent human expertise in a particular domain in order to act as assistants to human experts and assist people who do not have access to an expert.
2. The knowledge base of an expert system includes declarative and procedural knowledge, possibly in the form of production rules.
3. The inference engine of an expert system is the control structure that decides how the system executes.
4. An expert system's user interface may use natural language techniques to simplify communication between the computer and its user.
5. In the identification stage of expert system development, the knowledge engineer and domain expert determine the characteristics of the problem.
6. During conceptualization, the problem may be diagrammed to show the relationships among its parts.
7. In the formalization stage, the relationships depicted during conceptualization are analyzed to connect the problem to its proposed solution.
8. During the implementation stage, a prototype expert system is constructed and evaluated.
9. In the testing stage, the system is evaluated to determine if it was implemented correctly.
10. You typically use an expert system with a question-and-answer technique that also may allow the system to explain its reasoning.
11. A model-based expert system includes a model of a device, allowing it to reason from "first principles" to diagnose problems with the behavior of the device.

WHAT'S NEXT?

This chapter has introduced you to expert systems, currently one of the most popular and promising AI technologies. The next chapter discusses natural language processing, an AI technology that attempts to make computers much easier to use.

Quiz for Chapter 3

1. An expert system differs from a database program in that only an expert system:
   a. contains declarative knowledge.
   b. contains procedural knowledge.
   c. features the retrieval of stored information.
   d. expects users to draw their own conclusions.

2. Which of the following is a component of an expert system?
   a. Inference engine
   b. Knowledge base
   c. User interface
   d. All of the above
   e. None of the above

3. In a rule-based system, procedural domain knowledge is in the form of:
   a. production rules.
   b. rule interpreters.
   c. control rules.
   d. meta-rules.

4. A _____ is an integral part of developing an expert system.
   a. cognitive scientist
   b. domain expert
   c. knowledge engineer
   d. b and c above

5. A process that is repeated, evaluated, and refined is called:
   a. descriptive.
   b. diagnostic.
   c. interpretive.
   d. iterative.

6. A problem is first connected to its proposed solution during the _____ stage.
   a. identification
   b. conceptualization
   c. formalization
   d. implementation
   e. testing

7. Which of the following is being investigated as a means of automating the creation of a knowledge base?
   a. Simpler tools
   b. Automatic knowledge acquisition
   c. Discovery of new concepts
   d. All of the above
   e. b and c above

8. The explanation facility of an expert system may be used to:
   a. construct a diagnostic model.
   b. explain the system's reasoning process.
   c. expedite the debugging process.
   d. all of the above.
   e. b and c above.

9. A model-based expert system draws conclusions from knowledge of the _____ of a device.
   a. behavior
   b. expertise
   c. structure
   d. a and b above
   e. a and c above

10. The expert system developed at MIT to solve mathematical problems is known as:
    a. BUGGY.
    b. ISIS.
    c. MACSYMA.
    d. MOLGEN.
    e. TEIRESIAS.

Natural Language Processing

ABOUT THIS CHAPTER

When the first computers were invented, the only way that you could give them instructions was to connect and reconnect a series of wires, somewhat reminiscent of an old-fashioned telephone switchboard. Although today's computers have become much easier to use, communicating with a computer is not yet as simple as the most "natural" kind of communication: communicating with another *person*.

We don't have to use any kind of specialized, technical language to communicate with other people—we use *natural* languages, such as English. If computers could *understand* natural language, you could tell them what you wanted them to do in ordinary, everyday English. If computers could *generate* natural language, they could ask you questions and give you information in language that would be easy to understand.

This chapter explores *natural language understanding* and *natural language generation*, the two components of *natural language processing*—a technology with the ambitious goal of making it as easy to communicate with computers as it is with people.

The phrase *natural language processing* generally refers to language that is typed, printed, or displayed, rather than being spoken. Getting computers to understand spoken language is the focus of related AI technologies called *speech recognition* and *speech understanding*, which are discussed in Chapter 5.

NATURAL LANGUAGE UNDERSTANDING

Programming a computer to understand a natural language, such as English, should be easy because people can understand English with very little effort. However, it is difficult to accomplish because computers require more precision in communication than people do.

In building expert systems, scientists are attempting to have machines perform intelligent activities at a higher level than most people; after all, few humans are experts. On the other hand, in trying to create programs that allow computers to understand natural language, scientists are trying to teach computers to emulate a skill that nearly all of us perform without any trouble. Oddly enough, while expert systems already have been built that perform at the level of human experts, computers still cannot understand natural language as well as a typical four-year-old child.

Compared to people, computers require a great deal of precision in communication. For example, if you want someone to bring you something to drink, you might get the same result by saying any of the following.

- Please get me something to drink.
- Bring me a drink.
- Got anything to drink?
- I'm thirsty—can you get me something?

Unfortunately, a computer does not have that kind of linguistic flexibility. For example, a common "operating system" called MS-DOS™ requires the following command to instruct a computer to copy all files from one diskette to another:

```
COPY A:*.* B:
```

If you type "Please copy all the files on diskette A to diskette B" instead, the computer does not know what you are trying to tell it to do. The computer only accepts an instruction entered precisely in a form that it has been programmed to understand. If you misspell a word, misplace a colon, or omit an asterisk, the computer cannot execute your instruction properly.

What Is Understanding?

The goal of natural language understanding is not to have computers understand everything we say; after all, even people misunderstand each other occasionally. The goal of natural language understanding is to allow computers to understand people as well as *people* understand people.

What do we mean when we claim that other people understand what we say? As you might expect, it is not possible to define *understanding* with any more precision than that with which we were previously able to define *intelligence*. Rather than trying to develop a formal definition of understanding, let's consider one useful characteristic: understanding allows an appropriate action to be performed.

Consider our previous example of sentences that you might use to ask someone to get you something to drink. If saying any of the sentences resulted in an appropriate action (someone bringing you something to drink), you could certainly claim that you had been understood. If the person to whom you were speaking did not bring you something to drink, you may have been understood incorrectly or not understood at all (*Figure 4-1*).

> The goal of natural language understanding research is to enable computers to understand us well enough to perform an intended appropriate action.

**Figure 4-1.
Possible Results of
Different Levels of
Understanding**

Situation		Result
■ The other person understands you.	➡	You get what you requested.
■ The other person incorrectly understands you.	➡	You get something, but not what you requested.
■ The other person does not understand you at all.	➡	You don't get anything.

Similarly, when you give an instruction to a computer and it performs an appropriate action, the computer can be said to have understood your instruction. If, for example, you instruct a computer to copy files from one disk to another and it copies the files, you can say that the computer understood your instruction. If, on the other hand, it does nothing at all or if it erases the files instead of copying them, the computer has not understood you.

Why is it so easy for people to understand each other, yet so difficult for computers to understand people? Let's explore some of the characteristics of natural language that seem to cause no problems for people but which create great difficulties for computers.

Problems in Natural Language Understanding

Four problems that cause difficulties in natural language understanding are ambiguity, imprecision, incompleteness, and inaccuracy.

The natural language with which we normally communicate is informal and can be extremely ambiguous, imprecise, and incomplete—even when it is written correctly. When you add the problems of this inherent informality to the fact that we often use natural language "incorrectly"—that is, not strictly in accordance with rules of grammar and syntax—you may begin to understand why computers have so much difficulty understanding people.

Ambiguity

Natural language can be ambiguous due to multiple word meanings, syntactic ambiguity, and unclear antecedents.

Many of the things we say can be interpreted in more than one way. This ambiguity sometimes results in miscommunication between people and is one of the primary problems in programming computers to understand natural language. Some of the factors that contribute to the ambiguity of natural language are as follows.

■ Multiple Word Meanings—It is not uncommon for a single word to have more than one meaning, as in the following sentences.

The pitcher is angry.
The pitcher is empty.

Of course, the word "pitcher" in the first sentence refers to a baseball player, while the "pitcher" in the second sentence is a container designed to hold and pour liquids. Without knowing something about the characteristics of both kinds of pitchers, a computer could not determine which kind of pitcher is meant in each sentence.

- Syntactic Ambiguity—Some of the ambiguity in English is caused by peculiarities in its syntax. Consider the following sentence.

  I hit the man with the hammer.

How do you interpret the sentence? Did I pick up a hammer and hit a man, or did I hit a man who was holding a hammer? Unless it is able to understand the context in which the sentence appears, a computer may be unable to determine the intended meaning.

- Unclear Antecedents—We frequently use pronouns in place of previously used nouns. This can create occasional ambiguity, as in the following sentence.

  John hit Bill because he sympathized with Mary.

Is John or Bill the antecedent of "he"? In other words, who sympathized with Mary? As in the case of syntactic ambiguity, you cannot determine the antecedent of "he" without establishing a context for the sentence.

Imprecision

Concepts often are not described with precision. Your ability to understand what is being said may rely on your familiarity with a situation.

People often express concepts with vague and inexact terminology. For example, how long is "a long time"? Consider the following sentences.

- I've been waiting in the doctor's office for a long time.
- The crops died because it hadn't rained in a long time.
- The dinosaurs ruled the earth a long time ago.

If you read a story that included these sentences and then someone asked you about the length of the wait in the doctor's office, you might respond that it was no longer than a few hours because you are familiar with the concepts discussed in the sentences. Without that conceptual familiarity, a computer would not be able to differentiate between the three different lengths of time represented by the same phrase.

Incompleteness

We do not always say all of what we mean. Because we share common experiences, we usually can omit many details without fear of being misunderstood; we assume that our listeners can "read between the lines."

Because we expect other people to "fill in the details" when we tell them something, we often supply incomplete information.

As an example, Elaine Rich suggests the following story.

> **"John went out to a restaurant last night. He
> ordered steak. When he paid for it, he noticed that
> he was running out of money."**[1]

Did John eat the steak? Although it is not stated explicitly in the story, you probably assumed that he did; after all, why else would he have paid for it? Your expectations of likely events in that particular situation allowed you to understand information that was not included in the text. To be able to comprehend incomplete information, a computer must possess the same kind of situational expectations.

Inaccuracy

People usually can understand what they are told, even if it is not structured according to certain rules they know.

Adding to the problems inherent in understanding correctly structured natural language is the fact that natural language seldom adheres to rules. For example, the correspondence that you receive may include mistakes in any of the following areas:
- Spelling errors,
- Transposed words,
- Ungrammatical constructions,
- Incorrect syntax,
- Incomplete sentences, and/or
- Improper punctuation.

While too many mistakes may make a letter or a memo incomprehensible, people can overlook a variety of errors and quickly ascertain the intended meaning. A computer designed to understand natural language must be able to understand inaccurate uses of language at least as well as a person.

How People Overcome Natural Language Problems

People overcome natural language problems through an understanding of context, situations, and expectations.

With all the ambiguity and other problems inherent even in the correct use of language, and with all the additional problems created by the pervasive incorrect use of language, how do people ever understand each other? Several answers, including those summarized in *Figure 4-2* and explained below, were suggested by the preceding discussion.

Context

One way that we resolve linguistic ambiguity is by understanding an idea *in context*. For example, consider the following narrative.

> **There were two men blocking my escape. One held
> a hammer, one had nothing in his hands. I knew
> that I could not hit both of them. I hit the man with
> the hammer.**

[1] Elaine Rich, *Artificial Intelligence* (New York: McGraw-Hill, 1983), p. 236.

**Figure 4-2.
How People Overcome
Natural Language
Problems**

Problem	Solution
Ambiguity	Put the idea in context.
Imprecision	Relate the idea to a familiar situation.
Incompleteness	Complete the idea based on our expectations of likely events.
Inaccuracy	Infer the intended meaning by recognizing familiar patterns.

This narrative ends with the ambiguous sentence that we discussed previously. Because the sentence is presented here in context, you probably had no trouble determining its meaning.

Familiarity

We tend to identify with situations that are familiar to us, making it easier to understand language that deals with those situations. For example, if you have waited in a doctor's office or if you are familiar with others who have, you can give "a long time" a reasonable interpretation.

Expectations

Through our experiences, we have come to expect certain things in certain situations. As an illustration, select the ending that is most likely to complete the following narrative.

> **John went to a restaurant and ordered a steak.
> When the waiter brought his order to the table,
> John:**
> **1) recited the Gettysburg Address.**
> **2) ate the steak.**

While either of the selections is possible, most of us would select choice 2 based on our expectations of likely events in that particular situation.

Representing Knowledge

Natural language understanding research includes developing ways to represent the knowledge needed by the computer to enable it to understand our instructions. Two representation schemes are frames and scripts.

One important conclusion that can be drawn from investigating the ways in which people understand natural language is that a great deal of *knowledge* frequently is involved. Although knowing the formal rules of grammar, syntax, spelling, and semantics is important, early natural language understanding systems based solely on formal linguistic rules, such as several of the "machine translation" programs developed in the early 1960's, often produced comically inaccurate results. As we have discussed, a thorough understanding of contexts, situations, and expectations is essential to understanding natural language.

As in other fields of artificial intelligence, much research continues to be conducted on methods of representing knowledge for natural language understanding. Although it may be feasible to use any AI knowledge representation scheme (such as those discussed in Chapter 7), the two schemes that currently enjoy the greatest popularity for natural language understanding are frames and scripts.

Frames

Frames represent an object as a group of attributes. Each attribute in a particular frame is stored in a separate slot.

Some psychologists feel that when we mentally recall the image of a particular object, we recall a group of typical attributes of that object at the same time. The form of AI knowledge representation that attempts to emulate this cohesive grouping of attributes is called a *frame* and was first proposed by Marvin Minsky in the early 1970's.

For example, if a furniture salesperson were to say to you, "Follow me, I have a chair that I want you to see," the word *chair* would "trigger" a series of expectations in your mind. You would probably expect to see an object with four legs, a seat, a back, and possibly (but not necessarily) two arms. You would expect that it would be capable of serving as a place for you to sit. You might not have a preconception of any particular color, but you would probably have a general expectation of size.

All of your expectations about the attributes of a chair contribute to your ability to understand what the salesperson means by the word "chair." In an AI program, a *CHAIR* frame might include knowledge organized as shown in *Figure 4-3*.

Figure 4-3.
A Frame for the Word
"Chair"

FRAME: CHAIR	
Parts:	seat, back, legs, arms
Number of legs:	4
Number of arms: Default:	0 or 2 0
Color:	any

Size (in feet):
    Height:
    Width:
    Depth:
	
	2.5–5
	1–3
	1–3

Styles:	dinette, rocking, reclining, office, . . .
Function:	a place to sit

Each attribute of the object described in the frame in *Figure 4-3* is stored in a separate *slot*. For example, the *Number of arms* slot of the *CHAIR* frame is filled with either 0 or 2. Notice that the *Number of arms* slot has a *default*, an attribute value that is assumed to be in the slot unless there is evidence to the contrary.

While frames have proven to be valuable in many areas of AI, representing knowledge in the form of frames has proven to be especially useful in natural language understanding. When the word "chair" is input to a frame-based natural language system, all the attributes in the slots are immediately available, giving the system a set of expectations about what "chair" means. If the conversation later reveals that the particular chair being discussed has two arms, the number *2* is stored in the *Number of arms* slot for that particular chair, leaving the rest of the slots undisturbed.

Scripts

Scripts represent a situation as a sequence of scenes. Each event in a particular scene is stored in a separate slot.

Another knowledge representation system that is especially useful in the area of natural language understanding is a system called *scripts*, proposed by Roger Schank at Yale University. Scripts are composed of a series of slots that describe, in sequence, the events that we expect to take place in familiar situations. Just as the concept of *frames* is based on the assumption that we have a set of expectations about objects, the use of *scripts* assumes that we also expect certain sequences of events to occur in particular times and places.

In *The Cognitive Computer*, a book he co-authored, Schank uses a "restaurant script" as an example. During a typical visit to a restaurant you expect to see certain *props*, such as tables, chairs, menus, plates, utensils, and food. You expect to encounter people in certain *roles*, such as managers, waiters, waitresses, and cashiers. There are fairly predictable reasons that you are there: you are hungry and you have money. You also have assumptions about what you expect to have accomplished by the time you leave: you expect to be less hungry and you expect to have less money.

So far, the restaurant could be represented as a frame, but here Schank adds a critical concept: *scenes*. The script representing your experience in a restaurant is composed of a series of scenes that represent, in sequence, events that you expect to encounter. Your restaurant script might contain, for example, an *entering* scene, an *ordering* scene, an *eating* scene, and an *exiting* scene.

Each scene has its own script. The script that Schank suggests for *entering*, for example, appears in *Figure 4-4*. (As represented in an AI program, the script would contain considerably more detail.) Armed with the procedural expectations provided by a script, a natural language understanding program might be able to make sense out of incomplete information.

**Figure 4-4.
A Script for Entering a
Restaurant**
*(Source: Roger C. Schank and
Peter G. Childers*, The Cognitive
Computer, *Copyright © 1984,
Addison-Wesley)*

```
SCRIPT: RESTAURANT


SCENE: Entering
        Go into restaurant.
        Look at the tables.
        Decide where to sit.
        Go to table.
        Sit.
```

In the example provided by Elaine Rich that we discussed
previously, we were able to assume that John ate the steak that he
ordered although it was not stated explicitly in the story. We were able
to make that assumption because of our expectations of the usual
sequence of events in a restaurant. A script provides a natural
language understanding program with similar expectations, thus
enabling it to draw similar conclusions.

Natural Language Understanding Techniques

Techniques, like lexical,
keyword, syntactic,
semantic, and pragmatic
analysis, are used to
analyze text as
preliminary steps in
natural language
understanding.

We have seen that an analysis of grammar and syntax is insufficient
for a complete understanding of natural language. However, some
preliminary analysis is necessary to understand enough of the text to
take advantage of the more complex forms of knowledge
representation, such as frames and scripts.

In this section we examine several common AI language
analysis techniques from simple lexical and keyword analyses to more
sophisticated syntactic, semantic, and pragmatic analyses. In order to
understand natural language, a program may use one or more of these
methods of analyzing text.

Lexical Analysis

In lexical analysis, words
are looked up in a "dic-
tionary" to determine
their meaning.

To be able to attach meaning to words, a program must have access to
a *lexicon* (dictionary) containing symbolic definitions of the words and
phrases it is likely to encounter.

Keyword Analysis

Keyword analysis, which
finds keywords in the text
using pattern-matching
techniques, may overlook
many important details.

The simplest, but most shallow, method of analyzing the content of a
sentence is a pattern-matching technique called *keyword analysis*. A
program based on keyword analysis scans the text, looking for words
that it has been programmed to recognize. When it finds one of these
keywords, it responds by manipulating the text in some predetermined
fashion.

Joseph Weizenbaum's ELIZA program that was discussed in Chapter 2 is based on a clever keyword analysis scheme. ELIZA is programmed to find words like *I* and *my* and to parrot them back in questions as *you* and *your*. If you tell ELIZA, "I miss my family," ELIZA might respond, "Why do you miss your family?" The obvious shortcoming of keyword analysis is that, while it may grasp some of the essentials of a sentence, it also may overlook many important details.

Syntactic Analysis

Syntactic analysis separates a sentence into its component parts in order to analyze its form.

One way to ensure that none of the elements of a sentence is overlooked is to conduct a thorough analysis of the sentence's syntax. This *syntactic analysis* requires some kind of *parsing* technique (a method of separating a sentence into its component parts), which is the computer's equivalent of diagramming a sentence. Parsing takes advantage of inherent regularities in natural language to ensure that the computer understands the precise function of each word in a sentence, as well as its relationship to each of the other words.

Parsing techniques used for syntactic analysis include the following.

- Augmented Transition Network (ATN)—A method of breaking down a sentence into finer and finer parts until the sentence is completely parsed (*Figure 4-5*).

Figure 4-5.
An Augmented Transition Network for a Fragment of English
(Source: Elaine Rich, Artificial Intelligence, *Copyright ©* McGraw-Hill, 1983)

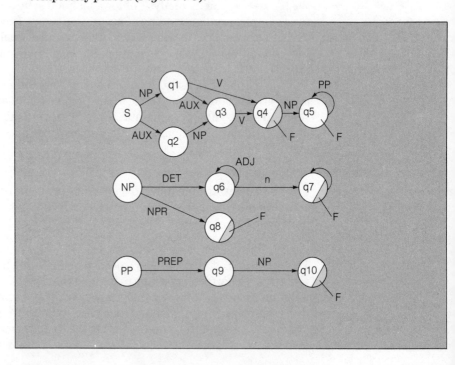

- Top-Down Parsing—Analyzing a sentence according to its anticipated structure.
- Bottom-Up Parsing—Analyzing a sentence by evaluating words from left to right, determining all possible syntactic structures as the analysis progresses.
- Semantic Grammar Parsing—Rewriting a sentence according to units of meaning, rather than adhering to traditional syntactic conventions.
- Grammarless Parsing—Abandoning traditional syntactic analysis in favor of other linguistic theories.

Semantic Analysis

Semantic analysis interprets a sentence based on its meaning. One approach is to use grammars that describe how sentences can be constructed.

Determining syntax only provides a framework for understanding. "Producing a syntactic parse of a sentence is only the first step toward understanding that sentence," notes Elaine Rich. "At some point," she adds, "a semantic interpretation of the sentence must be produced."[2] A *semantic analysis* is one that interprets a sentence according to meaning, rather than form.

Some methods of semantic analysis make use of various types of *grammars*, which are formal systems of rules that attempt to describe the ways that sentences can be constructed. A *semantic grammar*, for example, applies knowledge about classifications of concepts in a specific domain to the interpretation of a sentence in order to parse a sentence according to its meaning.

One system of semantic analysis is *conceptual dependency*. Developed by Roger Schank around 1970, this system attempts to classify situations in terms of a limited number of "primitive" (elemental) concepts. Conceptual dependency provides useful representations for conceptually equivalent sentences, such as "John sold Mary a book" and "Mary bought a book from John."

Schank uses conceptual dependency in conjunction with his system of scripts to determine meaning from an understanding of plans and goals. Just as people use expectations as an aid in understanding incomplete and ambiguous information, a program that tries to determine plans and goals from available information may be able to gain a deeper understanding of a passage of text than a program that does not take expectations into account.

Pragmatic Analysis

Pragmatic analysis attempts to determine what a sentence *really* means.

Possibly the most difficult task facing researchers in understanding natural language is *pragmatics*, the study of what people *really* mean. If you ask, "Why didn't the company show a profit last month?", the answer, "Because expenses were higher than income" is not acceptable; what you probably mean is something like "What mistakes did the company make to cause it to lose money?"

[2] Ibid., p. 320.

In order to understand sentences pragmatically, a natural language program requires a great deal of information, not only about the domain under discussion, but also about our perceptions of ourselves and our relationships with other people and with the world in general. Some researchers suggest that a successful natural language understanding program ultimately must include (or learn) a great deal of knowledge about its user in order to understand the pragmatics of a conversation and tailor its responses to the needs of an individual.

Uses of Natural Language Understanding

How can you use a computer that understands natural language? We have explored some of the methods that are used to develop programs that understand natural language. In this section, we discuss the applications for which such programs are being used. In *Figure 4-6*, Harry Tennant of Texas Instruments discusses his views on natural language understanding and describes how he believes it will be used in the future.

**Figure 4-6.
An Interview with Harry Tennant on "Natural Language Understanding"**

Q: Can you give me a simple definition of *natural language understanding*?
TENNANT: I guess it would be "understanding the language that people use in ordinary communication," but that definition doesn't work very well. People's language changes dramatically depending on what they're doing, to whom they're talking, and through what mode they're communicating, so that is not the definition that I've been operating on.

For the last 10 years or so, I've primarily been interested in interactive natural language systems, where a person is trying to communicate with a computer terminal through language. For interactive natural language, my working definition is something like "enabling the user to make use of sophisticated applications through a highly expressive interface that requires no learning time and is not forgotten over periods of disuse."

I think that communicating with a computer is always going to be a special-purpose kind of thing. Science fiction writers might not go along with this, but I don't think we are going to be "friends" with our computers; I think we're just going to use them to do things for us. The kinds of conversations we have with computers are always going to be for definite purposes, so you can structure the communication in ways that enhance that kind of interaction.
Q: On the old *Star Trek*® TV series, when Captain Kirk needs information, he talks to the computer just as if it were a person. The computer always understands him and responds with an answer. Do you think that that will ever happen? Is that kind of give and take possible?
TENNANT: Yes, that will happen, but it will be *better* than that—in the same way that when *people* communicate it is better than that. When you and I talk over the phone, not only our *words* go back and forth, we also get a little *intonation*, which helps. When we talk face to face, we get *gestures* into it; there are also the looks on our faces, body positions, and all those sorts of things. When we make formal presentations, we augment those things with pictures, diagrams, and maybe even demonstrations.

Figure 4-6.
An Interview with Harry
Tennant on "Natural
Language
Understanding"
(Continued)

What I'm trying to say is that the optimal communication link with a computer is not necessarily saying, "Computer, map a course to Andromeda." There is also the possibility of interacting with graphics and other enriching ways of expressing things that are enabled by the fact that you are talking to a computer. I'm all for natural language work, but I don't think that the ultimate way to communicate with a computer is simply through text; that is just *one* of the ways.

Q: Do you have an estimate as to when you expect that the *Star Trek* type of communication with a computer will be possible?

TENNANT: No, I don't have any dates; but I do have some feelings about sequence.

Three-year-old children understand the language pretty well, and their capabilities improve as they grow older (until they are teenagers, and then they don't use language well at all!). It is much later in life that they learn calculus and how to diagnose diseases and things like that. But it is much easier to build a computer system that can do calculus than to build one that can understand language. The reason is that understanding language requires a *vast* amount of knowledge: knowledge about language, knowledge about communication in general, but primarily knowledge about the world. Because of the amount of knowledge that it requires to communicate through language, my expectation is that *Star Trek* communication, where you assume that the computer can understand just about anything that anybody else can understand, will be one of the *last* problems solved by AI.

The question is, how is it going to be economically viable to put an enormous amount of knowledge into computers? It is highly unlikely, in my estimation, that anybody is going to pay someone to encode all the knowledge of a three year old—which is an awful lot of knowledge. Who wants to pay for that? What people *do* want to pay for is the knowledge of doctors and people who can do calculus. It is a lot more economically sensible to capture an expert's knowledge than to capture a three-year-old's knowledge, so there isn't the economic motivation to do this vast job at this point in time. Maybe some day it will happen as a by-product of some other process; but until it is done, we are not going to have *systems* that understand like *people* understand common, everyday things.

Natural Language Interfaces

One application of natural language understanding is natural language interface (NLI) programs, which allow you to communicate with a computer in English.

Much of the research that has been conducted on natural language understanding has been concerned with the development of *natural language interfaces* (NLI's), programs that allow you to "interface" (communicate) with a computer in everyday English. Also known as *natural language front ends*, NLI's usually include both understanding and generation capabilities so that they can both understand what you type and display text that is easy for you to understand.

In effect, an NLI "stands" between you and the computer as illustrated in *Figure 4-7*. Notice that you actually do not communicate directly with the computer; both you and the computer communicate with the NLI, which translates and forwards the communicated information.

For example, an NLI might enable you to enter a request in English to retrieve information stored in a database. Without an NLI, you must structure your request in a precise format.

One of the primary uses of NLI's has been to retrieve information from databases. Typically, to request information from a database, you must use a severely limited set of commands and structure your request in a precise format. For example, to request a list of magazine articles about automobile insurance from an information service, you might type the following request.

```
FIND (AUTO OR AUTOMOBILE OR CAR) AND (INSURANCE OR LIABILITY)
```

If any word is misspelled, or if the words are not entered in the correct order, or if any parentheses are misplaced, the program does not retrieve the desired information. However, if the service were equipped with a natural language interface, you might be able to request the same information in any of the following ways.

- Show me a list of articles about automobile insurance.
- What do you have about car insurance?
- Anythng about car insruance?

**Figure 4-7.
Communication with a
Computer Via a Natural
Language Interface (NLI)**

Notice that the last example contains two misspellings and is not a complete sentence. However, *you* were able to figure out what it meant, so a natural language interface theoretically should be able to do the same.

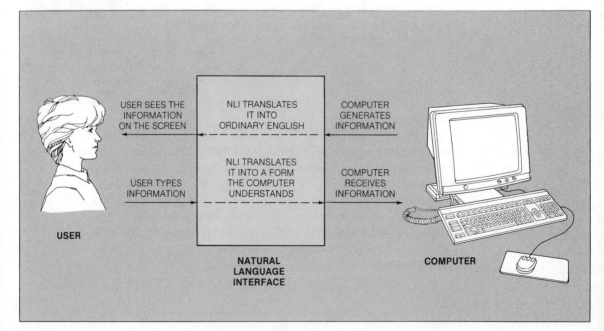

USER SEES THE
INFORMATION
ON THE SCREEN

NLI TRANSLATES
IT INTO
ORDINARY ENGLISH

COMPUTER
GENERATES
INFORMATION

NLI TRANSLATES
IT INTO A FORM
THE COMPUTER
UNDERSTANDS

COMPUTER
RECEIVES
INFORMATION

USER TYPES
INFORMATION

USER

**NATURAL
LANGUAGE
INTERFACE**

COMPUTER

Currently, an NLI does not exist that can interpret correctly every request entered in every format. However, natural language technology is improving rapidly, and programs do exist that allow wide flexibility in requesting information from databases.

Clout from Microrim is one NLI program.

One such program is Clout™ from Microrim™, the producers of the R:Base™ database program for microcomputers. When you use Clout in conjunction with R:Base, you can formulate requests such as the following.[3]

```
List the salespeople with salary greater than average.
```

Clout uses natural language techniques to parse the sentence and interpret the meaning of your request.

If you enter terms that Clout does not understand, you are given a chance to define them. For example, you might follow the previous request with one like this.

```
Are there any poor performers?
```

If Clout does not understand a term such as "poor performers," it asks you to define the term (or spell it correctly) as follows.

```
Did not understand: poor performers
Please enter a synonym or change spelling.
```

You then can define "poor performers" as follows.

```
salespeople with sales less than $10,000
```

Once you define the phrase, Clout understands it if you use it again.

Since natural language technology has not yet been perfected, Clout occasionally misinterprets requests. In one test, for example, Clout retrieved different information in response to the following two questions.

```
Whose address is NY?
Whose address is New York?
```

Another natural language interface, NaturalLink™ from Texas Instruments, uses an innovative "menu" technique to ensure that input is interpreted correctly. (NaturalLink is discussed later in this chapter.)

NaturalLink from Texas Instruments is another NLI program.

Although natural language interfaces have been most popular for retrieving information from databases, they also have been used with programs such as operating systems, spreadsheets, and tutorials. An NLI is also an important element of an expert system, ensuring that communication with the system is as simple as possible.

---

[3] Scott Mace, "Can Natural Language Sell?", *InfoWorld*, 12 November 1984, p. 39.

Text Understanding

Another use of natural language understanding that is being
investigated is the understanding of printed text. Computer vision
systems have been developed that can interpret letters and words
printed in many different type styles with great accuracy; but there is,
of course, an enormous difference between *recognizing* text and
understanding text.

Many text understanding programs have been devised that
can read and analyze text in limited domains, summarize the material,
and even answer questions about it. For example, Roger Schank's AI
group at Yale has developed programs that understand newspaper
accounts of subjects as diverse as automobile accidents and
international politics.

While text understanding programs currently do not offer
great utility, they do show much promise. A program that could scan
publications automatically for certain kinds of material and
summarize relevant articles would be of enormous value to a harried
businessperson, for example. The Defense Department also is
interested in programs that would find and summarize important
articles in foreign journals.

Natural Language Understanding Programs

This section briefly discusses several experimental and commercial
natural language understanding programs.

Intellect

A sophisticated natural language front end, Intellect is possibly the
most successful commercial natural language product currently on the
market. Intellect, a product of AI Corp., was developed in 1979 by the
company's founder and president Larry Harris, who describes his
company as "the foremost supplier of natural language technology."[4]

Intellect allows you to retrieve information by entering
requests in very informal English. For example, Intellect is designed to
respond correctly to a query such as the following.

```
I wonder how actual sales for last month compare to the
forecast for people under quota in New England.
```

LIFER

Designed by Gary Hendrix of Stanford Research Institute (SRI) in 1977,
LIFER is a natural language interface development tool (a program
designed to help develop natural language front ends). LIFER has been
used to develop NLI's for many systems, including databases and
expert systems.

[4] Larry R. Harris, "Natural Language Front Ends," in *The AI Business*, eds. Patrick H.
Winston and Karen A. Prendergast (Cambridge, MA: MIT Press, 1984), pp. 151-152.

LUNAR

Designed to help geologists evaluate data about moon rocks, LUNAR
was developed in 1972 at Bolt, Beranek and Newman (BBN) by
William Woods. LUNAR uses an augmented transition network (ATN)
to process natural language requests for information and to retrieve
the relevant data from a large special-purpose database.

MARGIE, SAM, PAM, and PEARL

Several interesting natural language understanding programs have
been created as part of a continuing development project under the
direction of Roger Schank at Yale, including the following.

- MARGIE (Memory, Analysis, Response Generation In English)—The
  first in Schank's series of experimental natural language programs
  designed to analyze simple text. "This was the first time," Schank
  claims, "anyone had created a system that could paraphrase
  meanings, translate, and draw inferences from English sentences."[5]
  (MARGIE was developed at Stanford in 1972, before Schank moved
  to Yale.)
- SAM (Script Applier Mechanism)—A program developed in 1975
  that reads, summarizes, and answers questions concerning
  newspaper stories about automobile accidents.
- PAM (Plan Applier Mechanism)—A program written in 1976 that
  uses a knowledge of plans and goals to interpret brief stories.
- PEARL—A commercial product of Schank's Cognitive Systems.
  PEARL, a natural language front end developed in the early 1980's,
  is based on work pioneered in SAM and PAM.

Savvy

A product of Excalibur Technologies, Savvy is an NLI for
microcomputers and is similar to Clout. However, while Clout
functions only as a data retrieval program, Savvy also includes
features that allow it to create and modify data.

SHRDLU

Named for the second half of the 12 most frequently used letters of
the alphabet, SHRDLU was developed in 1971 by Terry Winograd at
MIT. SHRDLU works in an imaginary limited domain called the
"blocks world," consisting of blocks of various sizes and shapes. You
can enter complex sentences to tell SHRDLU to manipulate the blocks
in its world. SHRDLU interprets your requests and executes your
instructions.

[5] Roger C. Schank and Peter G. Childers, *The Cognitive Computer* (Reading, MA:
  Addison-Wesley, 1984), p. 141.

For example, you might give SHRDLU the following instruction.

Find a block which is bigger than the one you are holding and put it into the box.

SHRDLU recognizes that there are two possible antecedents for "it" but is able to determine which is more likely and carry out your request.

As one of the first programs to combine linguistic knowledge with an understanding of human reasoning, SHRDLU clearly demonstrates the advantage of including more than linguistic knowledge in a natural language understanding program.

NATURAL LANGUAGE GENERATION

Natural language generation is the area of natural language processing research that is concerned with making it easier for you to understand a computer's output.

Natural language understanding is the area of AI that tries to make it easier for you to tell the computer what you want it to do. The field that studies ways of making it easier for you to understand what the computer is telling you is called *natural language generation*.

Although it may seem to be the "flip side" of natural language understanding, there has been relatively little research conducted in the area of natural language generation. One reason for the relative lack of attention may be that it does not seem to be as pressing a problem. Figuring out what the computer is telling you may be inconvenient, but it probably won't stop you from using the computer. However, you may not be able to use a computer at all if you can't make it understand what you want it to do.

A natural language generation program has the following three basic components, which are discussed in *Figure 4-8*.

- The program must decide when to say something.
- The program must decide what to say.
- The program must decide how to say it.

The natural language programs developed by Roger Schank's group at Yale generally have included both understanding and generation facilities. Schank uses generation to ensure that his programs actually understand the material with which they are presented; if a program can summarize a news story "in its own words," it may be safe to say that the program understands the story. Another major research project is being conducted at the University of Massachusetts under the guidance of David McDonald, who discusses his views on natural language generation in *Figure 4-9*.

Figure 4-8.
The Components of a
Natural Language
Generation Program

1) **The program must decide when to say something.**

   Obviously, when you ask a computer a question, you expect an answer as quickly as possible. There are also times when you do not ask a question that it still may be necessary for the computer to communicate, such as when you have made an error that must be corrected before you can continue.

2) **The program must decide what to say.**

   If you have made an error, for example, the program may be designed not only to alert you to the problem, but possibly to suggest a solution as well.

3) **The program must decide how to say it.**

   This is the most critical point in the natural language generation process and has proven to be the most difficult to implement. Not only must the communication from the computer be grammatically and syntactically correct, but it also must be written in a style designed best to be understood by the user of the program. In other words, a natural language generation program must include a great deal of knowledge about its user to be truly successful.

Figure 4-9.
An Interview with David
McDonald on "Natural
Language Generation"

Q: Why is less research being conducted into natural language generation than natural language understanding?
MCDONALD: It is probably harder.
Q: Why do you say that?
MCDONALD: The question is, where do you start from? When you are doing *understanding*, it's quite clear where you start from: there is some written text, and you just have to start going through it. With *generation* you don't know where you're starting from because no one knows how the human mind works.

The key problem in generation is—why do you say it *this* way instead of *that* way? Why do you use *active* voice instead of *passive*? Why do you put this phrase at the *beginning* of the sentence instead of at the *end*? Why do you put this sentence *here* in the paragraph instead of *there*? In understanding, that is not an issue.

In generation, you *must* worry about how you say it. You can't write down just one simple way to say it, make no decisions, and always use simple declarative sentences. That is *not* how people talk. You are confronted with this "how do I say it" problem that other work on language doesn't have to worry about.
Q: What's wrong with generating the same sentences each time?
MCDONALD: It's not sufficient because it's going to be used as the output facilities for some pretty serious programs. As soon as you can program a computer to use language, then the man on the street, the man using a weapons system, and the man in the financial office all think they're dealing with a person.

Figure 4-9.
An Interview with David
McDonald on "Natural
Language Generation"
(Continued)

The only language experience they've had is with people; they haven't had any experience with machines.

The way you say something carries a message about who you are, how you talk, how smart you sound. It's a question of perception. When you talk to someone who is not a native speaker of English, for example, you tend to think that they're dumber than they are because they don't use English quite right. You don't want people to think that the computers they're talking to are dumb. And you don't want people to think that the computers are smarter than they really are, either.

MACHINE TRANSLATION

Machine translation is the area of AI research that is concerned with using a computer to translate from one language to another, incorporating natural language understanding and generation research.

Early in the history of computers, attempts were made to use them to translate text from one language to another. It was assumed that if the computer had access to lexical and syntactic information about two different languages, it would not be difficult to translate text from one language to the other.

That approach to machine translation failed dismally. The best known example of the failure of this simplistic translation attempt was a translation of this sentence from English into Russian.

The spirit is willing, but the flesh is weak.

When the resulting Russian sentence was translated back into English, the shortcomings of the technique became obvious. The ambiguity inherent in natural language helps to account for this result.

The vodka is good, but the meat is rotten.

The unsuccessful early attempts at machine translation failed because they assumed that you could translate without first understanding. Current machine translation research combines the techniques of natural language understanding and natural language generation to try to ensure that text is translated more intelligently.

The research conducted by Roger Schank's group provides evidence of the promise of that technique. When one of Schank's programs summarizes or paraphrases a passage of text, it uses the following two-step procedure.

- First, a natural language understanding program reads and analyzes the text.
- Next, a natural language generation program creates a summary or paraphrase of the text.

If the generation program is designed to produce text in a language other than English, the summary or paraphrase becomes a translation of the original material.

Research on machine translation is being conducted largely outside the United States, especially in Europe where the presence of many languages in a relatively small area tends to increase the demand for such systems. One current European machine translation project, EUROTA, is sponsored by the European Common Market and is being conducted at 15 universities in eight countries. In Japan, the Nippon Telegram and Telephone Corporation has demonstrated an experimental system to translate between English and Japanese.

NATURALLINK

NaturalLink, an NLI program from Texas Instruments, displays information on the screen using menus and windows to make it easier for you to use personal computer software.

At some time in the future, you may be able to sit down at your computer and type "free-form" instructions in natural language, just as if you were communicating with another person. Some of the natural language understanding programs that currently exist can handle relatively large lexicons and grammars with varying degrees of success, but none of the current "free-form" programs can understand everything you type.

As an interim solution to the problem of natural language understanding, Harry Tennant and a team at Texas Instruments developed NaturalLink, an understanding system that uses *menus* (option lists) and *windows* (separate areas of the screen) to step you through the process of creating a sentence that the computer understands.

NaturalLink is designed to work with microcomputers, such as the Texas Instruments Professional Computer (TI PC) and the International Business Machines Personal Computer (IBM PC™). Serving as easy-to-use natural language interfaces, NaturalLink programs have been developed as front ends to many popular software packages, including MS-DOS, Lotus 1-2-3™, WordStar™, and dBASE II™. In addition, the NaturalLink Technology Package allows software developers to create NaturalLink interfaces for other programs.

When you use NaturalLink, you are presented continually with all of the valid options that are available to you. Each time you select an option, the display changes to indicate the new options that become available; if you'd like, NaturalLink can explain the options to you. As you select options, a natural language sentence is built on the screen.

Because NaturalLink only displays *valid* options, there is never a chance that you may enter something the computer does not understand. And because NaturalLink always displays *all* available options, you never have to consult a manual to determine the capabilities of the program at any time. These features make NaturalLink especially attractive if:

- You are unfamiliar with the use of a sophisticated program,
- You infrequently use obscure capabilities of a familiar program, or
- You are not interested in learning "computerese."

NaturalLink also is helpful in allowing you to take efficient advantage of sophisticated programs even if you are not a skilled typist.

NaturalLink Access to MS-DOS

A sample session demonstrates how NaturalLink is used with MS-DOS.

To demonstrate the features of NaturalLink, this section explores its use in conjunction with a popular microcomputer operating system, MS-DOS.

For this example, suppose that you want to instruct MS-DOS to display a listing of the current "directory" (group of files). You'd like MS-DOS to present the listing one screen at a time and in the "wide" format, in which the names of the files are listed horizontally across the screen rather than in a single vertical column. Without NaturalLink, you would have to know which command to enter to display a directory listing with those options; but with NaturalLink, all of the appropriate MS-DOS commands and options are displayed for your review, starting with the screen shown here.

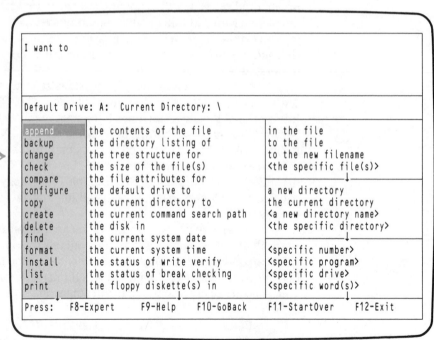

Notice that the beginning of a natural language command sentence is displayed in the upper-left corner of the top screen window. Also, various commands and options are listed in menus in the windows across the center of the screen. The left-most of these windows is highlighted, indicating that it is the "active" window;

therefore, you select a command from the menu in that window first. The arrow at the bottom of the window indicates that there are additional valid commands following those currently displayed in the window.

With NaturalLink, you press the arrow keys and the RETURN key to build a sentence representing an MS-DOS command.

Now you are ready to build a natural language sentence specifying your MS-DOS command. Each step is presented in this section, accompanied by several of the NaturalLink screens that you would see if you actually were executing this procedure on a computer.

1) Press the "down arrow" key until the "show" command is highlighted.

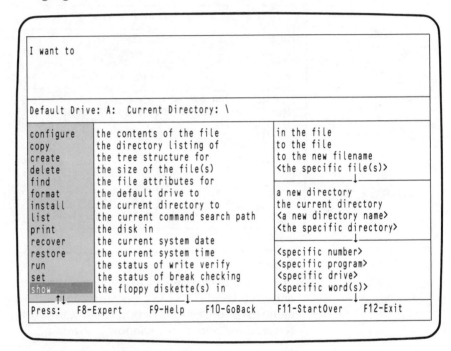

```
I want to



Default Drive: A:  Current Directory: \

configure    the contents of the file        in the file
copy         the directory listing of        to the file
create       the tree structure for          to the new filename
delete       the size of the file(s)         <the specific file(s)>
find         the file attributes for                      ↓
format       the default drive to            a new directory
install      the current directory to        the current directory
list         the current command search path <a new directory name>
print        the disk in                     <the specific directory>
recover      the current system date                      ↓
restore      the current system time         <specific number>
run          the status of write verify      <specific program>
set          the status of break checking    <specific drive>
show         the floppy diskette(s) in       <specific word(s)>
   ↑↓                         ↓                           ↓
Press:   F8-Expert    F9-Help    F10-GoBack   F11-StartOver    F12-Exit
```

(Note that if you were not certain that "show" is the command you wanted to select, the function key window at the bottom of the screen indicates that you can press F9, the "help" key, to display an explanation of any highlighted option.)

2) Press RETURN to accept the highlighted "show" command. Notice
that the word "show" is added to the command sentence in the top
window, and the next option window becomes active. The new
active window contains all the options that are available with the
"show" command.

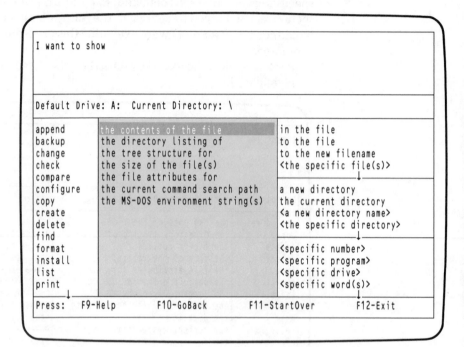

```
I want to show



Default Drive: A:  Current Directory: \

append      the contents of the file    in the file
backup      the directory listing of    to the file
change      the tree structure for      to the new filename
check       the size of the file(s)     <the specific file(s)>
compare     the file attributes for
configure   the current command search path   a new directory
copy        the MS-DOS environment string(s)  the current directory
create                                         <a new directory name>
delete                                         <the specific directory>
find
format                                         <specific number>
install                                        <specific program>
list                                           <specific drive>
print                                          <specific word(s)>

Press:   F9-Help        F10-GoBack      F11-StartOver       F12-Exit
```

3) Press the down arrow key to highlight "the directory listing of"
option and press RETURN. Because none of the options on the
menu in the upper-right option window are currently valid,
NaturalLink skips to the window below that.

4) Press RETURN to select "the current directory" option. A new
option window appears on the screen, containing a menu that lists
several additional options that currently are available.

*What
has been
selected
is added
here.*

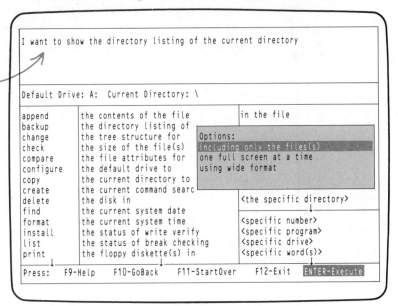

```
I want to show the directory listing of the current directory



Default Drive: A:  Current Directory: \

append      the contents of the file        in the file
backup      the directory listing of
change      the tree structure for      Options:
check       the size of the file(s)      including only the files(s)
compare     the file attributes for     one full screen at a time
configure   the default drive to        using wide format
copy        the current directory to
create      the current command searc
delete      the disk in                      <the specific directory>
find        the current system date
format      the current system time          <specific number>
install     the status of write verify       <specific program>
list        the status of break checking     <specific drive>
print       the floppy diskette(s) in         <specific word(s)>

Press:   F9-Help    F10-GoBack    F11-StartOver    F12-Exit   ENTER-Execute
```

5) Select the "one full screen at a time" option; then select the "using
wide format" option. Notice that you have now built a natural
language command sentence that states exactly what you want
MS-DOS to do.

```
I want to show the directory listing of the current directory
          one full screen at a time using wide format



Default Drive: A: Current Directory: \

append      the contents of the file        in the file
backup      the directory listing of        to the file
change      the tree structure for          to the new filename
check       the size of the file(s)         <the specific file(s)>
compare     the file attributes for
configure   the default drive to            a new directory
copy        the current directory to        the current directory
create      the current command search path <a new directory name>
delete      the disk in                     <the specific directory>
find        the current system date
format      the current system time         <specific number>
install     the status of write verify      <specific program>
list        the status of break checking    <specific drive>
print       the floppy diskette(s) in        <specific word(s)>

Press:   F9-Help    F10-GoBack    F11-StartOver    F12-Exit   ENTER-Execute
```

6) Press ENTER to execute the command. NaturalLink uses natural language techniques to parse the command sentence, convert it into an MS-DOS command, and execute it. The specified directory is displayed, looking something like this.

```
MS-DOS command: dir  /p /w


 Volume in drive A has no label
 Directory of  A:\

 COMMAND  COM    NLXSHELL INT    CHKDSK   COM    RECOVER  COM    NLXSHELL ES$
 NLXSHELL NM$    PRINT    COM    CONFIG   COM    FORMAT   COM    NLXSHELL HLP
 DISKCOPY COM    DISKCOMP COM    NLXSHELL EXE    SYS      COM    FIND     EXE
 FILCOM   EXE    LOGO     PIC    NLMSDOS  BAT    XUTOEXEC BAT    SORT     EXE
 BACKUP   EXE    TREE     EXE    FILATR   EXE    SIZE     EXE
         24 File(s)     17408 bytes free
```

Full directory →

```
                 Press the RETURN key to continue
```

Notice that the MS-DOS command ("dir /p /w") that is equivalent to your natural language command sentence is displayed at the top of the screen. If you had not used NaturalLink, you would have had to remember not only the name of the command ("dir") but also each appropriate option ("/p" and "/w") and what it does. MS-DOS does not provide any menus or other "hints"; all that appears on the screen is the MS-DOS "prompt" (A>) followed by a flashing "cursor," indicating that MS-DOS is waiting for you to type a command.

An NLI such as NaturalLink makes it easier to use a computer since you do not have to remember special commands.

If you are one of the many people who would like to use a personal computer but do not want to learn special computer commands or develop typing skills, you may find that a natural language understanding program such as NaturalLink is a valuable tool.

WHAT HAVE WE LEARNED?

1. The goal of natural language understanding is to allow computers to understand conversational, everyday language, instead of just specialized computer languages.
2. Ambiguity, imprecision, incompleteness, and inaccuracy create difficulties for the understanding of natural language by computers.
3. People overcome natural language problems by understanding ideas in context, identifying with familiar situations, and having expectations of likely events.
4. Many techniques of knowledge representation have been used with natural language processing; two techniques that currently are popular are frames and scripts.
5. For understanding, natural language may be analyzed at several levels, including lexical, keyword, syntactic, semantic, and pragmatic.
6. Two uses of natural language processing are natural language interfaces (NLI's) and text understanding.
7. The goal of natural language generation is to allow the computer to present information to you in a way that is easier for you to understand.
8. Machine translation combines natural language understanding and generation techniques to enable a computer to translate between languages.
9. NaturalLink, from Texas Instruments, is a natural language interface that uses menus and windows to facilitate the use of personal computer programs.

WHAT'S NEXT?

This chapter has introduced you to natural language processing, an AI technology that seeks to allow you to communicate with your computer in ordinary English, and has demonstrated how a natural language interface can simplify using a computer. The next chapter discusses speech recognition, computer vision, and robotics, three AI technologies that amplify specific human capabilities.

Quiz for Chapter 4

1. Natural language processing can be divided into the two subfields of:
   a. context and expectations.
   b. generation and understanding.
   c. recognition and synthesis.
   d. semantics and pragmatics.
2. Ambiguity may be caused by:
   a. multiple word meanings.
   b. syntactic ambiguity.
   c. unclear antecedents.
   d. all of the above.
   e. b and c above.
3. People overcome natural language problems by:
   a. grouping attributes into frames.
   b. identifying with familiar situations.
   c. understanding ideas in context.
   d. all of the above.
   e. b and c above.
4. A _____ is a series of slots that describes sequential events.
   a. context
   b. frame
   c. keyword
   d. script
5. A _____ analysis relies on a dictionary of symbolic definitions.
   a. lexical
   b. keyword
   c. syntactic
   d. semantic
6. A _____ analysis interprets a sentence according to meaning, rather than form.
   a. lexical
   b. keyword
   c. syntactic
   d. semantic
7. Natural language understanding is used in:
   a. natural language interfaces.
   b. natural language front ends.
   c. text understanding systems.
   d. all of the above.
   e. b and c above.
8. A natural language generation program must decide:
   a. what to say.
   b. when to say something.
   c. why it is being used.
   d. all of the above.
   e. a and b above.
9. Early attempts at machine translation failed because they assumed that translation without _____ was possible.
   a. experimentation
   b. summarization
   c. understanding
   d. verification
10. NaturalLink uses _____ to help you create sentences that the computer understands.
   a. explanations
   b. menus
   c. windows
   d. all of the above
   e. a and b above

Amplifying Human Capabilities

ABOUT THIS CHAPTER

In a sense, all areas of AI are related to the amplification of human capabilities. For example, an expert system can provide you with expertise that otherwise might require years of education and experience to acquire, and natural language processing lets you interact with sophisticated computer systems without first having to study their underlying principles.

Several AI technologies are related even more directly to specific human capabilities. This chapter explores the three areas of AI that seek to amplify our abilities to hear, see, and move. These AI technologies are:

- Speech Recognition,
- Computer Vision, and
- Robotics.

SPEECH RECOGNITION

The goal of natural language processing, as discussed in Chapter 4, is to make it easier to communicate with a computer by allowing you to type and read normal English instead of arcane computer jargon. Typing and reading, however, are not the methods that people use to communicate with each other most naturally; the most prevalent mode of communication between people is, of course, speech.

Just as natural language processing is divided into two areas (understanding and generation), speech processing consists of the following two fields:

- Speech Recognition—The recognition and understanding of spoken language by a computer, and
- Speech Synthesis—The generation of speech by a computer.

Research is being conducted in the area of speech recognition so that a computer can recognize the words we speak and can understand what the words mean.

Speech recognition is the process that allows you to communicate with a computer by speaking to it. (The term *speech recognition* sometimes is applied only to the first part of the process: recognizing the words that have been spoken without necessarily interpreting their meanings. The other part of the process, in which the meaning of the speech is ascertained, is called *speech understanding*. Note that it may be possible to understand the meaning of a spoken sentence without actually recognizing every word.)

By synthesizing speech, computers can speak to us. Determining what is to be said is part of natural language processing research.

Speech synthesis has proven to be a simpler process than speech recognition. The biggest problem remaining in speech synthesis is that of having the computer first determine what it wants to say, which is a natural language generation problem that was described in Chapter 4. Once it has decided what to say, having the computer speak the correct words and phrases is not difficult and does not seem to require any special ''intelligence'' on the part of the computer.

Advantages of Speech Recognition

Through enabling a computer to understand what we say, we can communicate with it more naturally, simplify using it, give it instructions faster, free our hands for other tasks, and access it remotely.

Although speech *synthesis* generally is not considered to be an AI technology, speech *recognition* continues to be a subject of AI research. The ultimate goal of speech recognition is to allow a computer to understand the natural speech of any human speaker at least as well as a human listener can understand it. In addition to being the most natural method of communication, speech recognition offers several advantages:

- Ease of Access—Many more people can speak than can type. As long as communication with a computer depends on developing typing skills, many people may not be able to use computers effectively. While natural language understanding may help to reduce the severity of the problem, it does not solve it completely.
- Speed—Even the most competent typists can speak quicker than they can type. It is estimated that the average person can speak twice as fast as a proficient typist can type.
- Manual Freedom—Obviously, communicating with a computer by typing occupies your hands. There are, however, many situations in which computers might be useful to people whose hands are otherwise occupied, such as product assemblers, pilots of military aircraft, and busy executives.
- Remote Access—Many computers are set up so that they can be accessed remotely by telephone. If the remote database includes speech recognition capabilities, you could retrieve information by issuing verbal commands into a telephone.

Potential speech recognition application areas range from entertainment to office automation.

In addition to those mentioned above, potential areas of speech recognition applications include:

- Clinical—Medical records, services for the handicapped;
- Entertainment and Education—Voice-controlled toys (*Figure 5-1*), interactive video games;
- Manufacturing Process Control—Machine operation, package sorting;
- Office Automation—Data entry, automatic dictation, automatic transcription; and
- Security—Voiceprint identification, building access.

Figure 5-1.
Verbot, a Voice-
Controlled Toy
(Photo Courtesty of TOMY)

Approaches to Recognition

Before speech can be
analyzed by a speech
recognition program, it
must be converted from
sound waves into speech
patterns.

As illustrated in *Figure 5-2*, speech, like all sound, is transmitted
through the air in the form of waves of various frequencies and
amplitudes. When these waves reach an electronic sensing device,
such as a microphone, they are converted into electronic *signals*
capable of being analyzed by a computer; analyzing the data from
sensing devices is sometimes called *signal processing*. Sophisticated
microprocessors designed specifically for signal processing, such as the
Texas Instruments TMS320, can analyze signal data quickly and
efficiently.

Due to differences in
speakers and in context,
recognizing speech is more
than comparing words to a
dictionary to obtain their
meaning.

You might think that a computer could have a "dictionary" of
the signal patterns of every English word and determine which words
had been spoken simply by comparing the spoken patterns to the
pattern "templates" in its dictionary. Unfortunately, there are no
"standard" patterns from which you could create such a dictionary
for two major reasons:

- No two people create exactly the same signal patterns when they
  speak the same word, and
- When you say the same word more than once, its pronunciation
  (and therefore its signal pattern) may differ dramatically,
  depending on the context and circumstances in which the word is
  spoken.

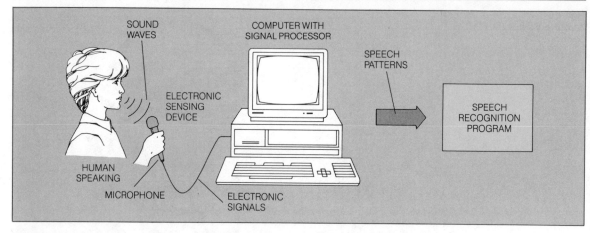

**Figure 5-2.
The Transmission of
Human Speech to a
Speech Recognition
Program**

These problems of speaker dependence and differences due to context have created varying levels of difficulty for speech recognition researchers and have caused them to divide their work along several avenues of research.

Speaker Dependence

Speech recognition researchers have developed two approaches to their research, speaker-dependent and speaker-independent recognition programs.

The variation between the speech patterns of different people has resulted in the following two approaches to speech recognition:

- Speaker-Dependent Recognition—A system designed to recognize the speech of a particular person. In a speaker-dependent system, you train the system to understand your voice by repeating the words and phrases that you want it to understand. The Texas Instruments Speech Command system, for example, is a speaker-dependent speech recognition system for personal and professional computers such as the TI PC.
- Speaker-Independent Recognition—A system designed to recognize the speech of *any* speaker. Speaker-independent systems have proven to be considerably more difficult to implement than speaker-dependent systems and currently are practical only in severely limited domains.

Context

Three approaches to handling words in different contexts are recognizing isolated words, connected words, and continuous speech.

The differences in the way words are pronounced according to context have resulted in the following three approaches to speech recognition:

- Isolated Word Recognition (IWR)—A system that uses pattern-matching techniques to recognize words only when they are spoken with short but distinct pauses between them, thus "isolating" each word from any context. By eliminating many of the problems in speech recognition that result from trying to interpret sounds that vary when words run together, IWR systems have enjoyed some success for about 20 years.

■ Connected Word Recognition (CWR)—A system designed to recognize words spoken in normal context without noticeable pauses between the words. Since the boundaries between connected words are often blurred, recognizing connected words requires more sophisticated AI techniques than recognizing isolated words, and the technology is not nearly as far advanced.

■ Continuous Speech Recognition (CSR)—A system designed to understand speech in typical conversations of normal durations. In addition to having to cope with all the problems facing the recognition of connected words, CSR faces the "real-time" problem of trying to process speech quickly enough to keep up with the rapid pace of normal conversation.

Experimental speech recognition systems have used various combinations of these approaches. Before 1970, most research focused on speaker-dependent IWR systems; currently, research on speaker-independent IWR systems is being conducted at CMU and MIT. It is unlikely that an effective speaker-independent CSR system with a large domain-independent vocabulary will be developed in the near future.

Analyzing Speech

To help analyze speech signal patterns, words can be broken into syllables, phonemes, or allophones.

Regardless of which speaker-dependence and context techniques are used, once the speech has been converted into an electronic signal, the signal patterns must be analyzed to determine what words they represent. The most common approach is to identify units of speech that are smaller than words, rather than trying to identify entire words from their signal patterns (although that approach has been used). These elementary linguistic units include syllables, phonemes, and allophones.

Syllables

Due to the number of syllables in the language, syllable identification is more difficult in English than it is in Japanese.

A *syllable* is a recognizable unit of speech consisting of a vowel and the surrounding consonants that are pronounced together. Individual syllables often can be isolated by analyzing the patterns of stress in a speech signal.

With over 10,000 syllables in English, individual syllables may be difficult to isolate. However, in other languages, such as Japanese, syllable identification may be easier, and hence more useful in speech recognition. Because there are only about 500 syllables from which all Japanese words are constructed, syllable identification plays an important role in the speech recognition techniques that are part of the Japanese Fifth Generation Project.

Phonemes

Words can be broken down into all of their individual sounds, called phonemes.

A *phoneme* is the *sound* of an individual consonant or vowel. For example, the word *sit* consists of three separate phonemes. However, a phoneme is not necessarily a single letter: the word *sought* also consists of three phonemes.

A particular letter combination may represent different phonemes in different words. For example, the *th* in *thigh* is a different phoneme from the *th* in *thy*. As shown in *Figure 5-3*, the English language includes nearly 40 phonemes.

**Figure 5-3.
The Phonemes of
American English**

Phoneme Symbol	Key Word	Key Word Transcription
p	pea	/pi/
b	bee	/bi/
m	me	/mi/
t	tea	/ti/
d	dot	/dat/
n	not	/nat/
k	cot	/kat/
g	got	/gat/
ŋ	sing	/siŋ/
f	fee	/fi/
v	vain	/ven/
θ	thigh	/θai/
ð	thy	/ðai/
s	sue	/su/
z	zoo	/zu/
š	show	/šo/
ž	measure	/mɛžɚ/
č	chain	/čen/
ǰ	Jane	/ǰen/
w	watt	/wat/
y	yacht	/yat/
l	late	/let/
r	rate	/ret/
h	hate	/het/
i	beat	/bit/
I	bit	/bIt/
e	bait	/bet/
ɛ	bet	/bɛt/
æ	bat	/bæt/
ʌ	but	/bʌt/
ɚ	Bert	/bɚt/
u	boot	/but/
ʋ	book	/bʋk/
o	boat	/bot/
ɔ	bought	/bɔt/
a	box	/baks/
ai	bite	/bait/
au	bout	/baut/
oi	boy	/boy/

Allophones

An allophone is a particular sound that occurs in a word based on the context in which the word is spoken.

In normal, fluent speech, the pronunciation of each phoneme is influenced strongly by its context. For example, the phoneme *t* is pronounced differently in *tale*, *late*, *later*, and *mountain*. An *allophone* is a distinct phonemic variation and represents a particular sound as it actually occurs in a word.

Speech Understanding

Even when the various elements of a speech signal have been analyzed and identified, the speech recognition process is far from complete. In normal, informal speech, we tend to speak somewhat indistinctly and imprecisely. Many words have similar sounds, and in continuous speech it may be difficult to determine where one word ends and another begins.

For computers to understand speech, they must select the most likely meaning of what has been said from several possible interpretations. Several techniques are used to make the selection.

This problem is hardly unique to computers; it is not uncommon for people to misunderstand each other in normal conversation (*Figure 5-4*). As with natural language understanding, we overcome many potential speech understanding problems through our expectations about familiar situations and an understanding of words in context. Similarly, a system that is to understand speech also must have a greater understanding of spoken English than is provided by signal processing: it must also have some knowledge of *meaning*.

**Figure 5-4.
A Note From the Author on Misunderstanding Speech**

An incident that occurred during the preparation of this book provides a vivid illustration of the difficulties involved in speech understanding. During my interview with David McDonald, he described an approach to an encyclopedic expert system. His approach sounded similar to a concept that I had explored previously with Doug Lenat, who had called the system the "knoesphere." I inquired whether McDonald was discussing the same concept, as follows:

> "Is that the same system that Doug Lenat calls the *knoesphere*?"

McDonald replied:

> "Yes, it's the same thing. I've gone back to calling it the *encyclopedia project*, but Doug likes *knoesphere*."

When I reviewed the transcription of the interview, I came across a baffling exchange. It took me a few minutes to realize that the transcriptionist, who was unfamiliar with *knoesphere*, had interpreted the term as well as possible. Without the knowledge required to recognize that word, she had entered:

> "Is that the same system that Doug Lenat calls the *Nose Fear*?"

> "Yes, it's the same thing. I've gone back to calling it the *encyclopedia project*, but Doug likes *Nose Fear*."

Although I suspect that Lenat would be surprised to learn of his affinity for this unusual olfactory phobia, I'm sure that a speech recognition system lacking specific knowledge of the knoesphere could not have done any better.

A method commonly used for speech understanding is to develop several possible interpretations and then use various AI techniques to select the most plausible one. Some of the interpretation techniques used for speech understanding are similar to those used for natural language understanding; analyses of syntax, semantics, and pragmatics may reveal that some possible interpretations are more likely than others. Patterns of stress and intonation in spoken language may provide additional clues that are unavailable in written language.

Some speech understanding programs begin with the first word in a sentence and attempt to interpret the words in sequence, just as you would do if you were reading the sentence. Although this technique has been used successfully, it can lead to problems if the first word happens to be misinterpreted.

In another technique, called *island driving*, the program selects the words within a sentence that are most likely to have been interpreted correctly. The program then tries to connect these "word islands" by selecting the most likely interpretations of the remaining words in context with the previously interpreted words. "This approach is useful," Elaine Rich points out, "because some words (often the most important ones, fortunately) are enunciated clearly, while other parts of the sentence are slurred."[1]

The DARPA Speech Understanding Research Project

Three programs in the DARPA Speech Understanding Research project have achieved recognition accuracy rates of 50% to 95%.

In 1971, the Defense Advanced Research Projects Agency (DARPA) initiated the five-year Speech Understanding Research (SUR) project. The SUR project, conducted at various AI labs, produced several remarkable speech recognition programs, including the following.

■ HEARSAY—Developed at CMU, HEARSAY consists of two successive programs. HEARSAY-I uses syllabic analysis and a knowledge of syntax and semantics to allow you to play chess against the computer using only spoken commands. HEARSAY-II analyzes a sentence on several different "levels" at the same time; the various analysis levels do not communicate directly with other, but share their conclusions in a common area called a *blackboard* in order to arrive at a final interpretation. The speaker-dependent HEARSAY programs achieved a recognition accuracy rate of over 90%.

---

[1] Elaine Rich, *Artificial Intelligence* (New York: McGraw-Hill, 1983), p. 350.

- HARPY—Also developed at CMU, HARPY uses a network of speech-pattern templates to understand speech in limited domains. In effect, the network structure used by HARPY can construct the patterns of all the sentences that HARPY can understand. The speaker-independent HARPY uses a heuristic technique called *beam search* to prune unpromising paths from the network and to achieve a recognition accuracy rate of over 95%.
- HWIM—Developed in the mid-1970's at Bolt, Beranek and Newman (BBN), HWIM ("Hear What I Mean") is designed to answer spoken questions about travel expenses. HWIM includes phonemic representations of words likely to be encountered in its domain and also implements *juncture rules* that specify the way word combinations are spoken. HWIM achieves a recognition accuracy rate of about 50%.

COMPUTER VISION

Developing computers with vision that also can understand what they see is a challenging area of AI research.

How do we understand what we see? The process of human vision, the primary sense through which most of us receive information about our world, is understood only dimly, at best. Just as we *hear* when sound waves reach our ears, we *see* when light waves reach our eyes. Just as sound waves reaching a microphone can be transformed into electronic signals, light waves similarly can be transformed by a camera that uses signal processing techniques to *digitize* visual images. However, processing these images intelligently so that they can be understood by a computer remains the subject of much investigation. Currently, computer vision is considered to be one of the most challenging of the fundamental areas of AI research.

Analyzing Visual Clues

Visual images have been stored in computers since the early 1950's, even before the formal advent of AI research. A visual image received by a camera can be *digitized* by an analog-to-digital (A/D) converter and stored in a computer as a matrix of individual dots called *pixels*. You can increase the accuracy of the digitized image by using a larger density of pixels, a process that also requires more computer memory.

On a computer, analyzing a visual image requires interpreting a group of dots.

Digitized images have tended to become more accurate as computer memory sizes have increased, but the problem of interpreting the digitized images remains difficult. To get an idea of the scope of the problem, compare *Figure 5-5* with *Figure 5-6*. The computer pictured in *Figure 5-5* is composed of dots, but they are arranged so densely that your brain interprets the dots as a recognizable shape. The dots in *Figure 5-6* are arranged much less densely, making the photograph more difficult to interpret. If the dots were even less dense, the photo might look like nothing more than a group of dots, not forming any recognizable image.

Figure 5-5.
The Texas Instruments
Professional Computer
Pictured Normally

*Fine dot
pattern*

Figure 5-6.
The Texas Instruments
Professional Computer
Pictured with Very Few
Dots

*Coarse
dot
pattern*

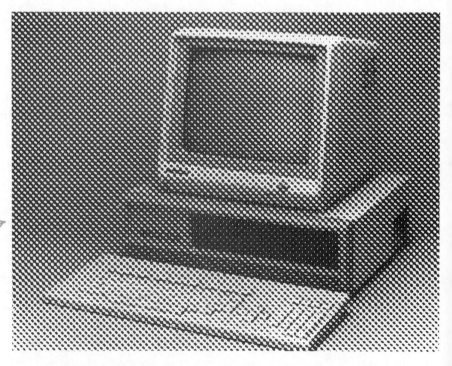

To a computer, a digitized image is *always* just a group of dots. No matter how many pixels are used to form an image, a computer cannot "step back" to gain a better perspective and somehow recognize patterns. Instead, AI techniques are used to analyze and interpret the digitized image. Computer vision systems analyze patterns to find visual "clues" that can help determine various features of the image. These clues include color, depth, texture, and motion.

Clues provided by the color and texure of an object, as well as the distances between objects, help a computer to analyze an image that it receives.

Color

Patterns of color (or, in a monochrome image, different shades of gray) can help to identify the features of objects in a visual image. An analysis of color can provide clues in the areas of hue (the color itself), saturation (the "purity" of the color), and density (intensity). In some systems, an image is divided into three separate color images—red, green, and blue—each of which can be analyzed separately to provide additional clues.

Depth

We perceive depth through a process called *binocular* (or *stereoscopic*) vision, which is possible because we have two eyes. Each of our eyes receives an image from a slightly different perspective and the dual images are processed by our brains, providing us with information about our relative distance from various objects. Using a similar process, images captured by two cameras can be analyzed by a computer to provide three-dimensional information that is unavailable through the use of a single camera.

Texture

The surface of every object has an inherent feature called its *texture*. Changes in texture may be indicated by variations in color and, if the texture is sufficiently coarse, depth; these changes may help to identify surfaces of objects.

Motion

Additional clues to the nature of objects captured by visual images can be provided by the motion of either the camera or the objects. A mobile camera capturing a series of images provides information about the same objects from various points of view; such information then can be analyzed using methods similar to those used to interpret binocular information. If one or more objects in an image are in motion, a series of images captured by a stationary camera can be used to help separate the foreground from the background and to offer clues about the features of each.

Interpreting Visual Images

Once a digitized image has been analyzed, the difficult task of identifying the components of the image begins. Several different interpretation techniques commonly are used to help the computer understand the visual image. These techniques include *edge detection* and *model-based vision*.

Edge Detection

In edge detection, a computer needs to determine where an object's edges are in order to identify it; however, various factors make it difficult to recognize the edges.

As discussed, one of the fundamental problems in speech recognition is determining where one word ends and another begins. Similarly, a basic problem in computer vision is determining where one object ends and another begins. It is difficult to identify an object if you cannot recognize its edges.

Edges that are marked by distinct changes in color (hue, saturation, and/or intensity) are relatively easy to find. However, not all edges are identified easily for reasons including the following.

- Some edges are not entirely distinct, and actually may be quite blurred.
- Because a single object may contain more than one color, every change in color does not signify the edge of an object. The boundary between colors may be so distinct that a computer may have difficulty distinguishing it from an edge.
- A shadow may cause a change in shading without necessarily signalling the edge of an object.
- An object may include different planes at various angles to the camera. Each plane may reflect a different shading depending on the direction and strength of the light source.
- All the edges of an object may not be visible. All portions of any three-dimensional object usually are not visible from any one vantage point, and parts of objects often are hidden from view by other objects.
- Determining the orientation of a vertex (a point where edges meet) is also a challenge.

Although these considerations make it more difficult for the computer to find edges, they actually may make it easier for the computer to find lines. Finding the edge of an object is not the primary goal of every computer vision system. If the system is inspecting printed circuit boards for defects, for example, it may be examining surfaces to find lines rather than attempting to identify objects. The difficulty in knowing the difference between an edge and a line may or may not be a problem, depending on the purpose of the particular vision system.

The most successful AI edge detection techniques are those that have been developed for specific domains, where the types of objects likely to be encountered are well known in advance. Research into general-purpose edge detection techniques continues in AI labs, such as those at MIT and VPI (Virginia Polytechnic Institute). Although general-purpose edge detection has not met with the degree of success enjoyed by special-purpose systems, research in that area has led to advances that have improved the quality of all types of computer vision systems.

Model-Based Vision

In model-based vision systems, the computer may use templates or descriptions of features to identify an object.

One of the speech recognition techniques mentioned previously consists of matching received sound patterns with templates of various words. Similarly, in *model-based vision*, the computer may use image templates that describe selected objects in terms of their digitized image patterns. In more sophisticated model-based vision systems, the computer uses descriptions of important *features* of selected objects, providing greater flexibility in object identification.

Model-based vision has proven to be especially effective in limited domains where the vision system is expected to recognize a restricted number of objects. However, even in limited domains, model-based vision presents several problems. The object must be isolated using edge detection and other vision techniques. Knowledge representation is also a problem because a universally acceptable method for constructing computer vision models has not yet been discovered. Generally, different forms of knowledge representation are developed for different types of applications.

Two notable model-based vision systems are:

- ACRONYM—A Stanford University system that uses algebraic and geometric reasoning to identify objects such as airplanes from aerial views, and
- VISIONS—A University of Massachusetts system that uses the "blackboard" approach developed for HEARSAY (the previously discussed speech recognition system) to identify components of typical outdoor scenes (such as streets and houses).

Applications of Computer Vision

Computer vision has been used in such applications as military navigation, inspection and testing by robots, and monitoring gauges.

In the United States, much of the computer vision research has been for military applications, including navigation and target identification. Computer vision also is being used in *robot vision* systems appearing in manufacturing environments in the U.S. and in Japan. Robot vision applications include material handling, inspection, and testing; several examples of robot vision systems are discussed later in this chapter.

Other current computer vision applications include:
- Reading printed text aloud by combining computer vision with synthesized speech;
- Monitoring gauge and sensor information, such as strip charts produced by seismographs; and
- Generating maps from aerial photographs and satellite images.

ROBOTICS

The majority of present-day robots have been programmed to perform a variety of industrial tasks.

Of the three AI technologies discussed in this chapter, *robotics* is the most advanced in terms of its actual implementation in applications that solve real problems. Robotics is the study of *robots*, which are machines that can be programmed to perform manual tasks.

The vast majority of robots in use today are designed for industrial applications, such as spot welding, spray painting, and material handling. Robots have proven to be especially useful in the automotive and electronics industries. Currently, Japan is far ahead of the United States in the implementation of robot technology; some estimates indicate that over half of the world's industrial robots currently in use are in Japan.

According to NASA's William Gevarter,[2] robots help industry achieve a variety of goals, such as:
- Increasing productivity,
- Reducing costs,
- Overcoming shortages of skilled labor,
- Providing flexibility in manufacturing operations,
- Improving product quality, and
- Freeing human beings from boring and repetitive tasks, or operations in hostile environments.

The Parts of a Robot

Most robots consist of only an "arm" and a "hand"; some also include a sensor device to tell them about their environment.

In science fiction, a robot is often a mobile machine in humanoid form. In actual practice, however, most robots emulate just a single human limb: the arm. These robots generally consist of a *manipulator* (arm), an *end effector* (hand), and a control device that *actuates* (powers) the mechanism. An "intelligent" robot also contains a sensor mechanism that allows it to receive feedback from its environment.

Manipulator

The joints (degrees of freedom) in a robot manipulator (arm) give the robot its flexibility.

The *manipulator* is the arm itself, which may be inflexible or *articulated* (jointed) with a sliding or rotary joint, like the elbow of a human arm. Each joint provides a robot with one *degree of freedom* (DOF); the more DOF's a robot has, the more potentially flexible is its operation.

---

[2] William B. Gevarter, *Intelligent Machines* (Englewood Cliffs, NJ: Prentice-Hall, 1985), p. 159.

For example, a typical manipulator might have 3 DOF's: at the "shoulder," "elbow," and "wrist" (*Figure 5-7*). A more flexible manipulator might have three DOF's in the wrist alone (*Figure 5-8*).

**Figure 5-7.
A Robot Arm with Three
Degrees of Freedom
(DOF's)**

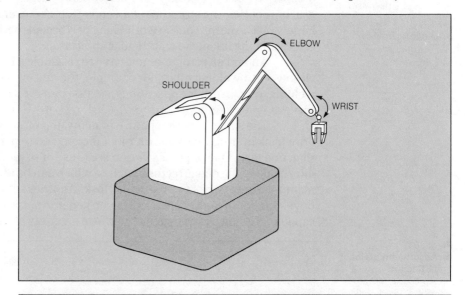

**Figure 5-8.
A Robot Wrist with Three
DOF's**

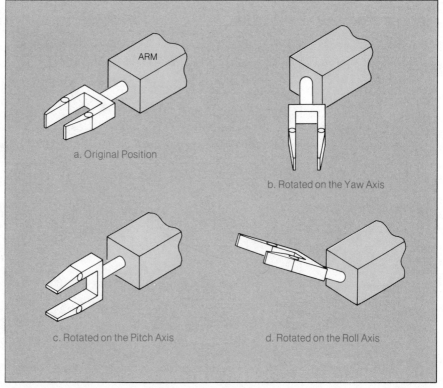

End Effector

The end effector (hand) on many robot arms is designed for a particular purpose, but can be changed to enable the robot to perform a variety of functions.

The hand attached to the manipulator is called an *end effector* or a *gripper*. While the development of a general-purpose end effector is a goal of robotics, the structure of an end effector currently depends largely on the nature of the work being performed, with each end effector being unique to a particular application.

An end effector does not have to resemble a human hand closely. On a welding robot, for example, the end effector is simply a welding tong. In other applications, suction cups or magnets may serve as end effectors (*Figure 5-9*).

The single-function nature of many end effectors can be a drawback in situations where a robot is expected to perform more than one task. One popular solution is the use of several interchangeable end effectors, each of which can be attached to the manipulator to perform a particular task. Another approach is the development of multi-function or even general-purpose end effectors, capable of being programmed to perform a variety of tasks.

Figure 5-9.
An Assortment of Robot End Effectors
(Source: Schmitt, N.M. and Farwell, R.F., Understanding Automation Systems, © 1984, Texas Instruments Incorporated)

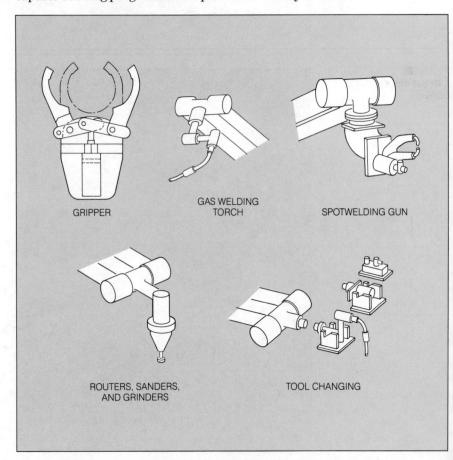

GRIPPER

GAS WELDING TORCH

SPOTWELDING GUN

ROUTERS, SANDERS, AND GRINDERS

TOOL CHANGING

One obvious method of designing a general-purpose end effector is the use of several "fingers," possibly jointed with "knuckles" like human fingers. Multifingered end effectors remain largely in the research stage. The University of Utah, the MIT AI lab, and Stanford University currently are experimenting with three- and four-fingered end effectors (*Figure 5-10*).

AI researchers are attempting to design a general-purpose end effector, possibly with several fingers.

Actuators

The device that provides the power to move the robot is known as an *actuator*. Most actuators fall into one of three categories:

- *Pneumatic* actuators tend to be clean and inexpensive. However, it is difficult to control the movement of a pneumatically actuated robot with precision.
- *Hydraulic* actuators can generate a good deal of power, but they may be messy. Like pneumatic actuators, hydraulic actuators tend to be difficult to control.
- *Electric* actuators are inexpensive, clean, precise, and reliable. However, they tend to be considerably less powerful than hydraulic actuators.

An actuator is a control device that powers the robot. The type of actuator used depends on the robot's application and environment.

**Figure 5-10.
A Multifingered End
Effector**

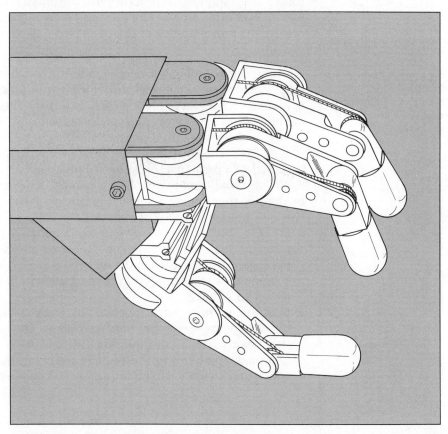

As you can see, each type of actuator has its advantages as well as its drawbacks. Thus, the type of actuator chosen for a particular application depends on the requirements of, and the environment for, that application.

Controlling a Robot

There are several different methods of controlling the *trajectory* (motion) of a robot. Depending on the nature of its control technique, a robot is classified as either a *non-servo* robot or a *servo* robot.

Non-Servo Robots

Non-servo robots may move in a straight path until something physically blocks that path.

If the trajectory of a robot is controlled strictly by inflexible, mechanical means, the robot is classified as a *non-servo* robot. This type of robot does not include a *servomechanism*, which is a device that can correct a robot's performance.

The most common type of non-servo robot uses an *open loop* technique to move from one location to another. In this technique, the robot moves at full speed in a predetermined direction until something physically blocks its path. To modify the trajectory of an open loop robot, you simply adjust the location of the physical restraints. Non-servo robots often are used for *pick-and-place* applications, which involve the transportation of objects between fixed locations.

Servo Robots

Servo robots can be given a path to follow by moving them along the path or by controlling them with a computer.

The other class of robot is a *servo* or *programmable* robot. This type of robot includes a servomechanism, which may be programmed in one of several ways. A servo robot is considered to be *intelligent* only if it can alter its own trajectory in response to feedback from a sensing device, which is typically a camera.

There are two primary techniques of programming the trajectory of a robot: *playback control* and *computer control*.

Playback control involves "training" a robot to perform a motion and then having it repeat ("play back") that action. There are two basic methods of playback control.

- *Point-to-Point Control* involves programming a sequence of points through which you want the robot to move, possibly by physically placing the robot in each of the selected positions. The robot computes the trajectories that connect the selected points and moves accordingly.
- *Continuous Path Control* involves physically moving the robot through the trajectory you want it to follow. The robot "records" the motion so that it can duplicate the trajectory subsequently. Continuous path control is especially useful for applications in which smooth motion is important, such as painting.

Although computer-controlled robots may be programmed with the continuous path method, the current trend is to program them with programming languages specifically developed for robotics. These languages include:

- WAVE—A high-level interactive language developed at Stanford University in 1971;
- AL—An experimental language developed in 1972, also at Stanford;
- VAL—A commercial implementation of WAVE developed in 1979 by Unimation, a leading American commercial robot manufacturer; and
- AML—A relatively easy-to-use language, based on AL, that was developed by IBM™ in 1980.

Other robotics programming languages include HELP (General Electric), JARS (Jet Propulsion Laboratory), MCL (McDonnell-Douglas), RAIL (Automatix), and RPL (SRI).

Intelligent Robots

Intelligent robots can alter their motions to adjust to changes in their environment by actually touching an object or using computer-vision technologies.

The primary difference between non-intelligent and intelligent programmable robots is that a non-intelligent robot simply executes pre-programmed motions, while the AI techniques used in programming an intelligent robot allow it to understand its environment and to take appropriate intelligent actions in response to various external situations.

Because it receives information about the status of its environment from a camera or other external sensing device, an intelligent robot is also called a *sensor-controlled* robot. Intelligent robots formulate and execute plans and monitor their own operation.

There are two basic types of sensory information that can be supplied to a robot.

- *Contact sensing* involves a robot sensor that physically touches another object. A contact sensor might be as simple as a switch that is triggered when it comes into contact with an object. More sophisticated contact sensors respond to force, torque, and other tactile information. A contact sensor, for example, might prevent a robot from inserting a screw that is improperly aligned.
- *Non-contact sensing* involves a robot sensor that can detect objects with which it is not in physical contact. The primary method of non-contact sensing is computer vision, which is known as *robot vision* when it is incorporated into a robot.

Robot Vision

Robot vision is a commercial implementation of the computer vision technology discussed earlier in this chapter. Philippe Villers, president of Automatix, characterizes robot vision as "the first of the widespread uses of artificial intelligence on the factory floor."[3] Model-based vision is especially useful in robotics because an industrial robot generally is programmed to recognize only a limited number of different items.

Several robot vision systems are currently in use in industrial applications, including the following.

Some of the industrial applications for robots are welding, moving parts to different locations, inspecting products, and testing and sorting products.

- Autovision, an Automatix product based on research originally performed at SRI (Stanford Research Institute), is used for applications such as welding and inspection.
- CONSIGHT™, developed and used by General Motors (GM), transfers objects from a moving conveyor belt to various locations.
- KEYSIGHT™, also a GM system, inspects automobiles for assembly defects.
- The MIC Vision Module from Machine Intelligence Corporation (MIC) recognizes specified parts and is used for inspection and various manipulation tasks. Like Autovision, the MIC Vision Module is based on SRI research.
- VAM (Vision-Aided Manufacturing), a Texas Instruments robot vision system, tests and sorts calculators on a conveyor belt.

Other industrial applications of robot vision include selecting and sorting parts, deburring and finishing, riveting, and assembling products.

Mobile Robots

Mobile robots move from one place to another by rolling, walking, crawling, or hopping.

Like people, some robots are capable of moving from place to place on their own. These *mobile robots* use a variety of methods for locomotion: some roll on wheels, others "crawl" by being pulled along by their manipulators, some "hop" on one leg, and some actually walk on four legs. (Shakey, an experimental mobile robot developed at SRI, is pictured in Chapter 2, *Figure 2-10*.)

The Robotics Institute at CMU, which houses the largest American effort in mobile robots, developed the remotely controlled mobile robot that inspected the damaged Three Mile Island nuclear reactor. In addition, mobile robots are being considered for applications in areas such as oceanic and arctic exploration, office and factory cleaning, industrial security, and crop harvesting.

The Japanese are paying particular attention to the development of fully automated machine shops that feature manufacturing processes requiring no human intervention. These shops probably would require mobile robots to transport materials and products between the more traditional robot stations.

---

[3] Philippe Villers, "Intelligent Robots: Moving toward Megassembly," in *The AI Business*, eds. Patrick H. Winston and Karen A. Prendergast (Cambridge, MA: MIT Press, 1984), p. 208.

WHAT HAVE WE LEARNED?

1. The goal of speech recognition is to allow computers to recognize and understand human speech, the form of communication with which people are most comfortable.
2. Speaker-independent recognition, which involves recognizing the speech of any speaker, is considerably more difficult than speaker-dependent recognition, recognizing the speech of a single individual.
3. Recognizing isolated words is easier for a computer than recognizing words spoken in context.
4. Computer vision systems analyze clues in the areas of color, depth, texture, and motion.
5. Model-based vision relies on stored templates to identify objects in limited domains.
6. A robot commonly consists of a manipulator (arm), an end effector (hand), and an actuator that provides power for movement.
7. Intelligent robots can alter their own trajectories in response to feedback from a sensing device such as a camera.

WHAT'S NEXT?

This chapter has explored three basic AI technologies that amplify specific human capabilities. The next chapter discusses five areas in which AI technologies are being applied.

Quiz for Chapter 5

1. Which approach to speech recognition avoids the problem caused by the variation in speech patterns among different speakers?
   a. Connected word recognition
   b. Continuous speech recognition
   c. Isolated word recognition
   d. Speaker-dependent recognition

2. Which approach to speech recognition avoids the problem caused by the differences in the way words are pronounced according to context?
   a. Connected word recognition
   b. Continuous speech recognition
   c. Isolated word recognition
   d. Speaker-dependent recognition

3. Elementary linguistic units which are smaller than words are:
   a. allophones.
   b. phonemes.
   c. syllables.
   d. a and c above.
   e. all of the above.

4. A speech recognition technique called _____ begins with the parts of a sentence that are most likely to have been interpreted correctly.
   a. allophonic analysis
   b. beam search
   c. blackboard
   d. island driving

5. Visual clues that are helpful in computer vision include:
   a. color and motion.
   b. depth and texture.
   c. height and weight.
   d. a and b above.
   e. none of the above.

6. A computer vision technique that relies on image templates is:
   a. binocular vision.
   b. edge detection.
   c. model-based vision.
   d. robot vision.

7. A robot's ''arm'' is also known as its:
   a. actuator.
   b. end effector.
   c. manipulator.
   d. servomechanism.

8. Which type of actuator generates a good deal of power but tends to be messy?
   a. Electric
   b. Hydraulic
   c. Pneumatic
   d. b and c above
   e. None of the above

9. If a robot can alter its own trajectory in response to external conditions, it is considered to be:
   a. intelligent.
   b. mobile.
   c. non-servo.
   d. open loop.

10. Programming a robot by physically moving it through the trajectory you want it to follow is called:
    a. contact sensing control.
    b. continuous-path control.
    c. pick-and-place control.
    d. robot vision control.

Other Artificial Intelligence Applications

ABOUT THIS CHAPTER

Previous chapters have discussed applications of several "basic" artificial intelligence technologies: expert systems, natural language processing, speech recognition, computer vision, and robotics. This chapter discusses other ways in which AI technology can help solve "real world" problems.

The AI applications covered in this chapter are:

- Intelligent Computer-Assisted Instruction (ICAI),
- Software Development,
- Planning and Decision Support,
- Factory Automation, and
- Office Automation.

INTELLIGENT COMPUTER-ASSISTED INSTRUCTION (ICAI)

Computers have been used in education for about 25 years, contributing to activities such as:

- Teaching students to program computers and use computer software,
- Helping students discover problem-solving strategies that also are applicable to non-computer situations,
- Having students play educational games designed to make learning an enjoyable experience, and
- Involving students in computerized instruction that can be individualized for each of them.

Computer-Assisted Instruction individualizes the instruction that a student receives.

Although each of these activities is instructional, only the last one is specifically known as *Computer-Assisted Instruction* (CAI).

Frame-Based CAI

Early CAI programs essentially imitated previously existing instructional materials. For example, a common CAI technique mirrors a method called *programmed instruction*. In a programmed instruction text, students read brief instructional material and then are presented with short questions to test their comprehension.

Students turn to different pages of the book, depending on their answers to the questions, so that each student effectively "programs" a different path through the material based on individual comprehension abilities.

A frame-based CAI program is designed to present particular material based on the student's responses to the problems presented.

The CAI technique based on programmed instruction is known as *frame-based CAI*. (This use of "frame" predates the word's use as a type of knowledge representation and is not related to that usage.) In frame-based CAI, a student responds to problems presented by the computer. The computer is programmed to react differently to possible student responses. If the student's answer is incorrect, for example, the computer might display remedial material and then pose a simpler problem.

The effectiveness of a frame-based CAI program depends entirely on how well it is designed. Special programs called *authoring systems* are available to help instructors develop frame-based CAI programs without first having to acquire extensive computer programming knowledge. Although many successful programs have been developed, frame-based CAI programs use computers simply as electronic "page-turners" and do little to bring the enormous power of computers to bear on the instructional process.

Components of an ICAI Program

Intelligent CAI programs have three components: problem-solving expertise, student model, and tutoring model.

Adding AI techniques to CAI results in an effective, new instructional method called *Intelligent Computer-Assisted Instruction* (ICAI). The goal of ICAI is the development of instructional materials that actually analyze a student's performance in order to develop individualized tutoring strategies.

According to Avron Barr and Edward Feigenbaum,[1] the main components of an ICAI system are:

- Problem-Solving Expertise,
- Student Model, and
- Tutoring Module.

The relationship between these three components is illustrated in *Figure 6-1*.

Problem-Solving Expertise

The problem-solving expertise component is the knowledge base of an ICAI program.

The problem-solving expertise component of an ICAI program contains the knowledge that the system tries to impart to the student. This expertise is represented with techniques similar to those used in the knowledge base of an expert system. In fact, this component can be thought of as a specialized expert system that contains expertise in the domain of the ICAI program. Early ICAI programs stressed the ability to generate problems from this knowledge base, a technique called *generative* CAI.

[1] Avron Barr and Edward A. Feigenbaum, *The Handbook of Artificial Intelligence*, 3 vols. (Los Altos, CA: William Kaufman, 1981-82), 2:229-235.

**Figure 6-1.
The Relationship
Between the
Components of an
Intelligent Computer-
Assisted Instruction
System**

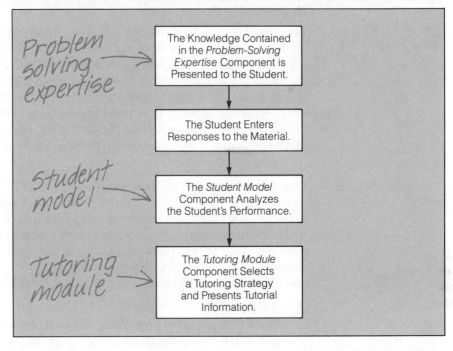

Student Model

The student model compo-
nent analyzes a student's
responses to the problems
presented.

The *student model*, a representation of the student's understanding of
the domain, is an important element of ICAI. If a student is
experiencing difficulty with certain material, the student model
analyzes the student's performance to ascertain the specific causes of
the problem. By identifying response patterns, the student model
determines the student's misconceptions and discovers the exact
causes of erroneous reasoning.

Tutoring Module

The tutoring module com-
ponent determines how
to present tutorial information.

Once the student model has determined the causes of a student's
problem, an ICAI program decides how to correct the problem. The
component of the program that selects the strategies for presenting
tutorial information to students is called the *tutoring module*. Various
strategies may be used to ensure that students understand both the
causes of their errors and the actions necessary to correct them. A
tutoring module generally incorporates natural language processing
techniques to communicate at the level of each individual student.

ICAI Programs

While the use of ICAI programs currently is not widespread, several
ICAI programs have been tested successfully in laboratory
environments. This section briefly describes four of these ICAI
programs: BUGGY, GUIDON, SCHOLAR, and SOPHIE.

BUGGY

BUGGY helps students
with arithmetic.

Developed at Bolt, Beranek and Newman (BBN) to diagnose a
student's problems with basic mathematics, BUGGY identifies and
explains a student's arithmetic misconceptions. BUGGY is based on
the assumption that many students who have difficulty solving
problems are not unable to follow procedures but rather are following
incorrect procedures. BUGGY provides a student with a series of
arithmetic problems, finds error patterns in the student's responses,
and analyzes those patterns to determine the cause of the errors.

GUIDON

GUIDON teaches medical
students.

Using the production rule knowledge base from MYCIN (see Chapter
3), GUIDON instructs medical students in the diagnosis and treatment
of bacteriological infections. Developed at Stanford University,
GUIDON conducts an interactive dialogue to present symptomatic
evidence that can help the student analyze the problem. Since it is
compatible with many rule-based systems, GUIDON can be adapted to
create instructional programs for other knowledge bases.

SCHOLAR

SCHOLAR provides in-
struction in South
American geography.

Created at BBN as part of an ongoing research project, SCHOLAR
provides instruction in South American geography. SCHOLAR uses a
semantic network (see Chapter 7) for internal knowledge
representation, where each node in the network contains properties
of a particular geographical unit. Using a *mixed initiative* natural
language interface, SCHOLAR can either respond to student questions
or initiate a line of questioning on its own.

SOPHIE

SOPHIE simulates an elec-
tronics lab.

Another ICAI program developed at BBN, SOPHIE (SOPHisticated
Instructional Environment) actually consists of two programs that
create a student learning environment. SOPHIE-I simulates an
electronics lab in which the student initiates interaction to diagnose
faulty electronic equipment. SOPHIE-II adds an educational game and
provides frame-based CAI techniques that offer the student
preliminary instructional material.

SOFTWARE DEVELOPMENT

The two primary components of a working computer system are:
- Hardware—The physical structure of the computer itself, including
  its electronic and mechanical parts; and
- Software—The programs that tell the computer what to do.

(Many computer systems also include a hybrid of hardware and
software called *firmware*, which is a program embedded in a
hardware component.)

Throughout the history of computing, the costs of computer hardware have declined continually at a dramatic rate, largely due to advances in integration (combining many electronic functions into a single component) and automated manufacturing techniques. In contrast, the development of software remains an expensive and time-consuming process because software development relies on the time and effort of professional programmers, who tend to be expensive resources.

Another area of AI research involves automating programming to reduce the time and expense involved in writing computer programs.

As computer programs have become more sophisticated, software development time has increased and programming costs have risen. The problem is especially acute in AI, which generally involves extremely sophisticated programming. It is not unusual, for example, for an expert system to require several years to develop and refine. Continual advances in the automation of hardware development have contributed greatly to the advancement of computer technology; to prevent software development from becoming a limiting factor in that advance, it too must be automated.

Artificial intelligence offers two related approaches to software automation:

- Intelligent Software Development Tools—AI programs specifically designed to help a programmer perform various phases of software development, and
- Automatic Programming—AI programs designed to develop other programs in response to a programmer's specifications.

Intelligent Software Development Tools

Some of the software development tools available to programmers are editors, debuggers, assemblers, compilers, and interpreters.

Programmers use special programs called *software development tools* to increase their productivity in various stages of the software development process. These tools include the following:

- Editors—Programs that help a programmer enter a program into the computer. Some sophisticated editors are similar to the word processing programs that are proving to be effective in office automation.
- Debuggers—Programs that help a programmer test a program, locate program "bugs" (errors), and "debug" (eliminate the bugs from) the program.
- Assemblers, Compilers, and Interpreters—Programs that translate other programs written in assembly language or in a high-level language into machine-language programs.

Although all of these tools can simplify various aspects of software development, they still may require a large amount of effort on the part of the programmer. As AI researchers themselves are often programmers, they are acutely aware of the scope of the problem from first-hand experience. It is hardly surprising, then, that one focus of artificial intelligence has been the development of *intelligent* software development tools that incorporate AI techniques into the programming process.

The Programmer's Apprentice

One project that is developing intelligent tools is the Programmer's Apprentice project, directed by Charles Rich and Richard Waters at MIT. The Apprentice concept is based on programming efficiency theories popular at IBM™ in the early 1970's. These theories suggest that a programming team should consist of an "expert" programmer and a group of programming "apprentices" and other support personnel. "We propose," says Charles Rich, "to provide every programmer with a support team consisting of intelligent computer programs."[2]

The intelligent tools being designed as part of the Programmer's Apprentice project include the following:

A knowledge-based editor, an interactive query feature, and automatic documentation are intelligent software development tools being developed by the Programmer's Apprentice project.

- Knowledge-Based Editor—A program editor that includes knowledge of a specific computer language and programming in general. Because it knows a programming language, a knowledge-based editor can identify and correct syntax errors that are entered by the programmer before they cause program execution problems. Because it possesses programming knowledge, it can actually generate sections of the program in response to brief specifications by the programmer.
- Interactive Query—A feature that allows a programmer to ask the computer questions about the execution of the program. The interactive query system simplifies the process by which the programmer traces program execution, making it easier for the programmer to diagnose program errors and to ascertain that all elements of the program are functioning correctly.
- Automatic Documentation—An extension of the query system that generates program documentation (manuals and explanations) automatically.

Other intelligent tools are under development at various AI labs to assist in programming tasks such as design, testing, and maintenance.

Automatic Programming

Several techniques are being researched to allow computer programs to "write themselves."

In a sense, intelligent software development tools are merely interim measures on the road to the ultimate AI software development goal of automatic programming. If programs were able to "write themselves," there might not be any need for programmers at all, much less for tools to increase their efficiency.

[2] Charles Rich, "The Programmer's Apprentice," in *The AI Business*, eds. Patrick H. Winston and Karen A. Prendergast (Cambridge, MA: MIT Press, 1984), p. 121.

Currently, several different approaches to automatic programming are being investigated, including the following:

- Formal Specification—Uses formal logic methodology (as discussed in Chapter 7) to specify the relationship between program input and output. AI theorem proving techniques often are used to construct the specified program.
- Specification by Example—Uses examples of program input and output supplied by the programmer. The computer employs AI techniques to analyze the examples and discover the patterns necessary to construct the program (*Figure 6-2*).
- Natural Language Specification—Uses a specification written in ordinary English, perhaps through interaction with queries from the computer. Currently, natural language specification has proven to be practical only in limited domains.

Automatic Programming Systems

Automatic programming systems assist in various stages of the software development process.

Although a general-purpose automatic programming system has yet to be developed, several systems have proven to be somewhat useful in various situations. Examples of automatic programming systems include the following:

- Protosystem I—A continuing project of the MIT computer science lab, Protosystem I is being implemented in five stages that correspond to five phases of software development: problem definition, specification analysis, implementation, coding, and compiling.

Figure 6-2.
A Sample of the "Specification by Example" Approach to Automatic Programming

Input

Output

INPUT:

NAME:		DONNA HARTLEY	JACK ADAMS	PAT FRENCH
INCOME:	JAN:	2000	2000	3250
	FEB:	2000	2100	3250
	MAR:	2000	2100	3800
	APR:	2000	2100	3800
	MAY:	2300	2100	3800
	JUN:	2300	2200	3800

OUTPUT:

EMPLOYEE NAME	—— INCOME ——		
	1Q	2Q	YTD
DONNA HARTLEY	6000	6600	12600
JACK ADAMS	6200	6400	12600
PAT FRENCH	10300	11400	21700

An Automatic Programming System Using *Specification by Example* Might Be Able to Write a Program to Produce the Necessary Transformations by Analyzing the Patterns in the Input and Output Presented Above.

- PSI—Developed by a group headed by Cordell Green at Stanford University, PSI combines several specialized programming modules into one integrated system. PSI can be thought of as a set of expert systems, each of which is designed to perform a specified portion of the software development task.
- SAFE—Developed at the University of Southern California (USC), SAFE constructs a formal program specification from an informal natural language specification written in a limited, domain-specific vocabulary. SAFE also contains a *transformation implementation module* that interactively transforms the formal specification into program code.

PLANNING AND DECISION SUPPORT

Helping you develop a plan to reach a particular goal is another area of AI research.

There is usually more than one way to solve a problem, whether in "real life" or on a computer. One of the most common and efficient problem-solving methods is to develop a *plan*, which is an ordered series of actions that are designed to produce a desired result.

If your goal is to take your family to the movies, for example, your informal plan might be to round up the family members, gather them into your car, drive to the theater, purchase tickets, enter the theater, buy refreshments, and watch the movie. If, however, your goal is to increase the revenue of your department by 10% in the next quarter, your plan is apt to be more formal; but it will nonetheless consist of a series of steps designed to lead you to your goal.

In general, AI research is devoted to discovering better ways of having computers make plans to solve problems. (The search techniques described in Chapter 7 essentially are designed to generate and investigate plans for reaching desired goals.) If AI techniques can be used to help *programs* make plans, it is not surprising that these techniques also have been used to help *people* make plans.

Planning Techniques

The two types of AI planning techniques are hierarchical, which starts at the highest level and works down to details, and non-hierarchical, which uses a single level.

The AI techniques used for planning are divided into two categories: hierarchical and non-hierarchical.

A *hierarchical* plan consists of successive representations of a plan. As illustrated in *Figure 6-3*, the "highest" representation is broad, abstract, generalized, and simplified; and the "lowest" representation is a detailed, step-by-step solution to the problem. For example, ABSTRIPS is a hierarchical planning program designed to help robots make simple plans.

A *non-hierarchical* plan is developed at only one level of representation. HACKER, a non-hierarchical program that acquires new skills, solves problems by applying procedures with which it is familiar and, if necessary, modifying those procedures.

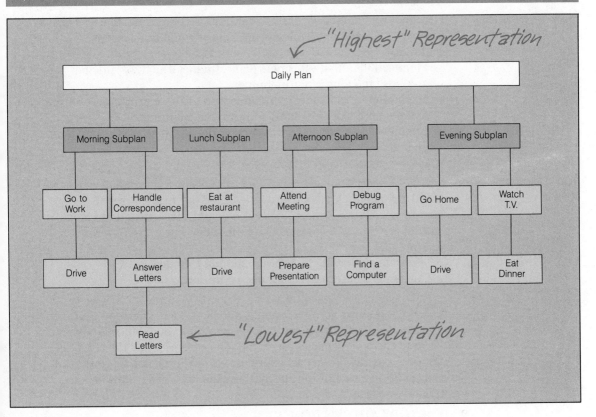

"Highest" Representation ✓

Daily Plan

Morning Subplan | Lunch Subplan | Afternoon Subplan | Evening Subplan

Go to Work | Handle Correspondence | Eat at restaurant | Attend Meeting | Debug Program | Go Home | Watch T.V.

Drive | Answer Letters | Drive | Prepare Presentation | Find a Computer | Drive | Eat Dinner

Read Letters ← *"Lowest" Representation*

**Figure 6-3.
A Hierarchical Plan of
Daily Activities**

Some decision support
programs use AI tech-
niques to help managers
evaluate information,
choose a goal, or reach a
conclusion.

Decision Support

Experimental planning programs have been designed to assist in tasks
from daily scheduling to sophisticated financial analysis. Specialized
planning programs that help managers make business decisions are
starting to become commercially available. These programs are known
as *decision support programs*.

There is not universal agreement that decision support
programs are part of AI. However, some decision support programs
use AI techniques to evaluate the relative importance of information,
choose between conflicting goals, and reach conclusions in spite of
incomplete information. A few expert system development tools are
specifically designed to help develop decision support programs; one
of these tools, Expert Ease™, is discussed in Chapter 8.

Arborist™, a decision support software package from Texas
Instruments, is designed for use with personal and professional
computers such as the TI PC and the IBM PC/XT™. Using operations-
research techniques to construct decision trees, Arborist lets you
evaluate all of the variables that contribute to the selection of the best

Arborist, a decision support software package, can help managers in a variety of business areas, including financial planning and marketing.

decision from among several alternatives. Arborist might be useful in a variety of fields that involve the making of complex decisions, including:

- Financial Planning—Business plans, financial analysis, pricing analysis, and long range planning;
- Marketing—Product introductions, corporate redirection, resource and personnel deployment, and strategic planning;
- Engineering—Risk evaluation and design approach determination; and
- Law—Questions of "litigate vs. settle."

Expert Choice is another decision support program that can help you make business decisions.

Expert Choice® , a product of Decision Support Software (DSS) of McLean, Virginia, also is designed to run on personal computers. To use Expert Choice, you build a tree-structured model of a problem (*Figure 6-4*) and specify the following:

- Your goal,
- The criteria that are factors in reaching your goal, and
- The possible alternatives for each criterion.

Then, for each alternative, Expert Choice lets you specify values for importance, preference, and likelihood. DSS feels that entering values for these intangibles amplifies your ability to make "seat of the pants" decisions—which they describe as "the ability of 'experts' to draw upon past experiences, intuition, and insight."[3] Expert Choice weighs the alternatives and offers its results in both tabular and graphic formats.

FACTORY AUTOMATION

Through AI research in factory automation, the computer can determine where decisions made in one part of the manufacturing process can affect other parts of the process.

Manufacturing is an activity in which theories of artificial intelligence are starting to be put to the test. The automation of factories is attractive as an AI "testing ground" because:

- The manufacturing process is composed of a variety of interdependent problems that have existed for many years and which are relatively well understood, and
- Factory owners often are willing to invest in the development and implementation of technology that will increase productivity and raise profits.

The power of artificial intelligence is being brought to bear on factory automation problems because, as in many human endeavors, manufacturing expertise is a scarce commodity. Because it is often difficult to achieve a comprehensive overview of the subtle interdependencies among the various manufacturing processes, decisions made in one component of the manufacturing process may have unforeseen consequences in another.

[3] *Expert Choice Office Relocation Model* (McLean, VA: Decision Support Software, 1983), p. 7-14.

Figure 6-4.
A Sample Screen from
Expert Choice Showing
the First Three Levels of
the Model for Selecting
an Office Location
(Screen Courtesy of Decision
Support Software, Inc.)

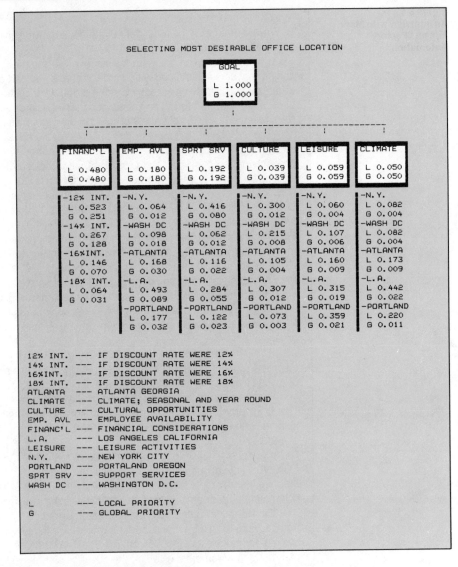

The Manufacturing Process

The seven stages of the
manufacturing process
are unique but interde-
pendent.

The manufacturing process consists of several distinct stages, each
with its own characteristics and problems. Not only does each stage of
the process have unique problems, but the interdependence of the
areas creates additional concerns. Mark Fox, head of the Intelligent
Systems Laboratory of the Robotics Institute at CMU (Carnegie-Mellon
University), discusses factory automation in *Figure 6-5.*

Figure 6-5.
An Interview with Mark
Fox on "Factory
Automation"

Q: What is the role of the Intelligent Systems Laboratory in respect to factory automation?

FOX: What we've been doing for the last five years is trying to understand how AI can impact decision making within organizations—in particular, manufacturing organizations. We've been looking at the product life cycle, because in order to understand manufacturing and decisions that take place in manufacturing, you have to understand the life of the product in the organization.

The first step is that somebody conceives of a product. Then, somebody designs a product based on that conception. Somebody then plans production to produce that product. Somebody then actually produces it. Somebody then distributes it to customers. Somebody then supports it or services it in the field. Now, all of that comes back to "how can AI impact that product life cycle?"

Q: If AI is applicable to decision making in general, why have you chosen to focus on manufacturing?

FOX: Because we understand manufacturing. The problems are very clear there, in many cases. Manufacturing has been around for a long time. You can clearly identify that there are a lot of problems with a lot of payoffs. Manufacturing is interesting because any type of problem that you could possibly conceive of exists somewhere in a manufacturing organization. There are high-level management decision makers, engineers, professionals, technicians, hourly workers—every type of skill exists somewhere in the organization.

If I had focused my attention solely on the decision making of the *directors* of an organization, I would have failed because I would have broken a cardinal rule of AI: if you can't define the inputs for the decision, can't define the outputs, or don't have an expert, it is going to be very difficult for you to build the system. That is the problem of high-level management decision making—the inputs are ill-defined, the outputs may be ill-defined, and there may not be demonstrated expertise.

Q: Do you plan to use expert systems to solve manufacturing problems?

FOX: Very little of our work is in expert systems. Our work focuses on AI theories. For example, we conduct research in the area of job-shop scheduling—theories of *constraint-based reasoning* are the focus of our work.

Think about all of the different types of information that somebody uses in trying to construct a factory schedule: who's here today, what tooling is available, what are the cost constraints from the controller, what are the marketing requirements, what are the advance planning requirements that certain facilities be used, what is the status of the jobs on the factory floor—all these factors go into the decision as to what your schedule is going to be. We call these factors *constraints* because they *constrain* the decision that you're going to make.

Fox divides the manufacturing process into the stages shown in *Figure 6-6*. As illustrated, project management is a challenge that relates to each stage of the manufacturing process and to the process as a whole. (Note: The remainder of this section is adapted from

**Figure 6-6.
The Stages in the
Manufacturing Process**

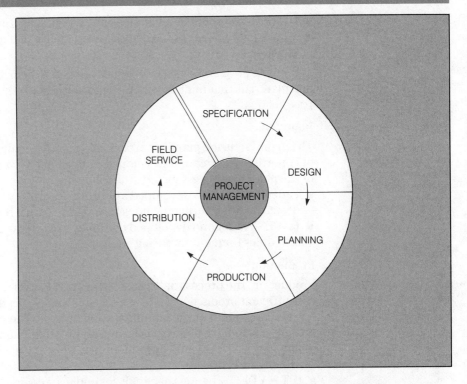

material presented in *Artificial Intelligence in Manufacturing* by
Mark S. Fox.[4])

Specification

With AI programs, the
specification stage, which
defines the product to be
manufactured, can be
conducted interactively.

Specifications, which define the function and form of products, are
frequently poorly executed. This results in problems throughout the
remainder of the steps in the manufacturing process. XCALIBUR and
XSEL, a pair of AI programs jointly developed by CMU and DEC
(Digital Equipment Corporation), use AI natural language techniques
to help develop specifications interactively.

Design

AI programs can aid in
design, a creative stage of
the process.

Design, "the mapping of function onto form,"[5] is a creative process
that is often poorly structured. Artificial intelligence programs, such
as the following, continue to be developed to assist in various phases
of the design process.

- EL™—An MIT program that analyzes and checks electronic circuit
  design.

[4] Mark S. Fox, *Artificial Intelligence in Manufacturing* (Pittsburgh: Intelligent
  Systems Laboratory, Robotics Institute, Carnegie-Mellon University, 1984).
[5] Ibid., p. 8.

- HI-RISE—A program developed at CMU that helps design buildings.
- VT—A joint project of CMU and Westinghouse that assists in elevator design.

AI programs also are being developed to help select designs and materials that minimize manufacturing costs without sacrificing product quality.

Planning

In the planning stage, programs can help in many ways. Factory layout and maintenance schedules are examples.

The manufacturing planning process frequently requires a good deal of expertise. AI programs developed to assist in the various elements of the planning process include the following.

- Fades—A program developed at Purdue University that helps design manufacturing facilities to maximize work-floor utilization.
- RACE—A program developed by Honeywell to plan maintenance schedules for manufacturing equipment.

Production

Robots and other AI products are improving production efficiency.

Production, the process of "transforming raw materials into a quality, cost-efficient product,"[6] is the most visible and perhaps the most critical component of the manufacturing process. The field of robotics is beginning to have an increasing impact on production efficiency. AI technology also is affecting production in other ways, as indicated by the following programs.

- IDT—A DEC program that analyzes and tests computer systems.
- IMACS—A program developed by CMU and DEC for scheduling and monitoring production operations.
- ISIS—A factory scheduling system developed by CMU and Westinghouse that evaluates conflicting factors and constructs job-shop schedules. (ISIS is described briefly in Chapter 3.)

Distribution

AI programs can help organize the distribution of products.

No matter how well a product is specified, designed, planned, and produced, it will not remain a viable product for long if it is poorly distributed. INET, a joint project of CMU and DEC, uses AI simulation and analysis techniques to help organize product distribution.

Field Service

AI programs also provide customer service support.

The manufacturing process does not end once the product has been sold. The continued servicing of the product and the customer is a critical element of the manufacturing cycle. AI programs that assist in product installation, maintenance, and repair include the following.

- ACE—A program developed by Columbia University and Bell Labs to diagnose problems with telephone transmission cables.

[6] Ibid., p. 21.

- CATS—A program used by General Electric (GE) to diagnose problems in locomotives.
- Dart—A joint project of Stanford University and IBM that diagnoses computer system faults at customer sites.
- PDS—A Westinghouse program that monitors sensors to identify process problems.
- XSITE—A program developed by CMU and DEC to help plan the installation of computer systems at customer sites.

Management

Project management programs based on AI technologies are available.

All of the aforementioned manufacturing activities have one thing in common: to succeed, they must each be managed effectively. AI programs have been developed to assist in various aspects of project management, including forecasting and short- and long-range planning. Callisto, a joint project of CMU and DEC, helps perform various management activities, including the following:

- Generating plans,
- Creating schedules,
- Monitoring project status,
- Allocating resources,
- Managing inventory, and
- Evaluating decisions.

OFFICE AUTOMATION

AI programs to automate offices are starting to be developed.

Unlike *factory* automation, where AI already is beginning to have a presence, the impact of AI in *office* automation is not yet a commercial reality. Because it is such a large potential market, however, it is likely that AI office automation products will start to appear in the near future.

According to Boston-based Brattle Research Corporation,[7] there are five "product opportunity areas" for AI in office automation:

- Administration and Managerial Support,
- Job Training and Support,
- Improved Man/Computer Dialogue,
- Intelligent Information Management and Text Searching, and
- Speaker-Independent Speech Understanding Systems.

Administration and Managerial Support

AI programs could help with budget preparation, resource allocation, and employee evaluations.

AI can be used for project management in an office environment just as it is being used in factory automation. Expert systems with natural language interfaces could expedite and objectify the processes of preparing budgets, allocating resources, and evaluating employees, to name just a few areas that tend to be extremely time-consuming and

---

[7] Brattle Research Corporation, *Artificial Intelligence and Fifth Generation Computer Technologies* (Boston), p. 236.

subjective. AI programs also might help to avoid delays by suggesting new schedules and alerting managers to unanticipated problems.

Job Training and Support

ICAI programs might have an impact in educating people at all levels.

The progress in ICAI discussed earlier in this chapter has yet to make its way into the commercial marketplace. However, the Department of Defense is investigating the use of intelligent tutors to train administrative personnel. Such programs also may be used in office automation for employee training, especially in areas requiring technical skills. In fact, the impact of ICAI programs may be greater in corporate environments than in educational institutions, as corporations often have greater financial resources at their disposal.

Improved Man/Computer Dialogue

Natural language interfaces could make it easier for managers to use computers.

As discussed in Chapter 4, natural language processing can make computers much easier to use. In an office environment, where managers typically may not be knowledgeable about computers, natural language interfaces might encourage more managers to take advantage of the power of computers by making computers appear to be "less arbitrary, inflexible, and inscrutable."[8]

Intelligent Information Management and Text Searching

AI programs have the potential to evaluate information and give managers only what is pertinent.

As personal computers continue to proliferate throughout the business world, the amount of information available to businesspeople grows proportionately. Personal computers actually may be contributing to "information overload" instead of helping to solve it. Experimental projects are investigating the implementation of AI techniques to search through large amounts of data and "weed out" extraneous information, presenting managers only with items of predetermined interest.

Speaker-Independent Speech Understanding Systems

Speech understanding systems could be applied in several areas of an office environment.

As discussed in Chapter 5, a goal of AI technology is to build computers capable of understanding the natural speech of any individual. Although this goal may not be attainable in the near future, speech understanding systems may soon appear for limited applications, such as the following suggested by Brattle Research:[9]

- Information entry and access,
- Processing commands,
- Directory assistance,
- Message routing,
- Scheduling,
- Voice mail addressing, and
- Dialing.

[8] Ibid., p. 239.
[9] Ibid., p. 242.

WHAT HAVE WE LEARNED?

1. An intelligent computer-assisted instruction (ICAI) program analyzes a student's performance and develops individualized tutoring strategies to identify and correct learning problems.
2. Although intelligent software development tools assist programmers in various stages of the programming process, the ultimate goal of automatic programming is to allow programs to "write themselves."
3. Decision support programs can help managers make intelligent business decisions.
4. AI theories are being applied to several areas of factory automation, including specification, design, planning, production, distribution, field service, and project management.
5. Although the use of AI techniques in office automation is not yet a commercial reality, there may be large potential markets in several product opportunity areas.

WHAT'S NEXT?

This book now has discussed the basic concepts and history of artificial intelligence and has provided overviews of prominent areas of AI applications. The next chapter explores the technical aspects of AI and focuses on symbolic processing, including discussions about AI programming, knowledge representation, and search techniques.

Quiz for Chapter 6

1. The CAI technique based on programmed instruction is:
   a. frame-based CAI.
   b. generative CAI.
   c. intelligent CAI.
   d. problem-solving CAI.

2. The component of an ICAI program that selects strategies for presenting information to the student is the:
   a. problem-solving expertise.
   b. student model.
   c. tutoring module.
   d. all of the above.
   e. none of the above.

3. Which of the following are examples of software development tools?
   a. Editors
   b. Debuggers
   c. Assemblers, compilers, and interpreters
   d. All of the above
   e. None of the above

4. Which technique is being investigated as an approach to automatic programming?
   a. Generative CAI
   b. Specification by example
   c. Non-hierarchical planning
   d. All of the above
   e. None of the above

5. Which kind of planning consists of successive representations of different levels of a plan?
   a. Hierarchical planning
   b. Non-hierarchical planning
   c. Project planning
   d. All of the above
   e. None of the above

6. Decision support programs are designed to help managers make:
   a. visual presentations.
   b. budget projections.
   c. business decisions.
   d. vacation schedules.

7. What part of the manufacturing process relates to each stage of the process and to the process as a whole?
   a. Design
   b. Distribution
   c. Field service
   d. Project management

8. What stage of the manufacturing process has been described as "the mapping of function onto form"?
   a. Design
   b. Distribution
   c. Field service
   d. Project management

9. In which of the following areas may ICAI programs prove to be useful?
   a. Corporations
   b. Educational institutions
   c. Department of Defense
   d. All of the above
   e. None of the above

10. For speech understanding systems to gain widespread acceptance in office automation, they must feature:
    a. speaker independence.
    b. speaker dependence.
    c. isolated word recognition.
    d. all of the above.
    e. none of the above.

Symbolic Processing

ABOUT THIS CHAPTER

The first computers were built to process *numbers* in order to perform mathematical calculations with speed and accuracy far surpassing human capabilities. Yet nearly from the beginning of the computer revolution, computer scientists have been trying to improve the performance of computers in an area that has proven to be significantly more difficult than "number crunching," something that many think is a key element of human intelligence: processing *symbols*.

This chapter explains the difference between *symbolic* processing and the more traditional *numeric* processing, and discusses symbolic processing programming languages specifically designed for artificial intelligence applications. Special attention is focused on LISP, the programming language invented by John McCarthy in 1958 which is the most popular symbolic processing language currently in use.

Some of the techniques used by AI programmers to represent knowledge in a computer are introduced in this chapter; and the important concept of *search*, the systematic exploration of possibilities, is discussed.

PROCESSING NUMBERS

Numeric processing is performed on digital computers, which are based on the binary number system. In this system, instructions are sent to the computer as a series of zeros and ones.

At the most basic level, all information in a modern electronic computer is represented by the presence or absence of voltage in a circuit. At any given time, a circuit in a computer either has an electrical current flowing through it or it does not. A computer circuit is like a *relay*, an electrical switch that can be either on or off, *not* half on (or half off).

A system like this, featuring separate and distinct states, is called a *digital* system; computers based on this system (as all modern electronic computers are) are called *digital computers*. The two states of a circuit—off and on—often are represented by the digits zero and one, the two digits of the binary number system. Even the most powerful and sophisticated computers are based on this binary system. Therefore, the inner workings of all computers can be analyzed, at the lowest level, in terms of zeros and ones.

Binary Systems and Digital Computers

Alan Turing created a machine based on Boole's binary system of mathematical logic. The same concepts were applied to the first computer, Harvard's Mark I, and to the current generation of computers based on VLSI (Very Large Scale Integration) technology.

In the middle of the 19th century, George Boole developed the system of mathematical logic that bears his name. One of the features of Boolean algebra is that it is a binary system, representing logical processes with just two digits, zero and one.

In 1937, Alan Turing drew on Boole's work to show that a "binary" machine could be programmed to carry out any algorithmic task. This hypothetical "Turing Machine" could perform only two actions, drawing and erasing a mark on a paper tape. In the same year, Claude Shannon concluded that you could achieve similar results with electrical relays. In fact, the first computer, Harvard's Mark I built in 1943 (*Figure 7-1*), used relays to perform mathematical computations.

Electronic technology has improved tremendously since 1943. ENIAC, the second digital computer, took advantage of the electronic switching capability of vacuum tubes to replace the relays used in Mark I; computers based on vacuum tubes are called *first generation* computers. The second generation of computers was based on transistors; the third generation featured integrated circuits (IC's). The "fourth generation" of computers is based on the sophisticated integrated circuit techniques of VLSI (Very Large Scale Integration) technology.

Figure 7-1.
The Mark I Computer
(Photo Courtesy of Cruft Photo Lab, Harvard University)

A single, tiny VLSI "chip" may contain hundreds of thousands of circuits—each of which either does not have current or has current, is off or on, zero or one. As you can see, although the *technology* has improved, the *concept* remains the same. The digital binary system of logic proposed by Boole and extended by Turing and Shannon remains the theoretical basis of every digital computer, from the "primitive" Mark I to today's most sophisticated supercomputers.

PROCESSING SYMBOLS

To be truly intelligent, digital computers must be able to process symbols.

The binary number system lends itself very nicely to numerical calculations. However, even before the first computer was built, scientists had speculated about using binary computing devices to process information "intelligently." Numeric processing, the first stage of computer evolution, was not seen as an especially intelligent activity; after all, it had been accomplished on crude mechanical devices, like the abacus, for centuries. To be truly intelligent, it was felt that a computer must be able to process not only numbers, but also symbols.

If a digital computer can only "understand" binary numbers, how can we use computers to process letters and words? How can a computer process symbols?

Character Codes

Symbols are represented with codes which use only zeros and ones, the digits in the binary number system.

One simple way in which a computer can process symbols is by using a system of codes to represent letters and other characters. You already may be familiar with Morse code, a coding system that is widely used to represent letters. Morse code uses various combinations of just two symbols, a dot and a dash, to represent all the letters of the alphabet (*Figure 7-2*).

**Figure 7-2.
The Alphabet in Morse Code**

Letter	Code	Letter	Code
A	• —	N	— •
B	— • • •	O	— — —
C	— • — •	P	• — — •
D	— • •	Q	— — • —
E	•	R	• — •
F	• • — •	S	• • •
G	— — •	T	—
H	• • • •	U	• • —
I	• •	V	• • • —
J	• — — —	W	• — —
K	— • —	X	— • • —
L	• — • •	Y	— • — —
M	— —	Z	— — • •

Computers use a binary code system to represent letters and other symbols. The code most commonly used today is called *ASCII* (American Standard Code for Information Interchange); another computer code system, used mostly by IBM™, is called *EBCDIC* (Extended Binary Coded Decimal Interchange Code). In ASCII, for example, each eight-digit binary number is also a code representing a letter or other character.

Programming languages such as COBOL, which were developed for numeric processing, include limited capabilities for symbolic processing.

When computers began to be used in the business world, it was important that a *programming language* be developed that could process letters as well as numbers. COBOL (COmmon Business Oriented Language), the most widely used business programming language, has this capability; however, the symbolic processing capability of a language like COBOL is elementary, at best. It can compare two names to determine if they are identical, for example, and it can sort a list of names in alphabetical order. But we don't consider this crude kind of symbolic processing to be much more intelligent than numeric processing. The computer may be able to put names in order, but what does it really "know" about those names? Does it even "understand" that they are names? Or what a "name" is?

Clearly, to perform the kind of symbolic processing that we would consider "intelligent," it would be helpful to have a programming language with greater symbolic capabilities than COBOL. Before we explore some of the programming languages that were developed specifically for sophisticated symbolic processing, let's briefly discuss exactly what a programming language is.

Programming Languages

The three levels of programming languages are machine language, assembly language, and high-level language.

A *program* is a list of instructions that a computer follows in order to perform a specific task. A program must be written in a *programming language*, a set of symbols that can be processed by the computer. Programming languages usually are grouped into the following three levels.

- Machine Language—Programming a computer by giving it instructions in the 0's and 1's of binary code is called *machine language* programming because you are programming in the only language that the machine directly "understands."
- Assembly Language—To simplify the task of programming, an *assembly language* uses short words and numbers that are translated into the 0's and 1's of machine language by a special program called an *assembler*. Assembly language is called a *low-level language* because each individual assembly instruction is "assembled" into one machine language instruction.

- High-Level Languages—In a *high-level language*, the instructions you give the computer more closely resemble English, making it easier for you to tell the computer what you want it to do. Each program instruction may be translated into many machine language instructions, further expediting the program-writing process. Commonly used high-level languages include BASIC (Beginner's All-purpose Symbolic Instruction Code), COBOL (COmmon Business Oriented Language), FORTRAN (FORmula TRANslator), and Pascal.

Samples of computer instructions written in each of the three levels of programming languages are provided in *Figure 7-3*.

Compilers and Interpreters

Programs written in a high-level language typically are coverted into machine language by a compiler or an interpreter.

There are two types of special programs that generally are used to translate programs written in high-level languages into machine language so that they can be executed by the computer.

- A *compiler* generates a new copy of the entire program in machine language. Then, the compiled program can be executed by the computer, one instruction after another.
- An *interpreter* translates each instruction into machine language one at a time when that instruction is ready to be executed by the computer.

Each method has its advantages. Using a compiler is somewhat slower during the process of developing a program because the entire program must be compiled each time you change or add to the program. However, a compiled program is executed quicker than an interpreted program because it has previously been converted into machine language in its entirety. An interpreted program must be translated at "run time" (while the program is being executed).

PROGRAMMING FOR ARTIFICIAL INTELLIGENCE

A particular programming language usually is designed for a specific type of application.

Although it may be *possible* to write many programs in any programming language, certain languages are designed to execute certain kinds of programs with maximum efficiency. FORTRAN is useful especially for mathematics and science; COBOL is intended for business use; BASIC has a combination of simplified features specifically designed to be attractive to beginners.

**Figure 7-3.
Samples of Machine-Language, Assembly-Language, and BASIC Instructions**

Language	Instruction
Machine Language	1010001011000110
Assembly Language	ADD R6,R11
BASIC	LET GRAND.TOTAL=GRAND.TOTAL+PREVIOUS.TOTAL

In general, the languages devised for other purposes have not proven to be especially efficient for writing AI programs. The techniques of numeric programming, for example, are not very useful in simulating intelligence. For the most part, AI programmers have had to develop their own programming languages to allow them to manipulate symbols more efficiently.

The languages designed for AI programming are referred to as symbolic processing programming languages.

These special AI languages are known as "symbolic processing programming languages" or some variation thereof (such as "symbol processing languages," "symbol manipulation languages," "list processing languages," or just "AI programming languages"). The most prominent AI language is John McCarthy's venerable LISP, but there are other important languages used in AI. Although LISP has a lengthy history for a computer language, it was not the first programming language developed for artificial intelligence—that distinction is reserved for IPL.

IPL (Information Processing Language)

The first language developed for AI programming was IPL.

The Logic Theorist, often considered to be the first AI program, was developed by Allen Newell, J. C. Shaw, and Herbert Simon in early 1956. Before they could create the Logic Theorist, however, Newell, Shaw, and Simon had to find a programming language that would let them represent the symbolic concepts they were trying to program.

The only language that seemed even remotely suitable was a language that they had created earlier for writing a program to play chess—a language that they had informally named IPL (Information Processing Language). Following the success of the Logic Theorist, Newell, Simon, and Shaw wrote another classic AI program in IPL: the General Problem Solver.

Five versions of IPL—dubbed IPL-I through IPL-V—were actually developed at various times. IPL, a fairly low-level programming language, was somewhat difficult to use; widespread use of IPL has since been supplanted by a higher level, more convenient AI language: LISP.

Several popular features of symbolic processing languages originated with IPL. One such feature is that of a *generator*, a process that computes or retrieves a series of values, one at a time. For example, if you construct a generator to retrieve the names of customers in Georgia from a database, the generator retrieves the name of a different Georgia customer each time you use it (until all the names of your Georgia customers have been retrieved).

A critically important symbolic programming concept that was first implemented in IPL is *association*. In our minds, we relate groups of symbols to each other in various ways. An intelligent program also must be able to establish associations between symbols, not merely store them as unrelated pieces of data.

Lists

Symbolic processing languages associate symbols by representing them as a list, which consists of a series of cells.

The technique used by IPL to represent associations between symbols is a structure called a *list*. The processing of symbols in list structures, an arrangement that originated with IPL, is perhaps the most important concept of symbolic processing. In fact, the name of the most popular symbolic processing language, LISP, is an acronym for "LISt Processor." Symbolic processing languages in general are sometimes referred to as "list-processing" languages.

A list is represented in the memory of a computer as a series of *cells* (*Figure 7-4*). Each cell can contain two parts, or *fields*. In a simple list, one field contains a symbol and the other field contains a pointer to the next cell in the list. In a more complex list (such as in LISP), each cell can contain a *pointer* to a symbol or to the next cell.

Because each cell can contain a pointer to the next cell, the cells that comprise a list do not have to occupy consecutive locations in the computer's memory. The cells actually can be scattered throughout the memory of the computer; yet because each cell points to the next cell, the symbols in the list are firmly associated.

Figure 7-4.
Lists as They are
Represented by Cells and
Pointers

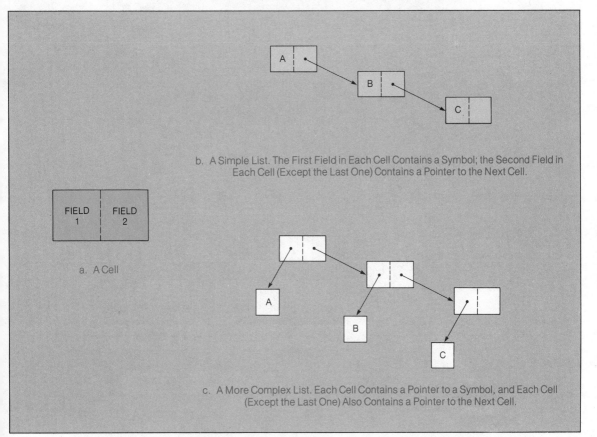

b. A Simple List. The First Field in Each Cell Contains a Symbol; the Second Field in Each Cell (Except the Last One) Contains a Pointer to the Next Cell.

a. A Cell

c. A More Complex List. Each Cell Contains a Pointer to a Symbol, and Each Cell (Except the Last One) Also Contains a Pointer to the Next Cell.

In symbolic processing, a list can change in size and shape as a program executes.

One problem that was solved neatly by using lists is that of not knowing the size or "shape" (structure) of your data at the time you write a program. Many programming languages require that you identify in advance the exact size and structure of the data that will be processed by the program so that the computer can allocate memory for that data. However, because each cell can point to other cells, a list can be *dynamic*; that is, its size and shape can change continually throughout the execution of the program (*Figure 7-5*).

**Figure 7-5.
A Dynamic List**

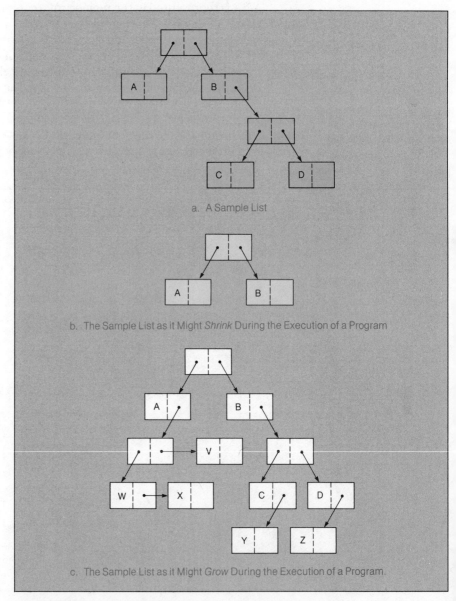

a. A Sample List

b. The Sample List as it Might *Shrink* During the Execution of a Program

c. The Sample List as it Might *Grow* During the Execution of a Program.

LISP (LIST PROCESSOR)

At MIT in 1958, John McCarthy proposed the development of an AI program, the Advice Taker, that would use the techniques of formal mathematical logic in order to make deductions and exhibit "common sense." Because the Advice Taker could not be implemented efficiently in any existing programming language, McCarthy designed his own programming language.

Although its specification has provided direction for many AI researchers, McCarthy's Advice Taker program actually has never been implemented. However, the programming language he created to facilitate the development of the Advice Taker has developed into the premier AI programming language and the most widely used symbolic processing language in the world; it is now the second oldest programming language (after FORTRAN) currently in widespread use. That language is, of course, LISP.

The Features of LISP

The original versions of LISP provided several features that made it an extremely attractive programming language for artificial intelligence, including, of course, its use of the list as a data structure. As LISP has continued to develop over the years, additional features have been implemented that have further increased its usefulness.

Recursion

A *list* in LISP is a sequence of *elements*, where each element may be either an *atom* (a single object) or another list. Notice that the word *list* is part of its own definition; that is, a *list* may be a sequence of *lists*. When a definition of a term includes the term itself, that definition is said to be *recursive*; in more general terms, an item is recursive if it includes itself.

LISP is not only recursive in the definition of its data structure but also in the programming techniques it allows. For example, the two-part mathematical definition of the factorial of a positive integer is as follows.

- The factorial of 1 is 1.
- The factorial of an integer greater than 1 is that integer multiplied by the factorial of the next lower integer (the integer minus 1).

Note that to calculate the factorial of a number, you must first calculate the factorial of the next lower number; to calculate the factorial of *that* number, of course, you must first calculate the factorial of the next number lower than *that* number, and so on. The recursive factorial process ends when you reach the factorial of 1, which is defined as 1. At that point, you can finish calculating the rest of the factorials and obtain the desired result (*Figure 7-6*).

**Figure 7-6.
The Recursive
Calculation of the
Factorial of 3**

Assume that you want to calculate the factorial of 3. According to the definition, the first problem you would have is

$$3! = 3 \times 2!$$

To solve this, you would first need to solve the following:

$$2! = 2 \times 1!$$

Since by definition the factorial of 1 is 1, you can now work your way back up, substituting as you go.

$$2! = 2 \times 1! = 2 \times 1 = 2$$
$$3! = 3 \times 2! = 3 \times 2 = 6$$

Therefore, the factorial of 3 is 6.

Some programming languages do not allow recursion; that is, you could not use the above technique to calculate the factorial of a number. LISP, on the other hand, facilitates the use of recursion, an important technique in intelligent problem solving.

Programs as Data

The design of LISP allows one LISP program to be used as data for another LISP program.

A LISP program is itself a LISP list. This means that a LISP program can be treated as data by another program or even by itself. The benefits of this unique approach include the following.

- Because LISP data and program instructions are in exactly the same format, information about the properties of an object (*declarative* knowledge) can be integrated easily with information about what actions to perform (*procedural* knowledge).
- A LISP program can actually modify its own program instructions— or add entirely new instructions to itself. It even is possible for a given LISP program to write an entirely new LISP program. This is especially helpful in an AI program that is learning to perform a new task.
- LISP programs can easily keep track of which instructions have been executed, how often each has been executed, and in what order they have been executed. This is a valuable feature for expert systems, because they often are expected to explain how they have arrived at their conclusions.

Interactive Interpreter

LISP programs are interpreted as they execute. Since AI programming is a trial-and-error process, this expedites the development of AI software.

Since LISP is an *interpreted* language, the LISP interpreter translates each instruction into machine language as it is needed to execute the program. This eliminates the waiting time that would be required if it were necessary to *compile* the entire program each time a change were made. As the development of intelligent programs is frequently a trial-and-error process, being able to test program changes quickly is an important benefit. (To allow a completed program to execute more quickly, LISP compilers also are available.)

LISP also was designed as an *interactive* language. Before LISP, the typical method of executing a program was for you to run a stack of punched cards through the computer's card reader. The computer would execute your program and provide you with a printout of the results. In contrast, a LISP program interacts with the programmer in every phase of development, greatly facilitating experimentation with new programming techniques. LISP programs also can be interactive while they are executing, so they can obtain any additional information needed to solve a problem.

Programming Environment

Many development tools exist for LISP, thus expediting the development process further.

One enormous advantage that LISP enjoys over other symbolic languages is that it has been around for a long time and has been used extensively in a large number of AI research labs. This has resulted in the development of programming "environments"—groups of programs that expedite program development and execution—that are unmatched by any other AI programming language.

Features of a programming environment include software "tools" such as a text editor (to enter program instructions), a debugger (to help find and correct programming errors), and a windowing system (to display various aspects of the program at the same time). Numerous sophisticated LISP software tools are available for several programming environments, many of which were developed by ingenious AI "hackers" to assist in their own advanced research. (See Chapter 9 for a more detailed discussion of LISP programming environments.)

The Elements of LISP

Although LISP has been used to create some of the most sophisticated computer programs ever written, the basic structure of LISP is fairly straightforward.

Atoms

An atom, which is a number or symbol, is the smallest unit in LISP.

The smallest unit in LISP is the *atom*. An atom may be a number or a symbol. For example, the following may be LISP atoms.

```
5            +      CONS           TEXAS_INSTRUMENTS
65.7         *      CDR            IS_SMARTER_THAN
.00786       R      INTELLIGENCE   QWERTYUIOP
```

The atoms in the first column are *numeric atoms* or just *numbers*. The rest of the atoms listed above are *symbolic atoms* or *symbols*.

Lists

Lists in LISP consist of atoms or other lists.

A *list* is a series of atoms or lists, enclosed in parentheses. The following are examples of LISP lists.

```
(+ 5 954)
(.00786 N CHAIR TEXAS-INSTRUMENTS)
(ANIMALS (HERBIVORES (COWS SHEEP) CARNIVORES (LION TIGER)))
```

In the last list, notice that the lists (COWS SHEEP) and (LION TIGER) are themselves elements of this larger list.

```
(HERBIVORES (COWS SHEEP) CARNIVORES (LION TIGER))
```

That list, in turn, is one of the two elements of the main list (the atom ANIMALS is the other element). Atoms and lists collectively are often called *symbolic expressions* or just *expressions*.

Procedures

A procedure is the element in a list that indicates what is to be done; the other elements are the arguments for the procedure.

A *procedure* is an element in a list that specifies how something is to be done. If present, a procedure is always the first element in a list. The remaining elements, the data with which the procedure is to work, are the *arguments*. A LISP *program* is simply "a collection of procedures intended to work together."[1]

Some procedures, called *primitives*, are built into LISP. For example, in the list (+ 3 5), + is a primitive that specifies the action to take with the arguments 3 and 5. Of course, the procedure + indicates addition; the result of evaluating the expression (+ 3 5) is 8.

Other procedures are defined by the programmer with the DEFUN (DEfine FUNction) primitive. For example, the following expression is the definition of FACTORIAL, a procedure that uses the recursive method we discussed previously to compute the factorial of a positive integer.

```
(DEFUN FACTORIAL (N)
(COND ((= N 1) 1)
(T (* N (FACTORIAL (- N 1)))))))
```

[1] Patrick Henry Winston and Berthold Klaus Paul Horn, *LISP* (Reading, MA: Addison-Wesley, 1984), p. 17.

Once you have defined the FACTORIAL procedure, LISP can evaluate expressions that use that procedure. For example, the result of evaluating the expression (FACTORIAL 5) is 120.

Symbol Manipulation

Some of the LISP primitives used for symbol manipulation are CAR, CDR, SET, and CONS.

Although it is far beyond the scope of this book to teach you how to write LISP programs, a quick introduction to a few basic symbol-manipulation primitives will give you some idea of how you can use LISP to work with lists.

> **NOTE: Each expression in the following examples includes at least one quote mark ('), which has an important purpose in the evaluation of LISP expressions. However, the use of the quote mark is not explained in this discussion and should be ignored.**

CAR: The CAR primitive retrieves the first element of a list, as in the following examples.

Expression	Value
(CAR '(A B C))	A
(CAR '((A B) C))	(A B)
(CAR (CAR '((A B) C)))	A

In the second example, notice that CAR retrieves the list (A B), which is the first element of the list ((A B) C). Also notice, in the final example, that you can use more than one CAR at a time; "nested" expressions are evaluated one at a time, starting from the innermost parentheses and working out (*Figure 7-7*).

**Figure 7-7.
Evaluation of a CAR
Example**

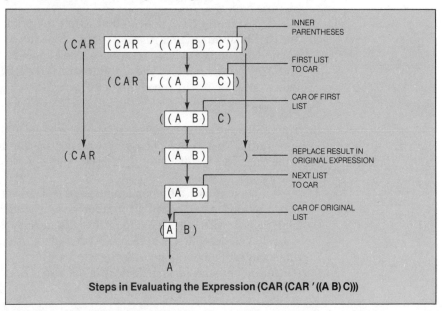

Steps in Evaluating the Expression (CAR (CAR '((A B) C)))

CDR: The CDR primitive, the complement of the CAR primitive, retrieves all but the first element of a list, as in the following examples.

Expression	Value
(CDR '(A B C))	(B C)
(CDR '((A B) C))	(C)
(CDR (CAR '((A B) C)))	(B)

Notice that the final example includes both a CDR and a CAR. The CAR is evaluated first because it is in a deeper level of parentheses.

SET: The SET primitive assigns a value to a symbol, as in the following examples.

Expression	Symbol	Value
(SET X 'A)	X	A
(SET SIGNS '(STOP SLOW))	SIGNS	(STOP SLOW)
(SET JIM (CAR '(A B C)))	JIM	A

Notice that, in the final example, the CAR expression must be evaluated before a value can be assigned to the symbol JIM.

CONS: The CONS (CONStruct) primitive inserts a new element at the beginning of a list, as in the following examples.

Expression	New List
(CONS 'A '(B C))	(A B C)
(CONS '(A B) '(C D))	((A B) C D)
(CONS 'YIELD SIGNS)	(YIELD STOP SLOW)

Notice that, as illustrated in *Figure 7-8*, the final example assumes that the symbol SIGNS has the value assigned to it previously in the SET examples.

(You may have noticed that, while the primitive names CONS and SET bear an obvious relation to the procedures they perform, the names CAR and CDR have no apparent relevance to their tasks. CAR and CDR are remnants of the architecture of the IBM 704 computer on which John McCarthy developed LISP.)

Dialects of LISP

The various versions (dialects) of LISP are divided into two groups, called "East Coast" LISP and "West Coast" LISP.

The LISP programming language is being revised and improved constantly. Frequently, changes are made in different places at the same time; as a result, several different versions of LISP currently are in widespread use.

Just as with a human language, different versions of a programming language are often referred to as *dialects*. The various LISP dialects all have basic similarities, but most of them are not entirely "compatible." Therefore, a program written in a particular dialect of LISP does not necessarily work with any other LISP dialect. (Different versions of a particular dialect also may not be entirely compatible.)

**Figure 7-8.
Evaluation of a CONS
Example**

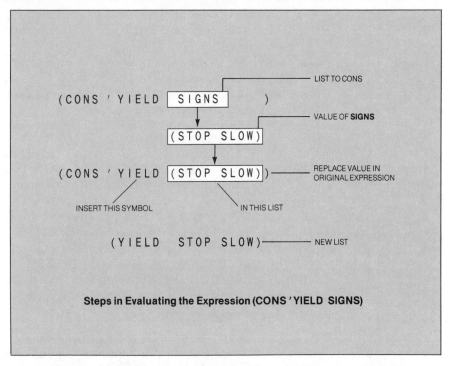

Steps in Evaluating the Expression (CONS 'YIELD SIGNS)

The currently popular LISP dialects can be divided into two major groupings: "East Coast" LISP and "West Coast" LISP.

East Coast LISP

The East Coast LISP dialects are based on a version of LISP developed at MIT. The standard dialect for East Coast LISP is Common LISP.

The East Coast LISP dialects descended from a version of LISP, called *MacLISP*™, created in the MIT AI Lab. (*MAC*, the name of an early MIT AI project, stands for Machine-Aided Cognition or perhaps Man And Computers. "The acronym was deliberately ambiguous," according to AI historian Pamela McCorduck, "because no one knew which direction the research would take."[2])

In an attempt to ensure that the developing East Coast LISP dialects maintain at least a modicum of compatibility, a standard LISP called *Common LISP* has been proposed and widely accepted in the East Coast LISP community. *ZetaLISP*™, a widely-used extension of Common LISP, runs on several popular "LISP machines," including the Symbolics 3600™ and the LMI Lambda™. Lower cost and more compact Common LISP's, such as *GC-LISP*™ (Golden Common LISP), have been developed for the IBM PC™ and PC "compatibles."

---

[2] Pamela McCorduck, *Machines Who Think* (New York: Freeman, 1979), p. 247.

Other current East Coast LISP's include:

- C-LISP (Conversational LISP), from the University of Massachusetts;
- Franz LISP™, from the University of California at Berkeley;
- NIL (New Implementation of LISP), from MIT;
- PSL (Portable Standard LISP), from the University of Utah;
- SCHEME™, from MIT; and
- T (True), from Yale University.

West Coast LISP

Although the West Coast LISP dialects are based on a version of LISP developed by a company in Boston, the developers of that version moved to the west coast.

West Coast LISP originated, oddly enough, in the Boston-area AI firm of Bolt, Beranek and Newman (BBN). When a large portion of the BBN organization headed west to work at the Xerox™ Palo Alto Research Center (PARC), they took their LISP development effort with them.

The best-known version of West Coast LISP is a Xerox product called *InterLISP*™ (INTERactive LISP). Designed to run on the Xerox 1100 series of LISP machines and on the DEC™ VAX™, InterLISP features an outstanding programming environment with many convenience features for the experienced AI programmer.

OTHER AI PROGRAMMING LANGUAGES

LISP is not the only language used for AI programming.

LISP is currently the overwhelming favorite among the programming languages used for artificial intelligence, especially in the United States. There are, however, other AI languages that enjoy varying degrees of popularity, both in the United States and abroad. These languages include:

- POP-2, from the University of Edinburgh;
- PROLOG (PROgramming in LOGic), from the University of Marseilles;
- SAIL (Stanford Artificial Intelligence Laboratory), from Stanford University; and
- Smalltalk™, from Xerox PARC.

These AI programming languages and others have been developed to implement specific techniques of solving AI problems. PROLOG is the only AI language other than LISP that is widely used.

PROLOG (PROgramming in LOGic)

Another symbolic processing language is PROLOG, which uses predicate calculus to solve problems.

Developed in France in 1973, PROLOG is a popular language for AI research in Europe. PROLOG also is used extensively in Japan, where it has been adopted as the official AI programming language of the Fifth Generation Project.

As its name implies, PROLOG relies on the use of logic to solve problems. PROLOG is basically what is known as a "theorem-proving system," using a formal logic technique known as "predicate calculus" to prove the truth of propositions from a set of axioms. PROLOG is a much simpler programming language than LISP, but many programmers do not feel that PROLOG offers the tremendous flexibility that is one of the hallmarks of LISP.

In the United States, PROLOG often is used as an "add-on" to LISP, offering several features that can help LISP programs resolve certain types of problems. Many American AI researchers do not believe that PROLOG is an acceptable general-purpose substitute for LISP in serious AI research. In *Figure 7-9* and *Figure 7-10*, Bruce Buchanan of Stanford University and Doug Lenat of MCC discuss the choice between LISP and PROLOG.

**Figure 7-9.
An Interview with Bruce Buchanan on "LISP vs. PROLOG"**

Q: Why is PROLOG used in Europe and Japan?
BUCHANAN: In Europe, they have not had the tools we've had for the last 20 years. They've had to work with much smaller machines; LISP requires much more memory than PROLOG.

The Japanese have a somewhat different reason. LISP was so identified with AI research in the U.S. over the last 25 years that, as a matter of national pride in their flagship Fifth Generation Computer Project, they had to find some other vehicle. I don't think that is a good scientific reason at all.
Q: Doug Lenat says that the Japanese have spent the last two years adding extensions to PROLOG so that it looks just like LISP. Was that a reasonable way to proceed?
BUCHANAN: That was a silly exercise as far as I'm concerned. I had a similar experience with a person who worked for me. He said that he could create AI systems in FORTRAN, and he did. But one of the first things he did was implement list processing and recursion in FORTRAN; he needed the tools that LISP already provides.

Leonard Bernstein was once asked what the difference was between his music and Beethoven's, and Bernstein said, "Well, we use the same notes—just in a different order." That applies to AI too. We are using data structures and programming techniques that are well known in computer science, but there is a somewhat different approach to problem solving in LISP.

People who have been programming in FORTRAN for 25 years don't think that there is anything new that they can't do. And, of course, the answer to that is that they're right. Of *course* you can do any of this in other languages—it just may take twice as long.

**Figure 7-10.
An Interview with Doug
Lenat on "LISP vs.
PROLOG"**

Q: How does PROLOG differ from LISP?

LENAT: There has been a constant dream in AI, by a large fraction of people in the field for 25 years, of the form: there really ought to be some way of formalizing and axiomatizing human thought and reason. But time and time again, all attempts at axiomatizing things have led people to trivialize them, to the point where they no longer apply to what they originally were modeled after in the real world.

There are a lot of people in the field who want to be *sure*, who want to believe that they can get absolutely precise, logically guaranteeable models that are close to what is going on in the real world. If you believe that, then the kinds of operations you want as primitives are *logical* operations, those involved simply in *theorem proving*. Those are the sort of operations that are present in PROLOG.

Q: Why is PROLOG used more in Europe than in the United States?

LENAT: In most European countries, you have very rigid hierarchies of "ancient" professors, and then younger professors, and then research associates—and then it filters down about seven levels to the people actually writing the programs. It is the people at the top who decide what research is going to get done, not the people at the bottom who have experience with what is actually happening.

The people at the top—who want to be believe in a nice, simple, mathematical, axiomatizable universe—basically determine the kind of research that is going to get done. The experiences that would lead them to change their minds are simply not occurring to them; they are occurring to the people at the bottom, who have no say.

Q: Is PROLOG used in the Japanese Fifth Generation Project for the same reason?

LENAT: In Japan, they use PROLOG mainly because it is not an American language; it adds to their national spirit and pride to be removed from what is going on in America. But if you look real hard, what the Japanese have done is to build LISP-like functions on top of PROLOG so that by now it is hard to tell what language they are using. They would have probably been about two years ahead if they had used LISP to start with instead of PROLOG.

KNOWLEDGE REPRESENTATION

One feature common to all AI programs is that they all involve *knowledge*. Knowledge is just as essential an ingredient to the artificial intelligence of a computer as it is to the natural intelligence of a person. In the simplest terms, if you don't know much—whether you're a person or a computer—you simply are not very smart.

The two types of knowledge that need to be represented in a computer are declarative knowledge and procedural knowledge.

What kinds of things do we know? Or, in other words, what kinds of knowledge do we have?

- Declarative Knowledge—We know facts about objects, about events, and about how they relate to each other.
- Procedural Knowledge—We know how to do things, how to use our declarative knowledge, and how to figure things out.

If computers are to be as intelligent as humans, they also must contain a great deal of declarative and procedural knowledge. The nature of human knowledge is only poorly understood, making it difficult to synthesize on a computer; and indeed, the problem of how best to represent knowledge in a computer has been a key question throughout the history of artificial intelligence.

At the present time, there is no acknowledged "best" way to represent knowledge. "It is not yet possible to prove that one scheme captures some aspect of human memory better than another," claim Barr and Feigenbaum. "There is no *theory of knowledge representation*. We don't know why some schemes are good for certain tasks and others not. But each scheme has been successfully used in a variety of programs that do exhibit intelligent behavior."[3]

Several common knowledge representation "schemes" are discussed in this section, including logic, semantic networks, and production systems. Frames and scripts, two methods of knowledge representation that are especially useful for natural language processing, are explored in Chapter 4.

Logic

The formal logic systems used to represent declarative knowledge in AI are propositional calculus, predicate calculus, and first-order predicate calculus.

Symbolic systems of mathematical logic were developed long before the computer was invented. Logic, the precise system of reason and deduction codified by the ancient Greeks, has proven to be relatively straightforward to implement on a computer; computers are, after all, based on theories of mathematical logic.

As you may remember from our discussion of PROLOG, logic-based AI systems are relatively easy to develop. Unfortunately, although computer architecture is conducive to the use of formal logic, logic is somewhat limited as a method of knowledge representation. As you probably recognize instinctively, people simply do not use logic alone to regulate their behavior; only a limited portion of intelligent human behavior can be described in terms of logic. (For example, the process of *instinctive recognition*, as suggested in the previous sentence, certainly is not based on logic.)

[3] Avron Barr and Edward A. Feigenbaum, *The Handbook of Artificial Intelligence*, 3 vols. (Los Altos, CA: William Kaufman, 1981-82), 1:147.

Essentially, an AI program that uses logic to represent knowledge views its domain as a group of logical formulas. By applying a strict set of *inference rules* to its knowledge base, the program may be able to draw the desired conclusions.

The systems that form the basis of formal logic in AI are *propositional calculus* and an extension of propositional calculus called *predicate calculus*. The formal logic system most often used for AI is a variant of predicate calculus called *first-order predicate calculus*.

Propositional Calculus

Propositional calculus is an elementary system of formal logic that is used to determine whether a given *proposition* is true or false. If you begin with statements with known "truth values" (true or false), propositional calculus provides a step-by-step inference system for proving the truth values of related statements (*Figure 7-11*).

Predicate Calculus

Propositional calculus helps you determine if a proposition is true or false. Predicate calculus adds the capability of specifying relationships and making generalizations (*Figure 7-12*).

**Figure 7-11.
An Inference in
Propositional Calculus**

Suppose that you begin with the following two statements.
■ Garfield is a cat.
■ If Garfield is a cat, then he is a mammal.

If we assume that both of these statements are true, then a propositional calculus *inference rule* called *modus ponens* tells us that the following statement also must be true.
■ Garfield is a mammal.

**Figure 7-12.
A Generalization in
Predicate Calculus**

Predicate calculus lets you start with statements like these.
■ Garfield is a cat.
■ All cats are bigger than all mice.
(Notice that the second statement includes generalizations: "All cats" and "all mice"; and a relationship: "are bigger than.")

If these two statements are true, predicate calculus lets you draw the following conclusion.
■ Garfield is bigger than all mice.

First-Order Predicate Calculus

Adding *functions* and several other analytical features to predicate calculus creates *first-order* predicate calculus. A *function* is a logical construct that "returns" a value; for example, an *is-owned-by* function applied to *Garfield* might return *John*. A list representing that knowledge might look like this.

```
(IS-OWNED-BY(GARFIELD JOHN))
```

Using first-order predicate calculus, you could create an AI program of which you might ask "Who owns Garfield?" If the system's knowledge base included the appropriate information and an *is-owned-by* function, it could tell you that John owns Garfield (Garfield *is-owned-by* John).

Logic in AI

The use of formal logic to represent knowledge was introduced in the very first AI program, the Logic Theorist. Less formal systems of logic also enjoy some degree of popularity in AI.

Fuzzy logic, for example, is designed to handle concepts that are relative and approximate, like *tall*, *expensive*, and *normal*. Fuzzy logic promotes constructions like "somewhat tall" or "moderately expensive," descriptions that are anathema to formal logic but which seem to be analogous to human thinking.

Semantic Networks

Declarative knowledge also can be represented graphically by a semantic network, where related facts are connected by links in the network.

When you're trying to define complex interrelationships in a knowledge base, the clearest way to represent those relationships may be to draw a graphic representation called a *semantic network* or a *semantic net*. For example, *Figure 7-13* is a simple semantic net depicting the knowledge about Garfield discussed in the previous section.

In structural terms, a semantic net consists of a group of *nodes*, representing facts, connected by *links* (or *arcs* or *edges*), representing relationships. The nodes of the semantic net in *Figure 7-13*, for example, are labeled GARFIELD, JOHN, CAT, MAMMAL, and MOUSE; the links are labeled IS-OWNED-BY, IS-A, and IS-BIGGER-THAN-A.

You can use a semantic net to simplify the process of deduction. For example, in *Figure 7-13* it is readily apparent that Garfield is a mammal and is bigger than a mouse, even though there is no direct link connecting the GARFIELD node to the MAMMAL and MOUSE nodes. In English, you might reason like this: "A cat is a mammal and is bigger than a mouse; Garfield is a cat; therefore, Garfield is a mammal and is bigger than a mouse." In a semantic net, discovering the relationships is considerably simpler: all you have to do is follow the arrows.

**Figure 7-13.
A Simple Semantic
Netwok**

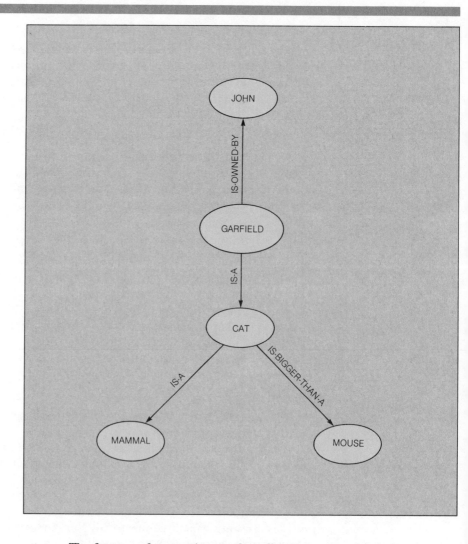

The feature of semantic nets that allows you to make that kind of obvious deduction is called *property inheritance*. A cat has the properties of being a mammal and being bigger than a mouse; since Garfield is a cat, he inherits those properties. An AI program using this semantic net for knowledge representation would have no trouble, for example, answering the question, ''Is Garfield bigger than a mouse?''

For a domain that includes a great deal of knowledge with complex interrelations, a semantic net can provide the foundation of a sophisticated inference system. Semantic nets have been used for knowledge representation in expert systems such as SRI's Prospector, which has proven to be successful in predicting the location of mineral ores.

Production Systems

Production systems represent procedural knowledge as production rules that tell these systems what to do with the facts in their knowledge base.

Logic and semantic networks are *declarative* or *object-oriented* systems of knowledge representation; they are useful for representing facts about objects and how those objects relate to each other. When you're trying to create an AI program such as an expert system that can recommend a course of action, it may be more efficient to use a *procedural* system of knowledge representation—one that contains not only facts but also includes knowledge of what to do with those facts.

Currently, the most popular procedural system of knowledge representation in expert systems is the *production system*, which uses *production rules* to represent procedural knowledge about the actions to take in specified situations. Expert systems that use production systems to represent knowledge are sometimes called *production-rule-based systems* or *rule-based systems*.

Production rules are formal representations of heuristics. For example, you might have a personal heuristic that could be stated as a production rule as follows.

IF the chance of rain is higher than 50%, THEN take an umbrella.

There are two basic clauses of every production rule.

Production rules consist of a condition clause and an action clause.

- The *condition* clause, or *left-hand side*, of a production rule begins with IF and specifies the condition that must exist. The condition in the example above is "IF the chance of rain is higher than 50%."
- The *action* clause, or *right-hand side*, of a production rule begins with THEN and specifies the action to take if the condition exists. The action in the example above is "THEN take an umbrella."

The current popularity of rule-based systems originated with MYCIN, the medical expert system discussed extensively in Chapter 3.

Production System Advantages

Some of the advantages of using a production system to represent knowledge in an expert system are:

- Explanation—All that is necessary to explain the "reasoning" of a rule-based system is to keep track of the rules that are "fired" (invoked) in the decision-making process.
- Modification—In a rule-based system, it is relatively simple to modify the knowledge base by adding, deleting, or changing the appropriate rules.
- Understanding—Knowledge in the form of production rules is extremely readable so that even someone who is unfamiliar with a program can often understand it.

SEARCH

When you have a problem to solve, you may consider several alternative solutions to determine the best way to attain your goal.

If the problem is relatively simple, your planning process may be largely subconscious and informal. If your goal is to cross a crowded room quickly, for example, you may just begin to walk in the approximate general direction, making quick decisions about avoiding obstacles as you go.

A more complex problem may demand a more conscious and formal planning process. If, for example, your goal is to drive from Los Angeles to New York, you might draw several possible routes on a highway map, consider the advantages and disadvantages of each route, and select a route after weighing the alternatives.

When solving a problem, AI programs start in an initial state and attempt to reach some goal state. To determine which path to follow to a goal, a search technique is used.

In an AI program, of course, there is no such thing as an "informal" planning process. Simulating any intelligent act, even one that is instinctively simple for a human, requires the definition of a formal procedure to determine a course of action. In artificial intelligence, you begin with an *initial state* and attempt to reach a *goal state*. The process of sifting through alternative solutions to proceed from the initial state to the goal state is called *search*; the realm of all possible avenues of exploration is the *search space*. Much of the history of AI research has been devoted to discovering more efficient search techniques, and many advances in AI have resulted from investigating new methods of limiting the search space.

Game Trees

One way to represent the area to be searched is with a search tree. A type of search tree is the game tree, where the starting position is at the top of the tree and the winning position(s) is at the bottom.

One common way of graphically representing search space is an inverted "tree" structure called a *search tree*. One typical search tree, known as a *game tree*, dates back to the early days of AI research when much attention was focused on computer game playing. Analyzing AI techniques in terms of game playing is a helpful tool because a game has a known starting position (initial state), a set of formal rules (search space), and a well-defined completion criterion (goal state). Unlike much intelligent activity, games are easily formalized.

For example, consider a relatively simple game such as tic-tac-toe (*Figure 7-14*). The initial state is an empty tic-tac-toe board, and the goal state is one of several winning positions consisting of three markers in a row. If you have the first move and you are playing X, there are nine possible places you can draw your first X. These nine *nodes* (possible moves) define the search space at the first *level* of the game tree.

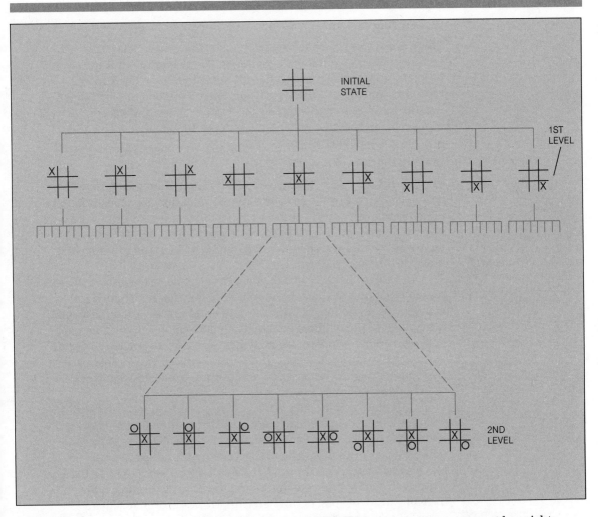

INITIAL
STATE

1ST
LEVEL

2ND
LEVEL

**Figure 7-14.
A Tic-Tac-Toe Game Tree
Through the Second
Level**

For each of your possible first moves, your opponent has eight places in which to draw an O. As you can see, the tree begins to *branch* very rapidly; on the second level alone, there are 72 (9 times 8) nodes, already making it difficult to represent the search tree graphically.

The progression advances more rapidly at each level; the third level consists of 504 (72 times 7) nodes. The problem caused by the geometric expansion of possibilities at each level of the tree is known as *combinatorial explosion*.

Search Techniques

There are several basic search techniques that you can use; the technique that you choose might depend on the nature of the problem. Just as there is no generally accepted ''best'' way to represent knowledge, there is no guaranteed method to select the most efficient search technique. Two of the considerations are:

- Whether to search breadth first or depth first, and
- Whether to chain forward or backward.

Breadth First vs. Depth First

A search can be breadth first, where all of one level is evaluated before the next level is searched, or depth first, where the search starts at the top and goes to a position at the bottom. In either type, the search ends when a goal state is reached.

In a *breadth-first* search, you evaluate every node at a given level before advancing to the next level. The evaluation may consist merely of determining if any of the nodes at the current level satisfies the goal state; if you reach the goal state, of course, the search is over. The tic-tac-toe game tree search illustrated in *Figure 7-14* is an example of a breadth-first search.

Due to the effects of combinatorial explosion, a breadth-first search is not practical when the goal state may not be attained for many levels. In tic-tac-toe, since no game can extend past nine levels, it is not out of the realm of possibility for a computer to consider each of the several hundred thousand nodes necessary to reach a goal state. In a game like chess, however, there are about 10^{120} different board positions (nodes); a computer conducting an extensive breadth-first search would never make a move.

If your search space is many levels deep, a depth-first search might be a better choice than a breadth-first search. In a *depth-first* search, you select a node at the first level, descend to one of the nodes that branches from that node to the next level, and so on, until you reach a terminal node (*Figure 7-15*). A *terminal-node* is a node from which you cannot proceed; in a tic-tac-toe game, a terminal node ends the game in a win, loss, or draw. If a depth-first search reaches a terminal node that does not satisfy the goal state, you return to the initial state and follow a different path to a new terminal node.

Forward Chaining vs. Backward Chaining

The search also can go forward from the initial state to the goal state or backward from the goal state to the initial state. Some programs use bidirectional search, starting at both ends and meeting in the middle.

In our tic-tac-toe example, we started from an initial state and progressed toward a goal state. This is an example of a search technique called *forward chaining*, which is generally considered to be a sensible approach when there are fewer possible initial states than goal states, as in tic-tac-toe.

Figure 7-15.
Depth-First Search on a
Tic-Tac-Toe Game Tree

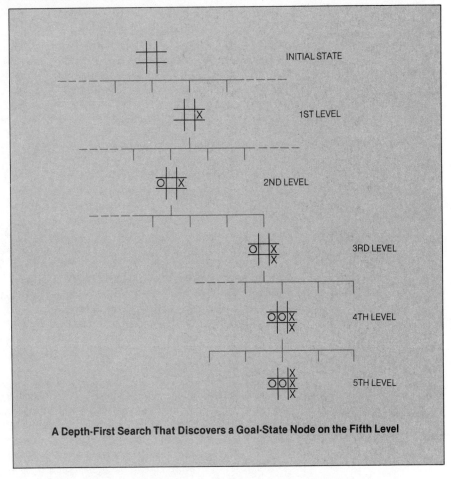

A Depth-First Search That Discovers a Goal-State Node on the Fifth Level

In the reverse situation, where there are few goal states and many initial states, it may make more sense to start from your goal and work back toward an initial state, a technique called *backward chaining*.

In actual practice, many AI programs use a combination of the two chaining techniques: a *bidirectional search*. Simultaneous searches are initiated from the initial state and the goal state; when the two searches meet at a common node, the search process ends.

Doug Lenat discusses the implications of forward and backward chaining in *Figure 7-16*.

**Figure 7-16.
An Interview with Doug
Lenat on "Forward and
Backward Chaining"**

Q: Can you explain the concept of *search*?

LENAT: Let's assume that at a given moment you have a particular goal. There are several actions that are open for you to take; after you take any one of those actions, you will be in a different state than you are in right now, and again there will be several actions open to you. You can think of achieving a goal as simply taking one action after another until that goal is achieved.

You would like to be able to plan the sequence of actions that you ought to take in order to reach your goal. For instance, in order to become a famous lawyer, you had better first become a lawyer; in order to do *that*, you had better go to law school; in order to do *that*, you had better go to undergraduate school, get good grades, take the right kinds of courses, and so forth.

Q: Is the process you just described an example of backward chaining?

LENAT: Yes, that's right. The most natural way for most people in a case like that would be to start with the goal and reason backward to the state you would have had to be in just before that, or to what *action* you would have had to take; then you have a new, shorter-term goal. Finally, you get down to "that means I really ought to study tonight instead of going out with the gang to see a movie."

Q: Could you use forward chaining in that situation?

LENAT: You could say, there are several things I could do tonight. One is to go to the movies. One is to watch TV. One is to study for this exam tomorrow. There are probably thousands of things you could do tonight; and, having done each of them, there are probably thousands of other things you could do tomorrow.

Q: And I would have to figure out which of them is most likely to lead me down the road to becoming a famous lawyer?

LENAT: You wouldn't know offhand, so you'd have to keep all those thousands of things in mind somehow; and for each one of those things, consider the thousand things you could do tomorrow—so now you are up to about a million. Finally, after something like 10 trillion or so of these thoughts, you are out 10 years in the future, and along one of the paths you are a famous lawyer. You look back and say, "Well, that all started when I studied tonight for my test."

So why is that silly? It is silly because its searches are very "branchy." If the branching factor (the number of options) is very, very high in one direction, you don't want to search in that direction; you want to search in the other direction so hopefully the branching factor won't be as high.

Pruning the Search Tree

Since a search tree can be very large, heuristic strategies have been developed to reduce the size of a tree by pruning it.

The search techniques that we have discussed are not necessarily intelligent. Whether you chain forward or backward, breadth first or depth first, if your search technique consists only of evaluating every node until you reach a goal state, you are using what is called the *generate-and-test* method to perform a *blind search*.

If your search space is small, a blind search may be an acceptable technique; as you have seen, it does not take a computer very long to explore all of the several hundred thousand possible nodes of a tic-tac-toe tree, for example. For a more complex game, such as chess, a blind search is not efficient. In a "real-life" situation requiring the emulation of human intelligence, conducting a blind search through an immense search space may be totally impractical.

Faced with complex situations and an abundance of alternatives in everyday life, we manage to reject certain avenues of exploration and concentrate on a few promising alternatives. In artificial intelligence terminology, we reduce the size of our search space by "pruning" the search tree. Even in chess, the experts do not consider every possible move; somehow, they are able to focus instinctively on a small number of moves in order to examine a relatively small search space.

Computers, of course, do not have instincts. Instead, AI scientists have devised *heuristic* strategies to help intelligent programs prune search trees and arrive more efficiently at intelligent solutions.

Heuristic Search

The concept of *heuristic search* is one of the foundations of artificial intelligence. A heuristic, of course, is a "rule of thumb"; the following definition shows how that term is applied to the search process:

> "**A *heuristic* is a rule of thumb, strategy, trick, simplification, or any other kind of device which drastically limits search for solutions in large problem spaces. Heuristics do not guarantee optimal solutions; in fact, they do not guarantee any solution at all;** *all that can be said for a useful heuristic is that it offers solutions which are good enough most of the time.*"[4]

Edward A. Feigenbaum and Julian Feldman, *Computers and Thought*

Four of the heuristic search techniques used in AI programs are difference reduction, hill climbing, minimax, and static evaluation.

The following are a few of the heuristic search techniques that are commonly used in AI programs.

- Difference Reduction ("Means-Ends" Analysis)—A *difference reduction* technique combines forward- and backward-chaining techniques to lessen the distance between the current node and the goal state by setting "subgoals."

For example, there may be a heuristic that you know (by backward chaining) would attain your goal state, but you might not be able to apply that heuristic from the current node. However, there may be a nearby node from which you *could* apply that heuristic. Using difference reduction, you would set aside your ultimate goal for the time being and concentrate on trying to reach the closer subgoal.

[4] Edward A. Feigenbaum and Julian Feldman, *Computers and Thought* (New York: McGraw-Hill, 1963), p. 6.

The difference reduction procedure is applied repeatedly to divide the problem into smaller and smaller subproblems. Each subproblem should have a much smaller search space than the original problem and thus be easier to solve. When all of the subproblems have been solved, the main problem also is solved.

- Hill Climbing—There are several ways to enhance the generate-and-test procedure to make it more intelligent than just a blind search. In the *hill climbing* technique, you begin by testing nodes in order, just as you would in a blind search. In a blind search, you merely check each node to see if you have reached a goal state; if you have not, you move on to the next mode.

  Using hill climbing, each time you discover that the node you are testing does not satisfy the goal state, you calculate the difference between that node and the goal state. By comparing the calculated differences, you can determine if you are moving closer to the goal state or further away from it. If you are moving away from the goal state, you can "backtrack" and select a new path.

- Minimax—The *minimax* procedure is a method of pruning a two-player game tree. In simple terms, nodes are evaluated according to both what would be of *maximum* benefit to you and result in *minimum* benefit to your opponent.

- Static Evaluation—Combinatorial explosion is a major problem in a breadth-first, forward-chaining search. However, if each node is somehow *evaluated* and the low-scoring nodes eliminated, the search space can be dramatically reduced.

  The type of evaluation depends on the particular problem. In chess, for example, a board position can be evaluated in terms of relative piece strength, control of the center, and other criteria.

By their very nature, heuristic search techniques are not foolproof: they do not *guarantee* the best solution—or even any solution at all. What heuristic searches do provide are intelligent methods of approaching problems, methods that are considerably more likely to bear fruit than the "trial-and-error" approach of a blind search.

WHAT HAVE WE LEARNED?

1. Although computers originally were developed to process numbers, the processing of symbols generally is considered to be a more "intelligent" activity.
2. Although many computer languages can be used for AI programming, special symbolic processing languages like IPL are designed specifically to expedite AI programming.
3. LISP, the most popular AI programming language in the United States, uses list structures and recursive techniques to facilitate the development of AI programs.

4. Other AI programming languages, such as PROLOG, are popular in the United States and abroad.
5. AI programs frequently represent a great deal of knowledge, in the form of both declarative and procedural knowledge.
6. There is no generally-accepted means of representing knowledge; instead, various forms of knowledge representation have been used, including logic, semantic networks, and production systems.
7. In artificial intelligence, a *search* is the process of proceeding from an initial state to a goal state.
8. AI search techniques include breadth-first and depth-first search, forward and backward chaining, and various forms of heuristic search that can be used to prune a search tree.

WHAT'S NEXT?

This book has discussed some of the technologies that comprise AI and has introduced you to symbolic processing, the technical underpinning of artificial intelligence. The next chapter introduces you to expert system development tools, software products specifically designed to expedite the process of developing expert systems.

Quiz for Chapter 7

1. The "Turing Machine" showed that you could use a/an _____ system to program any algorithmic task.
   a. binary
   b. electro-chemical
   c. recursive
   d. semantic

2. The first AI programming language was called:
   a. BASIC.
   b. FORTRAN.
   c. IPL.
   d. LISP.

3. In AI programming, a *list* may contain:
   a. cells.
   b. fields.
   c. pointers.
   d. all of the above.
   e. a and c above.

4. LISP was created by:
   a. John McCarthy.
   b. Marvin Minsky.
   c. Allen Newell and Herbert Simon.
   d. Alan Turing.

5. In LISP, the _____ primitive assigns a value to a symbol.
   a. CAR
   b. CDR
   c. CONS
   d. SET

6. PROLOG relies on _____ to solve problems.
   a. declarations
   b. logic
   c. schemes
   d. all of the above
   e. b and c above

7. Property inheritance is one aspect of a _____ that simplifies the process of deduction.
   a. fuzzy logic system
   b. production system
   c. semantic network
   d. none of the above

8. The clause on the right-hand side of a production rule is called the _____ clause.
   a. action
   b. condition
   c. IF-THEN
   d. procedure

9. Reasoning from a goal state towards an initial state is called a _____ search.
   a. backward-chaining
   b. bidirectional
   c. breadth-first
   d. heuristic

10. In which of the following situations might a blind search be acceptable?
    a. Complex game
    b. Real-life situation
    c. Small search space
    d. None of the above

Expert System Development Tools

ABOUT THIS CHAPTER

As discussed in Chapter 3, the process of developing an expert system can be extremely time consuming. This chapter explores special programs designed to expedite that process: expert system development tools. Several popular development tools are examined; and special attention is given to the Personal Consultant, a set of expert system development tools from Texas Instruments.

THE IMPORTANCE OF DEVELOPMENT TOOLS

Expert system development tools are needed to avoid expense and delays and to improve the efficiency of the development process.

"Building an expert system might best be described as an awesome venture," according to Chuck Williams, a founder and vice-president of Inference Corp., "best characterized by tedium, delays, and expense." In addition to providing a bleak assessment of this situation, Williams offers a solution. "What engineers need," he suggests, "is a *tool* (italics added) that gives them a foundation for designing the rules."[1]

Originally, expert systems were programmed in AI programming languages such as LISP. Until recently, expert systems have been largely experimental programs, implemented not as much to offer practical solutions to real problems as to explore the possibilities of the new technology. Now that expert systems increasingly are being developed for actual commercial applications, it is becoming less practical to develop each one "from scratch" in LISP. If the commercial potential of expert systems is to continue to increase, a more efficient means of developing them must be utilized.

Expert system development tools are programs that are designed specifically to turn expert system development into a more manageable task. These tools help to solve this problem in several ways, including rapid prototyping, imposed structure, and knowledge engineering.

---

[1] Chuck Williams, "Software Tool Packages the Expertise Needed To Build Expert Systems," *Electronic Design*, 9 August 1984, p. 153.

Rapid Prototyping

With tools that allow a
prototype system to be
developed rapidly,
developers can determine
earlier in the process if
their prototype is feasible.

One of the most difficult phases in the development of an expert
system is the construction of the first prototype. Even though it may
require a great deal of work to convert the prototype into a finished
system, a working prototype gives both the knowledge engineer and
the domain expert a tangible program that can be manipulated more
easily than the abstract concepts that existed previously.

By providing a development "framework," expert system
development tools greatly expedite the construction of a prototype
system. Rapid prototyping allows developers to ascertain quickly
whether or not they are on the right course and if they are using the
correct techniques and tools. It is not uncommon for a prototype to
reveal that the wrong development path is being followed; therefore,
if previous work must be discarded, it is obviously better to keep the
time invested in that work to a minimum.

Imposed Structure

The structure provided by
the tools enables a
developer to concentrate
on the content of an ex-
pert system, rather than
on its form.

One of the factors contributing to the rapid prototyping available with
development tools is the structure that they provide.

An expert system developed in LISP can be described as
"unstructured" in the sense that LISP itself does not impose any kind
of structure on the system. This can be seen as an advantage in that it
offers maximum flexibility. However, the lack of structure is often a
liability, forcing developers to resolve each new problem and
subproblem independently. While admittedly limiting flexibility, a
development tool resolves many questions of structure in advance,
allowing developers to concentrate on the more substantive issues of
content rather than dwelling on form.

If the imposed structure seems to be overly restrictive for a
particular system, many tools allow developers to write short
"subroutines" in LISP to address individual problems, such as
customized functions for graphics and access to databases or special
arithmetic operations. These tools offer the benefits of predetermined
structure without sacrificing the flexibility inherent in LISP.

Knowledge Engineering

In abstract terms, the process of developing an expert system can be
thought of as the transfer of expertise from a domain expert to a
computer program. Of course, the domain expert seldom interacts
directly with the computer that is being used to develop the system;
few domain experts have sufficient computer experience to allow
that. Instead, a knowledge engineer generally is required to interface
between the domain expert and the development computer.

Expert system development is complicated further by the fact that knowledge engineers are seldom experts in the domain of the expert system. Before they can begin the development process, knowledge engineers frequently must educate themselves to an acceptable level of domain knowledge, a task that can add considerably to the already time-consuming development process.

Expert system development tools reduce the amount of expertise needed by a knowledge engineer and some day may allow the domain expert to create the system alone.

A major reason that more expert systems are not available is the lack of skilled knowledge engineers to produce them. By effectively supplying some of the required knowledge engineering expertise, development tools help to reduce the level of skills required by developers. Although constructing an expert system using development tools is far simpler than constructing them in LISP, the process currently remains too complex for most domain experts to develop an expert system by themselves. Ultimately, the ideal development tools would allow a domain expert to create an expert system without the aid of a knowledge engineer.

DEVELOPMENT TOOL DESCRIPTIONS

Development tools are available for both LISP machines and personal computers. Typically, the tools for the smaller computers cost less.

A variety of expert system development tools are available at various levels of sophistication and cost. Until recently, development tools were designed only for sophisticated LISP machines such as those discussed in Chapter 9; some of these tools cost in excess of $50,000. Recently, useful but less ambitious development tools have been designed to work with microcomputers such as the Texas Instruments Professional Computer (TI PC); some of these tools can be purchased for less than $500. Several companies produce different levels of their development tools for different computers, providing less sophisticated versions of their products for smaller computers at a lower cost.

This section offers brief descriptions of several popular expert system development tools.

ART™ (Automated Reasoning Tool™)

ART, a development tool for LISP machines, allows forward and backward chaining, uses rule-based and production-rule programming, and displays graphic representations of its knowledge base.

Inference Corporation's ART enables programmers without extensive AI backgrounds to develop full-scale commercial expert systems for such application areas as resource scheduling, manufacturing planning, financial planning, and military command and control. ART is available for LISP machines such as those from LMI™, Symbolics™, and Texas Instruments.

ART represents facts and concepts, performs symbolic pattern matching, and can reason forward from facts and backward from goals. ART can use both logical rule-based programming and production-rule programming in a single application. Based on goals provided by the programmer, ART can evaluate several correct solutions to determine which is the "most correct."

ART includes a sophisticated display interface, comprehensive graphics facilities, and the capability for manual control and inspection of the expert system even while it is running. Recent enhancements include color graphics and an English-like language mode for rules and facts in the database (*Figure 8-1*). (Inference Corp., 5300 W. Century Blvd., Los Angeles, CA 90045, 213/417-7997)

Expert Ease™

Expert Ease from Human Edge Software (HES) is an expert system development tool designed primarily for decision support which runs on microcomputers such as the IBM PC™.

**Figure 8-1.
A Sample Screen from the Knowledge Base Development Environment for ART**
(Screen Photo Courtesy of Inference Corporation)

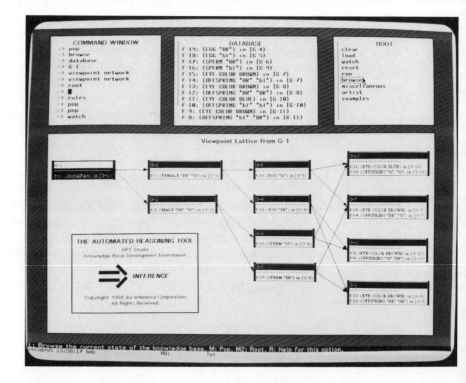

Expert Ease, a development tool for personal computers, is designed primarily to help non-programmers develop decision support applications.

Expert Ease infers its own production rules from examples entered by the developer. If the entered information is insufficient for the program to derive the proper rules conclusively, Expert Ease asks multiple choice questions to obtain the necessary data. Expert Ease is accompanied by several sample knowledge bases to help familiarize developers with the program. A sample of the Filer screen is illustrated in *Figure 8-2*.

Developed under the direction of Donald Michie, a respected AI researcher at Edinburgh University and director of the Turing Institute in Scotland, Expert Ease is designed specifically to be used by non-programmers who do not have any experience with knowledge engineering. HES recommends Expert Ease for applications including loan application evaluation, medical diagnosis, and employment application screening. (Human Edge Software, 2445 Faber Pl., Palo Alto, CA 94303, 800/624-5227)

EXSYS

EXSYS, also designed for personal computers, provides both a rule editor for entering production rules and an explanation facility. Also, it interacts with many spreadsheet and database programs.

The least costly of all the expert system development tools discussed here is EXSYS, a powerful program designed for use with personal computers. EXSYS uses a production rule approach and includes a *rule editor* to help developers enter the rules (*Figure 8-3*). On a "full-blown" personal computer with 640K RAM (over 640,000 bytes of memory), an expert system with over 5,000 production rules can be created.

**Figure 8-2.
A Sample Screen from Expert Ease Showing the Three Windows in the Filer Screen**
(Screen Photo Courtesy of Human Edge Software Corporation)

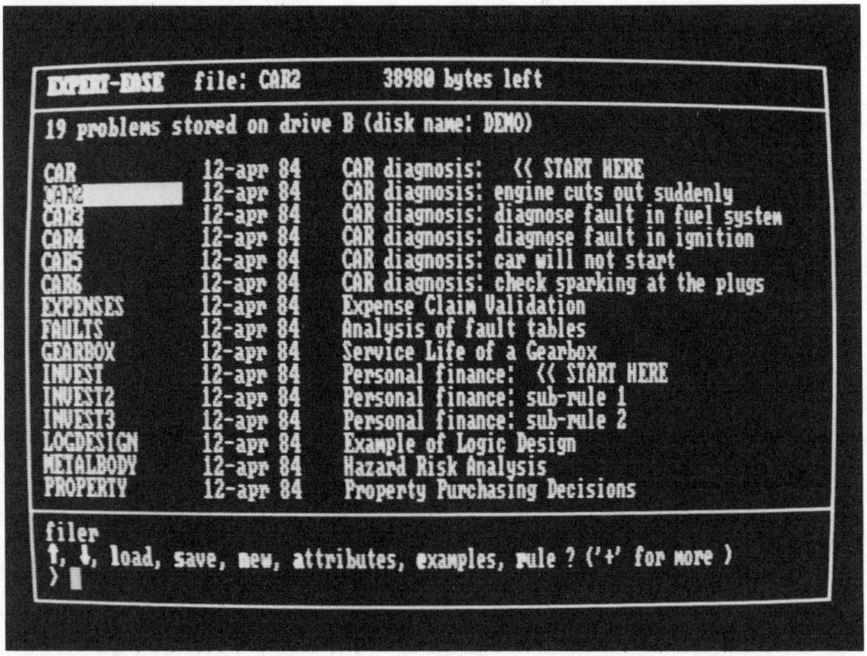

```
EXPERT-EASE  file: CAR2        38980 bytes left

19 problems stored on drive B (disk name: DEMO)

CAR         12-apr 84   CAR diagnosis:  << START HERE
CAR2        12-apr 84   CAR diagnosis: engine cuts out suddenly
CAR3        12-apr 84   CAR diagnosis: diagnose fault in fuel system
CAR4        12-apr 84   CAR diagnosis: diagnose fault in ignition
CAR5        12-apr 84   CAR diagnosis: car will not start
CAR6        12-apr 84   CAR diagnosis: check sparking at the plugs
EXPENSES    12-apr 84   Expense Claim Validation
FAULTS      12-apr 84   Analysis of fault tables
GEARBOX     12-apr 84   Service Life of a Gearbox
INVEST      12-apr 84   Personal finance:  << START HERE
INVEST2     12-apr 84   Personal finance: sub-rule 1
INVEST3     12-apr 84   Personal finance: sub-rule 2
LOGDESIGN   12-apr 84   Example of Logic Design
METALBODY   12-apr 84   Hazard Risk Analysis
PROPERTY    12-apr 84   Property Purchasing Decisions

filer
↑, ↓, load, save, new, attributes, examples, rule ? ('↑' for more )
>▮
```

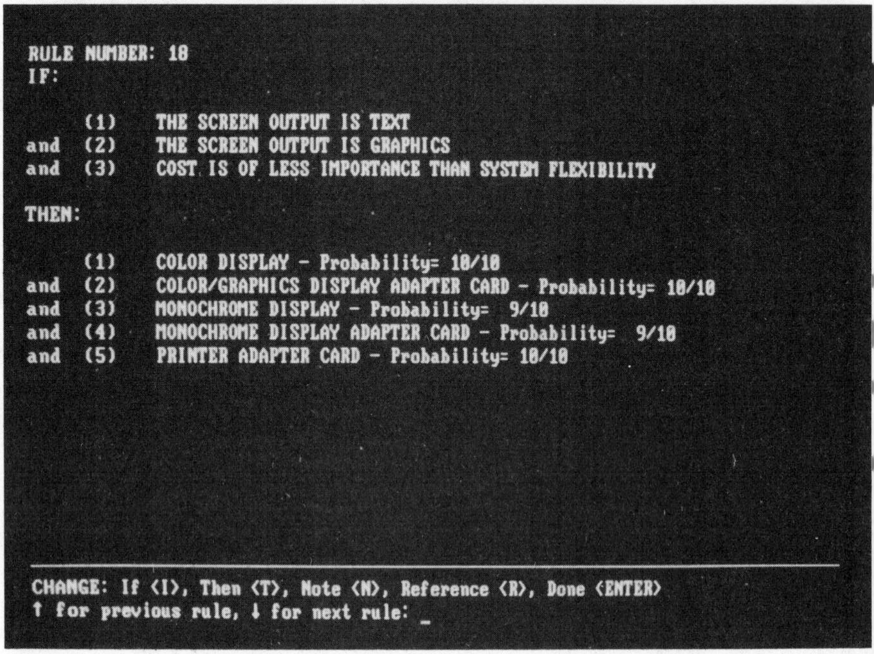

Figure 8-3.
A Sample Screen from
EXSYS Showing the Rule
Editor
(Screen Photo Courtesy of
EXSYS, Inc.)

```
RULE NUMBER: 18
IF:

      (1)    THE SCREEN OUTPUT IS TEXT
and   (2)    THE SCREEN OUTPUT IS GRAPHICS
and   (3)    COST IS OF LESS IMPORTANCE THAN SYSTEM FLEXIBILITY

THEN:

      (1)    COLOR DISPLAY - Probability= 18/18
and   (2)    COLOR/GRAPHICS DISPLAY ADAPTER CARD - Probability= 18/18
and   (3)    MONOCHROME DISPLAY - Probability= 9/18
and   (4)    MONOCHROME DISPLAY ADAPTER CARD - Probability= 9/18
and   (5)    PRINTER ADAPTER CARD - Probability= 18/18



CHANGE: If <I>, Then <T>, Note <N>, Reference <R>, Done <ENTER>
↑ for previous rule, ↓ for next rule: _
```

Featuring a full explanation facility, EXSYS can explain how it reached its conclusions and why it requires particular information. EXSYS enables you to change your answers to selected questions to determine the effects on the system's conclusions. Another valuable feature of EXSYS is that it allows you to interact with many spreadsheet and database programs so that data created with those programs can be analyzed further with EXSYS. (EXSYS, PO Box 75158, Contract Station 14, Albuquerque, NM 87194, 505/836-6676)

KEE™ (Knowledge Engineering Environment™)

KEE, designed for LISP machines, uses frames and production rules and includes windows and a graphics editor.

Perhaps the most sophisticated expert system development tool currently on the market, IntelliCorp's KEE is designed for LISP machines, such as the Explorer™ from Texas Instruments. KEE uses both frames and production rules for knowledge representation and includes a powerful windowing system that simplifies the process of making effective use of its varied capabilities.

KEE contains several unique features, including:

■ A graphics editor for designing and constructing models of objects such as meters and gauges to help explain the reasoning and behavior of the system, and

■ A fully customizable system so that the same techniques that are used to build and modify a knowledge base can be used to revise KEE itself according to the demands of the environment.

First produced in 1983, KEE has been used to develop diverse applications from diagnosing satellite malfunctions to managing heating and cooling resources. (IntelliCorp, 707 Laurel St., Menlo Park, CA 94025, 415/323-8300)

KES (Knowledge Engineering System)

KES, a product of Software Architecture and Engineering (Software A & E), includes a sophisticated set of expert system development tools. Different versions of KES are available to run on computers as large as a DEC VAX™ or as small as an "enhanced" personal computer, such as the IBM PC/XT™.

KES allows developers to select from one of three inference techniques: production rules, statistical pattern classification, or "hypothesize-and-test." According to Software A & E, regardless of the inference technique chosen, a KES knowledge base contains the following four kinds of information:[2]

- Schema—A list of attributes in the attribute hierarchy along with their value sets and other associated information,
- Associations—The network of associative links that relate the values of one attribute to those of another,
- Actions—Instructions to KES about how the knowledge base is to be organized, and
- Free Text—Supplementary free text such as definitions, references, etc.

The KES screen can be divided into windows as shown in *Figure 8-4.*

KES is available in different versions to run on LISP machines or personal computers. KES supports three inference techniques and includes a text editor for entering information.

**Figure 8-4.
A Sample Screen from KES Showing the Windowing Available**
(Screen Courtesy of Software A&E)

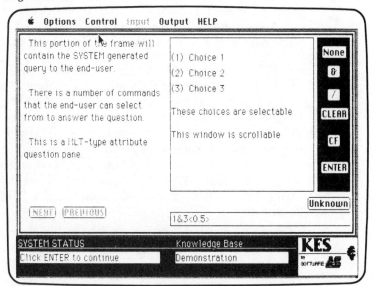

[2] Software A & E, *Knowledge Engineering System General Description Manual* (October 1984), p. 20.

To build a KES knowledge base, a developer uses a standard "text editor" program to enter information in a form consistent with the chosen inference technique. KES then parses the knowledge base, checking it for errors and converting it into a representation that can be processed by the computer. KES includes a tool called INSPECTOR that provides a great deal of useful information for creating and maintaining a production rule knowledge base.

The user of an expert system developed with KES interacts with the system by responding to a series of questions. A knowledgeable user also can enter special KES commands at any time to analyze the structure of the knowledge base or request explanations of questions and conclusions.

KES is based on knowledge management theories developed by James A. Reggia at the University of Maryland. (Software A & E, 1500 Wilson Blvd., Suite 800, Arlington, VA 22209, 703/276-7910)

M.1™

M.1, a set of expert system development tools for personal computers, uses a question-and-answer format to obtain knowledge about a problem.

A product of Teknowledge, M.1 is designed to run on personal computers such as the IBM PC. The features of M.1 include:
- Multiwindow display,
- Interactive knowledge base,
- Automatic question generation,
- Valid response checking, and
- Certainty factors.

After a knowledge base is developed, M.1 conducts a question-and-answer session to acquire knowledge about a specific problem. Then M.1 reasons from the knowledge base to draw conclusions and make specific recommendations. (Teknowledge, 525 University Ave., Suite 200, Palo Alto, CA 94301, 415/327-6600)

OPS5 +

OPS5 +, a tool for personal computers, uses menus and windows in the development of rule-based expert systems.

OPS5 + is an extension of OPS5, the CMU expert system development language that was used to create the R1 (XCON™) expert system (see Chapter 3). Designed to run on personal computers such as the IBM PC, OPS5 + uses a system of *menus* (option lists) and *windows* (divided screens) to help a knowledge engineer develop a rule-based expert system (*Figure 8-5*). OPS5 + can be used to create an expert system with as many as 1,500 production rules on a PC with 640K RAM. (Artelligence, 14902 Preston Rd., Suite 212-252, Dallas, TX 75240, 214/437-0361)

**Figure 8-5.
A Sample Screen from
OPS5 + Showing Four
Windows: Main Menu,
Interaction, Message,
and Conflict**
*(Screen Courtesy of
Artelligence, Inc.)*

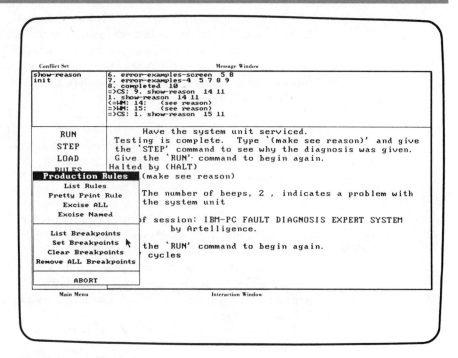

Personal Consultant™

Personal Consultant,
designed for use on per-
sonal computers, is
discussed later in this
chapter to illustrate ex-
pert system development
tools.

The Personal Consultant is a set of powerful expert system
development tools from Texas Instruments designed to run on
microcomputers such as the TI PC and the IBM PC/XT. These tools,
which are discussed in detail later in this chapter, have been used to
develop expert systems at corporations such as Campbell Soup and
Westinghouse and at several major universities. (Texas Instruments,
PO Box 809063, Dallas, TX 75380, 800/527-3500)

RuleMaster™

RuleMaster is available in
versions for mainframe
computers and personal
computers. RuleMaster
uses production rules and
can access information
from other sources such as
databases.

A set of expert system development tools from Radian Corporation,
RuleMaster is available for computers as large as mainframes or as
small as the IBM PC/XT. RuleMaster consists of the following two
major components:

■ RuleMaker—Infers production rules from examples, and
■ Radial—Interprets the production rules and executes the system.

RuleMaker uses a technique called *rule induction* to develop
production rules from examples provided by domain experts.
RuleMaker also can induce rules from *fault tables*, which are
diagnostic test results in tabular form.

In addition to executing the rules generated by RuleMaker, Radial can access information from external sources, such as database programs, other computers, and sensors and other instruments. Radial also supports the use of the *fuzzy logic* theory of knowledge representation developed by Lofti Zadeh of the University of California at Berkeley.

Like Expert Ease, RuleMaster was developed in conjunction with Donald Michie of the Turing Institute. WILLARD, an expert system built with RuleMaster that forecasts the chance of a severe thunderstorm occurring at a given location, is depicted in *Figure 8-6*. (Radian, 8501 Mo-Pac Blvd., Austin, TX 78766, 512/454-4797)

S.1™

S.1, designed for use on LISP machines, includes windows, a user interface, and an explanation facility.

Like M.1, S.1 is a product of Teknowledge. However, while M.1 is designed to run on personal computers like the IBM PC, S.1 operates on the Xerox™ 1100 series of LISP machines.

An S.1 knowledge base consists of three kinds of knowledge, each of which is encoded separately, as follows:

- Factual Knowledge—Assertions about objects and relationships between objects,
- Judgmental Knowledge—Heuristics in the form of production rules, and
- Procedural Knowledge—"Control blocks" consisting of sequences of problem-solving steps.

Figure 8-6.
A Sample Screen from WILLARD, an Expert System Built with RuleMaster
(Screen Courtesy of Radian Corporation)

```
*** Available data time, date ***

Enter available data time:  [00Z,12Z] 12Z
Enter available data date: 9 July 85

How is low-level moisture at 1000mb changing? [increasing, not_changing, decreas-
ing] not_changing
Expected 1800 CDT 9 July 85 values of near-surface dew points at Austin? [low, mo
derate,high] moderate
Is the 850 millibar dew point depression < 8 Deg C ? [yes,no] yes
Is a 550 millibar short wave trough approaching? [yes,no] no
Is a frontal boundary present? [yes,no] why

************************************************************
An investigation of a frontal boundary zone is being performed
     when an approaching 500 millibar short wave trough is absent
     in order to determine the vertical velocity field

     At <main>
     c)ont e)lab h)elp : e

Since a small 850 mb dew point depression, indicating the depth of the low-level
 moisture field, is present
     when near-surface dew point classification is moderate
     and the rate of change of low-level moisture at 1000 mbs is not_changing
     it follows that the low-level moisture field is marginal
An investigation of the vertical velocity field is being performed
     when the low-level moisture field is marginal
     in order to actually forecast the chance of severe thunderstorms

     At <main>
```

For the knowledge engineer creating an expert system, S.1 features a multiwindow development environment to facilitate the creation and modification of the knowledge base. S.1 also includes a user interface that conducts a dialogue in readable English and an explanation facility that can be probed to determine how any conclusion was reached. (Teknowledge, 525 University Ave., Suite 200, Palo Alto, CA 94301, 415/327-6600)

THE PERSONAL CONSULTANT

The Personal Consultant from Texas Instruments is one of the most powerful sets of expert system development tools designed for personal and professional computers, such as the TI PC and the IBM PC/XT.

Designed to assist knowledge engineers in the development of rule-based expert systems, the Personal Consultant is similar to EMYCIN (Essential MYCIN), the inference engine distilled from MYCIN at Stanford University. Knowledge bases developed with the Personal Consultant or EMYCIN are compatible in that a knowledge base developed with either system may be used with the other.

As illustrated in *Figure 8-7*, there are two major components of the Personal Consultant:

- Development Engine—Enables the knowledge engineer and the domain expert to develop and maintain a knowledge base, and
- Inference Engine—Enables the ''client'' (user of the expert system) to run the expert system using the knowledge base produced with the development engine.

Knowledge Base

The information in a Personal Consultant knowledge base can be divided into the following categories:

- Contexts,
- Parameters, and
- Production Rules.

Contexts

The problem areas of an expert system are divided into contexts and are solved according to the structure given in a context tree.

The various problem areas into which the domain of an expert system is divided are called *contexts*. A context associates a particular problem area in the domain with the information in the knowledge base needed to solve that problem. Contexts provide a convenient way of dividing a large problem into smaller and more manageable problems, each of which can be solved only if it is necessary to meet a specific goal.

Figure 8-7.
Personal Consultant
System Environment
(Source: Personal Consultant
Expert System Development
Tools Technical Report, *Texas*
Instruments Incorporated,
Copyright © 1985)

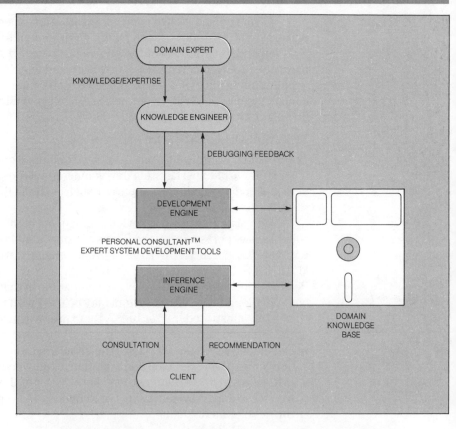

The contexts are arranged in a hierarchical structure known as a *context tree*. The structure allows you to control the flow of the system by specifying the number of contexts to be solved and the order in which the inference engine will process them. For example, a knowledge base concerned with the diagnosis of automobile problems might be structured into a context tree such as the one depicted in *Figure 8-8.*

Parameters

Parameters may be sup-
plied by the user or inferred
by the inference engine.

The facts whose values determine the system's conclusions are known as *parameters*. The user of the system may supply the values of some parameters in response to questions displayed on the screen. The inference engine may infer the values of other parameters from information in the knowledge base.

Figure 8-8.
An Example of an
Automotive Context Tree
(*Source:* Personal Consultant
User's Guide, *Texas
Instruments Incorporated,
Copyright © 1985*)

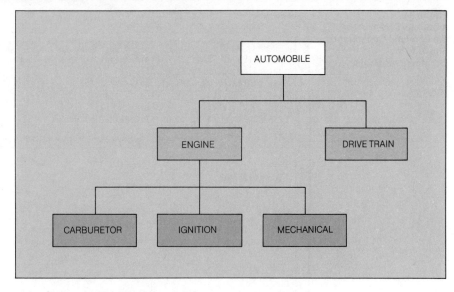

Production Rules

*The relationships among
the values of parameters
are in the form of production rules.*

The system's inference mechanism is encoded in the form of
production rules that specify the logical relationships among the
values of the various parameters. It is the production rules that give
the inference engine the ability to infer the values of parameters
instead of asking for them. Additionally, rules can assign different
certainty factors (CF's) which indicate the inference engine's level of
confidence in the parameter values it infers.

Screen Windows

*The Personal Consultant
presents information in
windows on the screen.*

The Personal Consultant's development engine divides the screen into
several windows, as shown in *Figure 8-9*. These windows are as
follows:

1) Header Stripe—Identifies the current knowledge base,
2) Upper Window—Displays the current prompt accompanied by
   several previous prompts and responses,
3) Prompt Support Stripe—Contains a brief explanation of the current
   prompt,
4) Lower Window—Displays a selection list or provides an area in
   which to respond to the current prompt, and
5) Function Key Stripe—Identifies the available function keys.

Selections are made by using the arrow keys to highlight the
desired option.

**Figure 8-9.
A Sample Screen from
the Personal Consultant
Showing the
Development Engine**

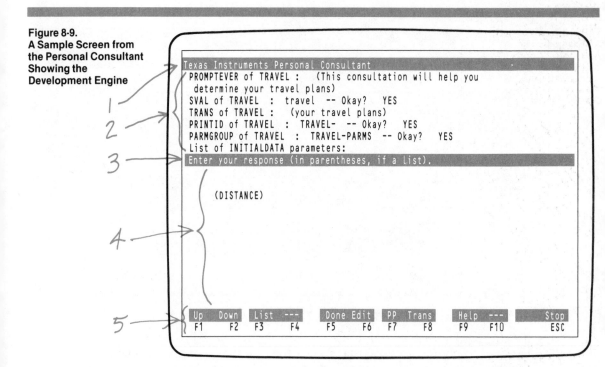

Developing an Expert System with the Personal Consultant

An expert system for making travel plans is used to illustrate the operation of the Personal Consultant.

Now let's explore the process of using the Personal Consultant to develop an expert system. As an example, assume that you are a knowledge engineer, and we'll step through a procedure that creates a simple expert system designed to help a client make travel plans. The finished system will prompt the client to enter information, such as the distance to be traveled, and will offer advice about which methods of transportation to use.

Preliminary Information

The first step in programming the expert system is to supply preliminary information, as prompted by the Personal Consultant.

When you use the Personal Consultant to develop a new expert system, the program first asks you for general information, such as the domain of the new knowledge base, the "root context" (main problem area), and the "PROMPTEVER" (a brief description of the root context).

Specifying Parameters

Next, you enter the parameters, their descriptions, and the type of value expected for each one.

The program then prompts you to enter information about the various parameters. In this example, we enter an "INITIALDATA" parameter (a parameter for which the client always is prompted) of DISTANCE; we also enter "GOALS" parameters (the parameters that the expert system is designed to obtain) of MODE and SUB-MODE, as shown here.

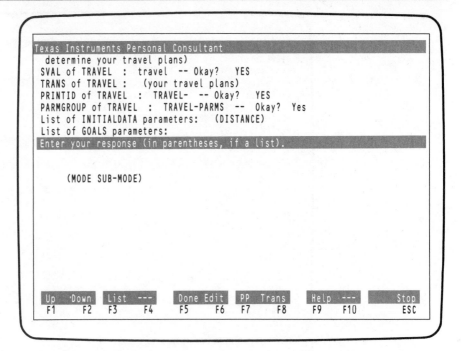

```
Texas Instruments Personal Consultant
 determine your travel plans)
SVAL of TRAVEL  :  travel  -- Okay?  YES
TRANS of TRAVEL :  (your travel plans)
PRINTID of TRAVEL  :  TRAVEL- -- Okay?  YES
PARMGROUP of TRAVEL  :  TRAVEL-PARMS  --  Okay?  Yes
List of INITIALDATA parameters:  (DISTANCE)
List of GOALS parameters:
Enter your response (in parentheses, if a list).



      (MODE SUB-MODE)






  Up   Down   List   ---       Done Edit   PP   Trans     Help  ---            Stop
  F1    F2    F3     F4         F5   F6     F7   F8        F9    F10            ESC
```

Next, the program allows you to enter additional information about the parameters, including descriptions and the types of values expected for each item. In this example, we enter the following descriptions:

- DISTANCE—The distance you wish to travel,
- MODE—The suggested mode of transportation, and
- SUB-MODE—The mode of transportation once you reach your destination city.

Although not all of the prompts displayed by the Personal Consultant are entirely self-explanatory, the Function Key Stripe indicates that F9 is the Help key. Therefore, you can press F9 to obtain additional information about any prompt that you do not understand. If you want an explanation of the "REPROMPT of DISTANCE" prompt, for example, pressing F9 displays the additional information shown here.

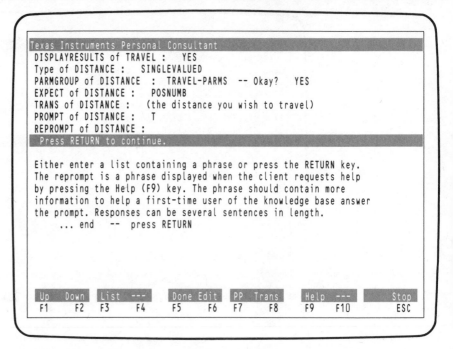

```
Texas Instruments Personal Consultant
 DISPLAYRESULTS of TRAVEL :   YES
 Type of DISTANCE :   SINGLEVALUED
 PARMGROUP of DISTANCE  :  TRAVEL-PARMS  -- Okay?  YES
 EXPECT of DISTANCE :   POSNUMB
 TRANS of DISTANCE :  (the distance you wish to travel)
 PROMPT of DISTANCE :   T
 REPROMPT of DISTANCE :
  Press RETURN to continue.

 Either enter a list containing a phrase or press the RETURN key.
 The reprompt is a phrase displayed when the client requests help
 by pressing the Help (F9) key. The phrase should contain more
 information to help a first-time user of the knowledge base answer
 the prompt. Responses can be several sentences in length.
      ... end   --  press RETURN



   Up    Down   List   ---      Done Edit   PP   Trans    Help   ---           Stop
   F1     F2     F3     F4       F5    F6    F7    F8      F9    F10            ESC
```

Main Development Activity Menu

The various capabilities of the Personal Consultant are listed on the Main Development Activity Menu.

Once you have entered all of the required preliminary information, the Personal Consultant displays its main development activity menu. A brief explanation of each item on the menu provides a quick overview of the development capabilities of the Personal Consultant.

- GO—Begin a consultation session with an expert system.
- QUIT—Exit from the Personal Consultant.
- LISP—Write routines directly in LISP.
- PARAMETERS—Add, delete, or edit parameters and their properties.
- RULES—Add, delete, or edit production rules.
- CONTEXTS—Add, delete, or edit information about contexts.
- VARIABLES—Add, delete, or edit information about variables.
- FUNCTIONS—Define your own Personal Consultant functions in LISP.
- LIST—Display or print a list of rules or parameters in LISP or English.
- SAVE—Store a knowledge base on a disk.
- TRACE—Record the logical flow of a consultation session.
- RECORD—Store a set of responses during a consultation session.
- PLAYBACK—Retrieve a previously stored set of session responses.

To make a selection, you use the arrow keys to highlight the appropriate option and then press RETURN.

Entering Rules

Production rules are entered by specifying the premise and the action to take based on that premise.

After you enter the parameters of the knowledge base, it is time to enter the production rules that tie them together. In the Personal Consultant, you enter a rule in two parts (premise and action) using a special language called Abbreviated Rules Language (ARL).

For example, suppose you want to enter a production rule that specifies that "If the distance to be traveled is greater than 400 miles, the best method of transportation is to fly." In response to the appropriate prompts, enter the following information:

- Premise—(DISTANCE > 400)
- Action—(MODE = FLY)

As indicated on the Function Key Stripe, you can check the results of entering production rules by pressing F8 to see an English translation (as in *Figure 8-10*); you also can press F7 to see the LISP version of RULE001, as shown here.

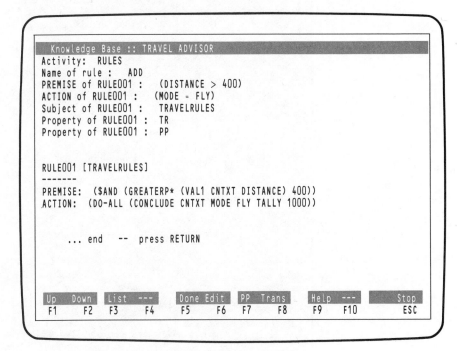

```
  Knowledge Base :: TRAVEL ADVISOR
 Activity:  RULES
 Name of rule :   ADD
 PREMISE of RULE001 :   (DISTANCE > 400)
 ACTION of RULE001 :   (MODE = FLY)
 Subject of RULE001 :   TRAVELRULES
 Property of RULE001 :  TR
 Property of RULE001 :  PP


 RULE001 [TRAVELRULES]
 -------
 PREMISE:  ($AND (GREATERP* (VAL1 CNTXT DISTANCE) 400))
 ACTION:  (DO-ALL (CONCLUDE CNTXT MODE FLY TALLY 1000))


     ... end   --   press RETURN




 Up   Down   List   ---       Done Edit   PP  Trans   Help   ---        Stop
 F1    F2     F3     F4        F5     F6   F7    F8     F9    F10        ESC
```

You can continue entering rules until your knowledge base is complete. For our example, we will create the simple five-rule system listed in both ARL and English in *Figure 8-10*. (Note that while this simple knowledge base is adequate for purposes of this demonstration, it is highly unlikely that you could represent any significant degree of expertise in five rules.)

**Figure 8-10.
The Five Rules in the
Sample Travel Advisor
Expert System**

RULE001

    Premise—(DISTANCE > 400)
    Action—(MODE = FLY)
    English—If   the distance you wish to travel is greater than 400,
          Then   it is definite (100%) that the suggested mode of
                 transportation is FLY.

RULE002

    Premise—(DISTANCE <= 400)
    Action—(MODE = DRIVE)
    English—If   the distance you wish to travel is less than or equal to
                 400,
          Then   it is definite (100%) that the suggested mode of
                 transportation is DRIVE.

RULE003

    Premise—(MODE = DRIVE)
    Action—(SUB-MODE = DRIVE)
    English—If   the suggested mode of transportation is DRIVE,
          Then   it is definite (100%) that the mode of transportation once
                 you reach your destination city is DRIVE.

RULE004

    Premise—(MODE = FLY AND FAMILIAR)
    Action—(SUB-MODE = RENTAL)
    English—If   1) the suggested mode of transportation is FLY, and
                 2) you are familiar with the city and surrounding area,
          Then   it is definite (100%) that the mode of transportation once
                 you reach your destination city is RENTAL.

RULE005

    Premise—(MODE = FLY AND ! FAMILIAR)
    Action—(SUB-MODE = TAXI)
    English—If   1) the suggested mode of transportation is FLY, and
                   2) you are not familiar with the city and surrounding area,
          Then   it is definite (100%) that the mode of transportation once
                 you reach your destination city is TAXI.

    The five rules of the sample TRAVEL ADVISOR knowledge base. Note the introduction in RULE004 of the FAMILIAR parameter, which is defined as "you are familiar with the city and surrounding area." The exclamation point (!) in the premise of RULE005 means "NOT" in ARL.

Using a Personal Consultant Expert System

To use an expert system developed with the Personal Consultant, you answer the questions the computer asks you.

Because they are based on the same inference engine, using an expert system developed with the Personal Consultant is very similar to the question-and-answer technique used in MYCIN (described in Chapter 3). For example, when you use the "travel advisor" system that we have been developing, the program first asks you to enter the distance you wish to travel. If you enter a number greater than 400, the program asks if you are familiar with the city and the surrounding area.

If you are unsure of how to answer a particular question, the Personal Consultant allows you to enter certainty factors (CF's) that indicate, as a percentage, how certain you are of your selection. The CF's are taken into account when the program reaches its conclusions.

Explanation Facility

The explanation facility allows you to ask the expert system to explain the information it is giving you.

Like MYCIN, the Personal Consultant contains an explanation facility. As indicated on the Function Key Stripe, you can press F7 to determine why the Personal Consultant is asking you a specific question; the program displays the rule that led it to ask that question, as shown here.

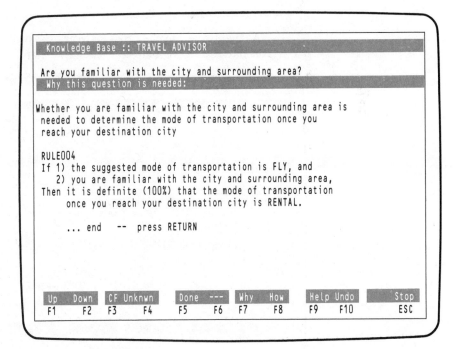

```
Knowledge Base :: TRAVEL ADVISOR

Are you familiar with the city and surrounding area?
Why this question is needed:

Whether you are familiar with the city and surrounding area is
needed to determine the mode of transportation once you
reach your destination city

RULE004
If 1) the suggested mode of transportation is FLY, and
   2) you are familiar with the city and surrounding area,
Then it is definite (100%) that the mode of transportation
     once you reach your destination city is RENTAL.

     ... end   --   press RETURN


 Up    Down   CF Unknwn    Done   ---    Why   How    Help Undo          Stop
 F1     F2    F3     F4     F5     F6     F7    F8     F9    F10           ESC
```

Once it has collected all the necessary information, the Personal Consultant displays its conclusions, as shown here.

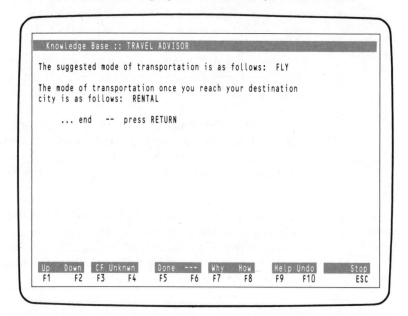

At that time, you can press F8 to ask the program to list the rules it used to reach its conclusions, as shown here.

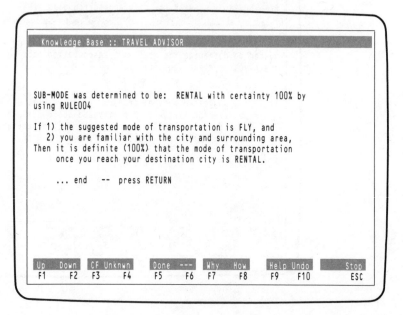

As you can see, although it may require some knowledge engineering expertise to use the Personal Consultant to *develop* an expert system, you only have to respond to the questions displayed on the screen to *use* the completed system.

WHAT HAVE WE LEARNED?

1. Expert system development tools are designed specifically to turn expert system development into a more manageable task.
2. The advantages of development tools include rapid prototyping, imposed structure, and knowledge engineering assistance.
3. Expert system development tools, some of which are available for both LISP machines and personal computers, include ART, Expert Ease, EXSYS, KEE, KES, M.1, OPS5+, Personal Consultant, RuleMaster, and S.1.
4. The Personal Consultant, a menu- and window-based development tool from Texas Instruments, helps develop rule-based expert systems on personal computers.
5. The knowledge base of an expert system developed with the Personal Consultant is divided into contexts, parameters, and production rules.

WHAT'S NEXT?

This chapter has discussed special software tools that expedite the development of expert systems and has demonstrated how these tools can be used. The next chapter explores LISP machines, computers with hardware and programming environments designed specifically to facilitate the development of AI programs.

Quiz for Chapter 8

1. Which of the following is an advantage of using an expert system development tool?
   a. Knowledge engineering assistance
   b. Imposed structure
   c. Rapid prototyping
   d. All of the above
   e. None of the above

2. ART is designed to be used on:
   a. LISP machines.
   b. microcomputers.
   c. personal computers.
   d. all of the above.

3. Expert Ease was developed under the direction of:
   a. John McCarthy.
   b. Donald Michie.
   c. Alan Turing.
   d. Lofti Zadeh.

4. KEE is a product of:
   a. Inference Corp.
   b. IntelliCorp.
   c. Teknowledge.
   d. Texas Instruments.

5. A KES knowledge base contains information in the form of:
   a. actions.
   b. associations.
   c. free text.
   d. schema.
   e. all of the above.

6. Two development tools from Teknowledge are:
   a. Expert Ease and EXSYS.
   b. KEE and KES.
   c. M.1 and S.1.
   d. OPS5 and OPS5 + .

7. OPS5, the forerunner of OPS5 + , was used to create the _____ expert system.
   a. MACSYMA
   b. MYCIN
   c. OPUS
   d. XCON

8. The Personal Consultant is based on:
   a. EMYCIN.
   b. OPS5 + .
   c. XCON.
   d. none of the above.

9. A Personal Consultant knowledge base contains information in the form of:
   a. contexts.
   b. parameters.
   c. production rules.
   d. all of the above.
   e. none of the above.

10. In the Personal Consultant, you use _____ to enter production rules.
    a. Abbreviated Rules Language
    b. Certainty Factor Recorder
    c. RuleMaster
    d. Window-Based Operating System

LISP Machines

ABOUT THIS CHAPTER

Until recently, most artificial intelligence programs were developed on multi-user computers. Computers simply were too expensive to allow a single programmer to monopolize all the resources of a computer during the lengthy program development process. Although the more economical personal and professional computers, such as the IBM PC™ and the TI PC, may be adequate for many types of programming, they often are not powerful enough to support the sophisticated AI software development commonly conducted in AI labs.

Now, a new type of single-user computer called a *LISP machine* is gaining popularity in AI labs. Because LISP machines are designed primarily for the development of AI programs, they are sometimes called "AI workstations"; however, LISP machines also have proven to be extremely useful in facilitating the development of software that is not related to artificial intelligence.

This chapter discusses the general features of LISP machines and describes several of the leading LISP machines in detail. Special attention is given to the Explorer™, a powerful but relatively inexpensive LISP machine from Texas Instruments.

COMPUTERS FOR AI PROGRAM DEVELOPMENT

When LISP was invented, programmers developed their programs on mainframe computers that had punched card inputs. If a large number of people used the same computer, they waited in line for it.

When AI pioneer John McCarthy invented LISP in 1958, he envisioned an interactive programming environment in which a programmer could enter a LISP statement and the computer would execute it immediately. Unfortunately, that environment did not exist then; the prevalent method of computer access at that time was a technique called *batch processing*.

In batch processing, a programmer develops a program on a series of "punched cards" that are created on a machine separate from the computer. The cards are "fed" into the computer, which then executes the program and prints the results. To modify a program, the programmer must re-punch the cards and resubmit them to the computer. If a large number of people use a single computer, as is frequently the case, much program development time actually is spent waiting to use the computer and the card-punch machines.

In time-sharing arrange-
ments, several people
share the use of the same
computer; however, each
of them works on a sepa-
rate terminal, thus giving
the illusion of a single-user
system.

To alleviate this problem, McCarthy invented *time sharing*, a
process that allows many people to use the resources of a single
computer at once—to "share its time." Since each user of a time-
sharing system accesses the computer from a terminal, they each have
the "illusion" of being the sole user of the computer.

The benefits of time-sharing were so obvious that it quickly
gained widespread use throughout the world of computing, not just in
AI labs. Since the late 1970's, the VAX™, a time-sharing "super"
minicomputer from DEC™ (Digital Equipment Corporation) that
features the power of a mainframe computer in a minicomputer
chassis, has been extremely popular for AI software development.

Single-user LISP machines
were developed first at
MIT and Xerox PARC.

Also in the late 1970's, experimental single-user LISP
machines were developed independently at MIT and Xerox™ PARC
(Palo Alto Research Center). Within a few years, both experimental
projects blossomed into commercial ventures.

- In 1980, Symbolics™ and LMI™, both spin-offs of the MIT project,
  began manufacturing LISP machines based on the MIT design; and
- In 1982, Xerox began to market their LISP machines.

The continual decline in the cost of computers and the
concurrent increase in computer power has resulted in the
development of these extremely sophisticated computers, which are
specifically designed to be used by one programmer at a time.
Computers with even more power than those with which McCarthy
was familiar finally are economically feasible for individual users.

Software developed on
LISP machines can be
designed for use on less
expensive LISP machines
or on personal computers.

Although LISP machines are designed primarily as
development systems (computers on which software is developed),
they often are used as *delivery systems* (computers utilized by users of
the completed software) as well. In other cases, however, software
that is developed on a LISP machine is designed to be delivered on less
expensive computers, such as lower-cost LISP machines or personal
computers.

FEATURES OF LISP MACHINES

Although the various LISP
machines are not iden-
tical, they do share a
number of common
characteristics.

Although the LISP machines offered by different companies have
different characteristics, there are a number of features that
programmers expect to find on any LISP machine, regardless of the
manufacturer. One obvious feature is that they are, with few
exceptions, designed to be used by only one individual at a time. In
addition, certain types of hardware and software have become
"standard" features on LISP machines.

Hardware

AI programs frequently require computers with sophisticated hardware.

Although it is possible to develop some AI software on machines as small as personal computers, many AI programs require extremely sophisticated computer hardware. The hardware features found on LISP machines include:

- High-Speed Processor,
- Large Memory,
- Bit-Mapped Display,
- Specialized Keyboard,
- Mouse, and
- Communication.

(Because *communication* is actually a combination of hardware and software features, it could be described as a *system* feature.)

High-Speed Processor

With high-speed processors, AI programs can execute more quickly and therefore achieve better results from a search.

In addition to their inherent single-user advantage over time-sharing computers, LISP machines are designed specifically to maximize the efficiency of symbolic processing. AI programs typically are more complex than algorithmic programs, due to their recursive natures and the elaborate search techniques they often use.

For example, an AI program performing a heuristic search may not be searching for an absolute solution, but rather for the best solution that can be obtained in a reasonable amount of time. The higher the speed of the computer, the more instructions it can execute in a given period of time. Therefore, faster computers may be capable of arriving at better heuristic solutions than slower computers.

The part of the computer that executes instructions is called the *processor*. The speed of the processor is one of the considerations that determines the speed of the computer. The processors of LISP machines are designed specifically to increase the execution speed of LISP programs. In the words of Brattle Research, "All LISP machines provide some form of hardware specialization to improve their performance in running LISP."[1] These specializations, which include high-speed LISP processors, can result in a LISP machine executing LISP programs 10 to 20 times faster than other computers.

Large Memory

AI programs usually require more random access memory and more storage space on disk drives than other programs do.

Not only do AI programs often require higher-speed computers, they also tend to be quite large and use more computer memory than other programs. Additional demands on memory are caused by the components of the sophisticated software environment (discussed later in this chapter) that AI programmers have come to expect. AI programs frequently require large amounts of the following two types of computer memory:

[1] Brattle Research Corporation, *Artificial Intelligence Computers and Software* (Cambridge, MA), p. 8.

- RAM (Random Access Memory)—The internal memory where the computer temporarily stores both the programs that it is executing and the data with which it is working, and
- Disk Drive—The external memory that serves both as the computer's "filing cabinet" for permanent storage of programs and data and as part of the computer's *virtual memory* (a system of managing RAM and disk space so that the computer appears to contain more RAM than it actually has).

In comparison to other computers, the large amount of memory that a LISP machine has is available to the single user of the machine at all times.

Until recently, the memory demands of AI program development could be satisfied only by large time-sharing computers. For example, *Figure 9-1* shows that a time-sharing computer such as the DEC VAX-11/785 "super" minicomputer features RAM and disk capacities far in excess of those offered by a typical personal computer, which may be of limited utility in the development of AI programs. Even "advanced technology" personal computers are too limited for sophisticated AI program development. However, a LISP machine offers an AI program developer "the best of both worlds": the memory of a large computer with the convenience of a computer designed for individual use.

A comparison of RAM and disk capacities might make it appear that a LISP machine such as the Symbolics 3670™ has only about half the power of a time-sharing computer such as the VAX-11/785. Remember, however, that all the memory of a LISP machine is available to an individual programmer, while a programmer using a time-sharing computer must share memory resources with all other users of the computer.

Figure 9-1.
Typical Memory Sizes of
Various Computers

Computer	RAM	Disk Drive
Personal Computers (TI PC)	640 Kbytes	18 Mbytes
"Advanced Technology" Personal Computers (TI Business Pro™)	1 to 2 Mbytes	20 to 30 Mbytes
LISP Machines (Symbolics 3670)	30 Mbytes	474 Mbytes
Time-Sharing Minicomputers (DEC VAX-11/785)	64 Mbytes	1 Gbyte

1 Kb (kilobyte) = 1 Thousand Characters
1 Mb (megabyte) = 1 Million Characters
1 Gb (gigabyte) = 1 Billion Characters

Bit-Mapped Display

The display on a LISP machine is a high-resolution, bit-mapped display, where individual pixels can be turned on or off. This type of display improves readability and allows more text and graphics to be displayed.

Most computer screens are designed primarily to display characters, such as letters and numbers. These characters are composed of a number of pixels (dots) forming a recognizable pattern, similar to the characters printed by a dot-matrix printer (*Figure 9-2*). The number of pixels on a screen determines the "resolution" of the screen: characters displayed on high-resolution screens are composed of more dots than those on medium- or low-resolution screens and thus appear to be sharper and clearer. The higher resolution also allows smaller characters to be displayed so that more characters can be displayed at one time.

High-resolution screens also are preferable for displaying graphics. To create graphics on a computer screen, a programmer must be able to turn each individual pixel on or off. A computer screen that is designed to provide this capability is called a *bit-mapped display*.

The resolution offered by personal and professional computers is usually sufficiently high for typical PC applications, but may be less than ideal for AI program development. The IBM PC, for example, features a resolution of 640×200 pixels (640 pixels wide, 200 pixels high); the resolution of the TI PC is 720×300. In contrast, the screens of some LISP machines, such as the Texas Instruments Explorer and the Xerox 1132, offer a resolution of 1024×808 pixels. The greater resolution available on LISP machines allows programmers to display a greater amount of text at one time, to create more complex graphics, and to use a display system based on windows more effectively.

**Figure 9-2.
Characters Printed by a
Dot-Matrix Printer**

Basic character matrix of 5 columns by 7 rows

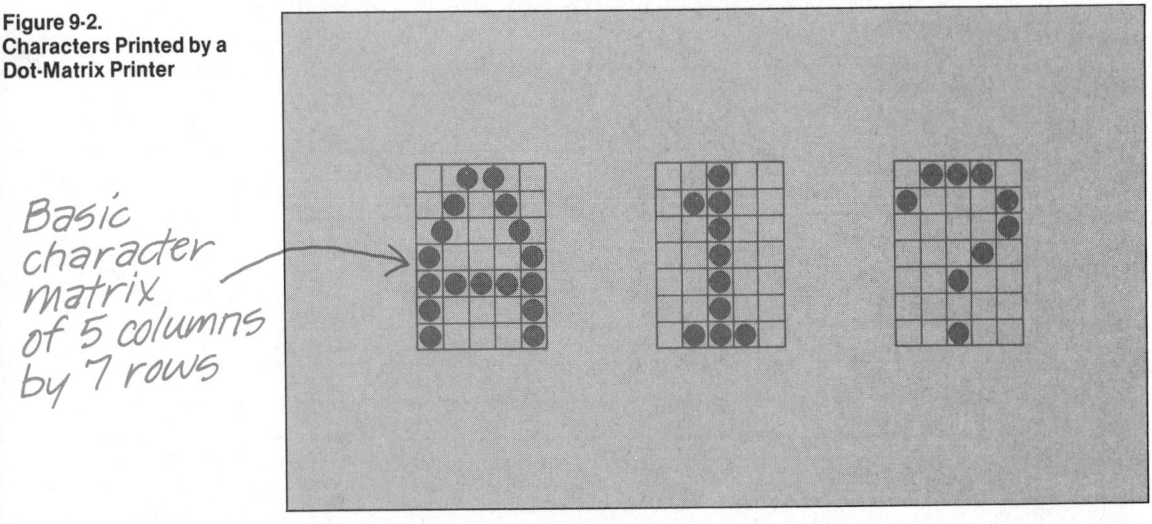

Specialized Keyboard

The keyboards on LISP machines are higher quality than on many other computers and include special single-keystroke function keys to assist in AI programming.

Since software developers generally spend a great deal of time typing on computer keyboards, it is hardly surprising that most programmers can be more productive on better keyboards. In addition to the physical quality of the keyboard itself, keyboards designed for AI use usually have more keys than typical computer keyboards (*Figure 9-3*); the extra keys serve special functions and allow programmers to invoke these functions with a single keystroke.

As you might expect, a sophisticated keyboard for a LISP machine can be quite expensive. For example, Brattle Research reports that an AI keyboard may cost over a thousand dollars, which is not much less than the price of a typical personal computer.

Figure 9-3.
The TI PC and Explorer Keyboards

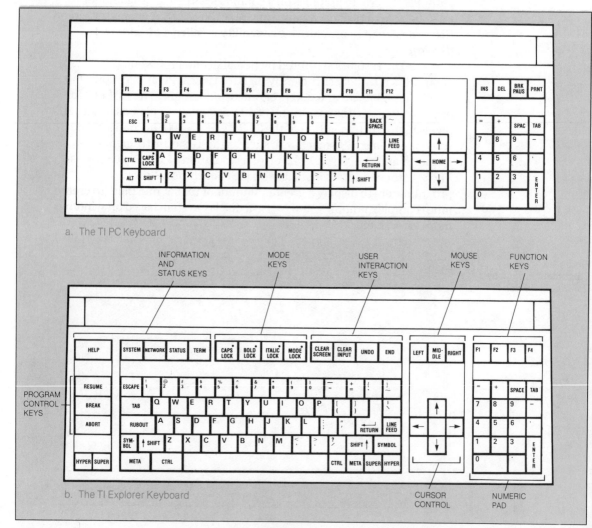

a. The TI PC Keyboard

INFORMATION AND STATUS KEYS   MODE KEYS   USER INTERACTION KEYS   MOUSE KEYS   FUNCTION KEYS

PROGRAM CONTROL KEYS

b. The TI Explorer Keyboard

CURSOR CONTROL   NUMERIC PAD

Mouse

A mouse allows you to use a computer by pointing to items on the screen instead of typing on a keyboard. The two basic kinds of mouse devices are mechanical and optical.

Typing on a keyboard is the most prevalent method of communicating with a computer; however, other methods of communication may be more suitable for various activities. *Pointing devices*, for example, may be useful for selecting among screen windows, "marking" blocks of text, creating graphics, and choosing program functions by pointing to graphic representations called *icons*.

The most popular pointing device used in conjunction with LISP machines is a small, sliding, handheld pointer called a *mouse* (*Figure 9-4*), which controls the movement of a pointer on the screen. By sliding the mouse on a flat surface, you move the screen pointer in a corresponding direction and distance. Once the screen pointer is in the desired location, you can press a button on the mouse to perform a specified action.

There are basically two kinds of mouse devices.

- A *mechanical* mouse glides on a roller mounted on its underside. The computer tracks the rotation of the roller to calculate the relative motion of the mouse, which generally can be used on any flat surface.
- An *optical* mouse uses an optical sensor to track its motion. The mouse must be moved on a special pad containing a grid that can be detected by its sensor.

Communication

LISP machines often are set up to communicate with other computers using a local area network (LAN) or telecommunication.

Even though LISP machines are designed specifically for individual use, it is not uncommon for them to be set up to communicate with other computers (possibly other LISP machines). More than one programmer may need to access the same knowledge base, for example, or a programmer might wish to transmit a particularly interesting program to another programmer.

Figure 9-4.
An Optical Mouse

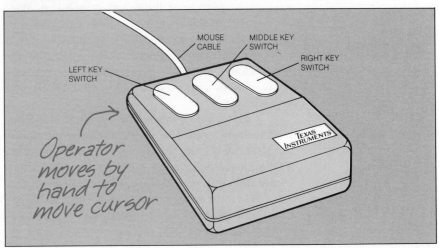

The two common ways in which LISP machines communicate are:

- Local Area Networks (LAN's)—Two or more LISP machines are physically connected by cables so that they can share information, and
- Telecommunication—A LISP machine communicates with another computer through the telephone lines.

A LISP machine may be configured for either or both of these communication techniques.

Software

Some of the software tools that a programmer expects to find on a LISP machine have been discussed in previous chapters. These tools include the following:

- AI Programming Languages (such as LISP and/or PROLOG)—To execute an AI program (Chapter 7),
- Editors—To enter and modify a program (Chapter 6),
- Debuggers—To help identify and correct program errors (Chapter 6),
- Expert System Development Tools (such as ART™ or KEE™)—To expedite the development of expert systems (Chapter 8), and
- Intelligent Software Development Tools—To assist in various phases of the programming process (Chapter 6).

Further descriptions of the software tools that are available for various LISP machines are included in the following discussions of the individual computers. One popular feature that warrants further discussion is a display technique known as *screen windows*.

Screen Windows

One major component of the software environment of any LISP machine is a system of dividing the screen into distinct sections called *windows*. The idea of screen windows, originally developed at Xerox PARC, is used not only on LISP machines but also is gaining popularity with personal computers such as the Apple Macintosh™ and Commodore Amiga™. Windows also form the basis of operating environments such as GEM™ for the IBM PC from DRI (Digital Research Inc.).

The window systems available for LISP machines allow programmers to use a sophisticated programming environment easily and effectively. As a programmer moves among the various development tools, the new contents of the screen can be displayed in a separate window, instead of replacing the original contents. It is possible to view several windows at the same time, with each window either representing the screen display created by a particular program

Many software tools are available for LISP machines to simplify and expedite writing an AI program.

With a window system, a programmer can display a variety of information on a single screen, further simplifying program development.

or performing a specific function. The flexibility created by a window system simplifies the process of "passing" data from one program to another so that various programs can manipulate a common set of data.

LISP MACHINE DESCRIPTIONS

The description of the features of several LISP machines follows.

This section offers descriptions of the following LISP machines:

- LMI Lambda™,
- Symbolics 3600™ series (3640 and 3670), and
- Xerox 1100 series (1108 and 1132).

Additionally, an in-depth discussion of the Texas Instruments Explorer system is presented in the following section.

These descriptions of LISP machines begin with a discussion of the MIT LISP machine, an experimental computer that was not marketed commercially, but which led directly to the development of several commercial products.

The MIT LISP Machine

Although the MIT LISP machine was not sold externally, people from the MIT AI lab started LMI and Symbolics, two companies that currently market LISP machines.

In the mid-1970's, a LISP machine was developed in the MIT AI lab to expedite the advanced research being conducted there. As with many other AI research projects, the MIT LISP machine project was funded by the Defense Advanced Research Projects Agency (DARPA).

The original MIT LISP machine, completed in 1976, was dubbed the CONS in honor of a LISP primitive. Two years later, the CONS was replaced by the CADR, an improved version of the CONS that also was named after a LISP primitive. In 1980, two companies, LMI and Symbolics, were formed by members of the MIT AI lab specifically to bring the CADR technology into the commercial marketplace.

In addition to developing hardware, the MIT AI lab also created sophisticated software as a programming environment for the CADR. For example, ZetaLISP™, a precursor of Common LISP (see Chapter 7), was developed at MIT for the LISP machine and is currently part of the software environment offered by LMI, Symbolics, and Texas Instruments.

LISP Machine Inc. (LMI)

The various LISP machines developed by LISP Machine Inc. are named the Lambda and come in sizes suitable for laboratory or office use.

LMI produces several versions of a LISP machine called the Lambda (after a LISP procedure). Most Lambda models include a five-foot tall cabinet containing most of the hardware and are designed specifically for use in a laboratory environment. The smallest model, the Lambda/E™ (a modified Texas Instruments Explorer), stands a little over two feet high and is designed primarily for office use.

Although some models of the Lambda can support up to four simultaneous users, the Lambda is not a time-sharing machine. A multi-user Lambda includes a separate processor for each user so that it is actually several computers in one; the processors share resources such as the disk, printer, and communication facility. According to LMI, a multi-user Lambda has "the lowest per-user cost of any fully configured high-performance LISP machine."[2] (A three-user Lambda is pictured in *Figure 9-5.*)

Processors and Operating Environments

The two processors available for the Lambda, the Lambda LISP processor and the MC68010 microprocessor, support different programming languages.

The Lambda offers a choice of two processors: the Lambda LISP processor or the Motorola MC68010™ microprocessor. The processor you select depends on which of the available operating environments you wish to use.

- The Lambda LISP processor supports both LISP (ZetaLISP-PLUS™ and Common LISP) and PROLOG (LM-PROLOG).
- The MC68010 microprocessor supports UNIX™, a popular "execution environment" developed by Bell Labs. With UNIX, you can develop programs in languages such as C, FORTRAN, and Pascal.

Figure 9-5.
The LMI Lambda 3 × 3, a Three-Processor LISP Machine
(Photo Courtesy of LISP Machine Inc.)

[2] *More Than Just a LISP Machine* (Los Angeles: LISP Machine Inc., 1984), p. 5.

To take maximum advantage of these features, you can configure a Lambda with both processors. A program called the Extended-Streams Interface™ enables the two processors, and the various software tools that accompany them, to work together smoothly.

Hardware Architecture

The Lambda combines two different hardware designs: the Multibus™ from Intel and the NuBus™ (developed at MIT) from TI. This flexible hardware architecture simplifies the addition of extra memory and peripheral devices to expand the Lambda system.

Memory

The various Lambda models differ somewhat in their memory sizes. Most models come with four megabytes of RAM and are expandable to 16 or 32 megabytes. Several different disk drives are available, with capacities of up to 515 megabytes. By "chaining" disk drives together, the Lambda can achieve a disk memory capacity of over one gigabyte.

Communication

The Lambda can communicate through Ethernet™, a popular LAN system developed by Xerox that has become an industry standard.

Software

The software development environment available for the Lambda includes components for creating a knowledge base, changing typefaces, using programs written in InterLISP-D, creating windows and menus, and more.

A wide variety of software is available for the Lambda, including the previously mentioned ZetaLISP-Plus, Common LISP, LM-PROLOG, and UNIX. The Lambda's software development environment includes the following components:

- AI-Base™—Facilitates the construction and management of a knowledge base and provides a natural language interface to LISP programs;
- Flavors—Allows you to develop "object-oriented" LISP programs similar to those developed with Smalltalk™ from Xerox;
- Font Editor—Lets you modify existing *fonts* (typefaces) or create new ones to vary the styles of characters that are displayed on the screen;
- Inspector—Helps you examine and modify complex LISP data structures;
- InterLISP™ Compatibility Package—Allows you to use many programs written in InterLISP-D, a dialect of LISP used on Xerox computers;
- Peek—Helps you examine various aspects of the status of system activities;
- PICON—Provides an expert system development tool for industrial process control applications;

- RTime™—Links a LISP program to an external "real-time" process for monitoring and control;
- Window System—Allows you to create and maintain customized windows and menus;
- ZMACS Editor—Expedites the process of entering a LISP program and helps to reduce errors; and
- Zmail—Adds electronic mail capability.

Many of these components are similar to features available with the Texas Instruments Explorer and are discussed in greater detail later in this chapter.

Symbolics

The two machines in the Symbolics 3600 LISP machine series are the 3640 for office use and the 3670 for laboratory use.

Like LMI, Symbolics is a spin-off from the MIT AI lab. In 1981, Symbolics introduced their first LISP machine, the LM-2, which was basically an MIT CADR with minor modifications. In 1983, Symbolics introduced the 3600 series of LISP machines, generally regarded as the most advanced LISP machines currently on the market. Symbolics refers to the 3600 series as "the premier symbolic processing system available for the development of solutions to complex problems,"[3] and calls the Symbolics 3670 "the most powerful symbolic processor available."[4]

Symbolics currently offers two computers in the 3600 series:
- The Symbolics 3640™, which is designed for office use and stands 2.5 feet high (*Figure 9-6*); and

Figure 9-6.
The Symbolics 3640 LISP Machine
(Photo Courtesy of Symbolics)

[3] *Symbolics Inc.* (Cambridge, MA: Symbolics).
[4] *The Symbolics 3670* (Cambridge, MA: Symbolics, 1984).

- The Symbolics 3670, which is designed for laboratory use and is available in a 4.5-foot tall cabinet.

Processor and Operating Environment

A single LISP processor is available for the Symbolics 3600 machines.

Unlike the multi-processor LMI Lambda, the Symbolics 3600 features a single LISP processor designed to run the Symbolics versions of ZetaLISP and Common LISP. However, the operating environment can be enhanced with "toolkits" that allow you to develop programs in other languages, including FORTRAN, Pascal, and PROLOG.

Hardware Architecture

The 3600 is built around the Symbolics LBus, which is slower and somewhat less flexible than the Multibus-NuBus combination in the Lambda's hardware architecture.

Memory

Both the 3640 and the 3670 come with two megabytes of RAM. The 3640 is expandable to eight megabytes, and the 3670 can be expanded to 30 megabytes. The 3640 includes a single 140-megabyte disk drive; the 3670 features disk drives with capacities of up to 474 megabytes. By chaining drives, the disk capacity of the 3670 can be expanded to over 3.5 gigabytes.

Communication

Like the LMI Lambda, the Symbolics 3600 supports Ethernet LAN communication.

Software

The software development environment for the Symbolics 3600 machines is similar to that of the LMI Lambda.

Because they both are based on the same software environment developed at MIT, the Symbolics 3600 series and the LMI Lambda offer many of the same software features, including:

- Flavors,
- Font Editor,
- Inspector,
- Peek,
- Window System,
- ZMACS Editor, and
- Zmail.

The InterLISP Compatibility Package offered by Symbolics is more flexible than the LMI version, allowing you to use programs written in InterLISP-10 and InterLISP-VAX as well as InterLISP-D. Symbolics also has a license from MIT to market MACSYMA, the mathematical expert system described in Chapter 3.

Xerox

The design and software environment of the Xerox 1100 LISP machine series differs from that of the Lambda and the Symbolics 3600 machines. The two machines in the series are the Xerox 1132 and the Xerox 1108.

In the mid-1970's, Xerox PARC conducted several pioneering research efforts with the aim of facilitating AI programming. The various research projects have had a profound impact on AI hardware and software development. However, although Xerox made good use of the results of their research internally, they were slow to recognize the external commercial potential of their developments. In the early 1980's, however, they began to market their LISP machines, which feature quite different designs from the MIT model offered by LMI and Symbolics. The Xerox software environment is also unique, although parts of it have been imitated by the other firms.

In 1973, programmers at Xerox PARC began to use a newly-developed personal computer called the Alto. Although its 64-kilobyte internal memory was tiny by current standards, it was a very advanced computer for its time. The Alto was the first computer to use a mouse as a pointing device and featured a high-resolution, bit-mapped display. Smalltalk, the Alto's programming environment, premiered the important concepts of windows and icons. Although the Alto enjoyed tremendous popularity at Xerox PARC, it never was introduced as a commercial product.

In 1978, Xerox PARC developed a LISP machine called the Dorado. This computer, featuring considerably more power than the Alto, again was used only internally until 1982, when it was introduced commercially as the Xerox 1132 (*Figure 9-7*). The Xerox 1100 series now also includes the less expensive Dandelion, officially known as the Xerox 1108.

Figure 9-7.
The Xerox 1132 LISP Machine
(Photo Courtesy of Xerox)

Processor and Operating Environment

The LISP processor of the Xerox 1100 series implements a version of LISP called InterLISP-D, which features a powerful and flexible programming environment.

Hardware Architecture

The Xerox 1100 machines are designed for different purposes and therefore have different architectures.

The two machines in the 1100 series do not share a common hardware architecture. The 1132 features an exceptionally high-speed bus, boasting a speed of over six times that of the LMI Lambda; the high speed is especially effective in displaying rapidly changing graphics. The 1108 hardware is slower, roughly comparable to that of the Lambda, because the 1108 is designed more for flexibilty than for speed.

Memory

The memory capacity of the Xerox 1100 series does not equal the LMI and Symbolics LISP machines. The 1108 features up to 3.5 megabytes of RAM; the 1132 comes with two megabytes of RAM, which can be expanded to 18 megabytes. The 1108 comes with a 42-megabyte disk drive, which may be supplemented by an additional 80- or 315-megabyte drive; the 315-megabyte drive also is available as an option for the 1132, which comes with an 80-megabyte drive as a standard feature.

Communication

Ethernet, the popular LAN system developed by Xerox, is available with either model in the 1100 series.

Software

The Xerox 1100 series software development environment is based on InterLISP-D and includes components for entering programs interactively, assisting in program debugging, creating windows, and more.

The software for the Xerox 1100 series is based on InterLISP-D, which features strong graphics capabilities (the *D* in *InterLISP-D* stands for *Display*). The Xerox history of using graphic interfaces to make complex computers easier to use dates back to the development of Smalltalk by Alan Kay, a PARC founder. With some justification, Xerox claims that the graphics features of InterLISP-D make the 1100 series "the easiest to use in the industry."[5]

The InterLISP-D software development environment includes the following components:

- Display Editor—Helps you enter programs interactively in accordance with the program's structure;
- DWIM ("Do What I Mean")—Automatically corrects typing and spelling errors;
- Inspector—Assists in the debugging process by allowing you to examine and modify complex program structures;
- Loops—Provides a set of knowledge programming tools;

[5] *The Keys To Artificial Intelligence Are At Xerox* (Pasadena, CA: Xerox).

- Masterscope—Analyzes a program's structure, answers questions about the program, and assists in the program modification process;
- Program Assistant—"Cooperates" in the software development process by monitoring interaction, analyzing errors, and acting as an "intelligent assistant"; and
- Windows—Lets you create a complex system of screen windows.

THE TEXAS INSTRUMENTS EXPLORER

To help you understand the use of a LISP machine, the Texas Instruments Explorer is described in detail.

The Explorer from Texas Instruments is a powerful but relatively low-cost LISP machine. Because the Explorer is based on technology developed at MIT for the CADR, it bears many similarities to the LISP machines produced by LMI and Symbolics; however, many new features have been added by TI.

In order to give you a better idea of what it is like to use a LISP machine, this section offers a discussion of the features of the Explorer and includes illustrations of several Explorer screens. Because there is a great deal of similarity in the features of the various LISP machines, this section can help familiarize you with the features of any LISP machine. (Much of the information presented in this section is adapted from material appearing in the *Explorer Technical Summary* manual.[6])

Hardware

The Explorer uses the NuBus architecture, which allows a variety of devices to be attached to the system, and a single-slot LISP processor.

The Explorer is a compact system designed primarily for use in an office environment. The system enclosure stands just over two feet high and weighs only 60 pounds. Even with a disk drive mounted on top of the system enclosure, the combined unit is just 2.5 feet tall and weighs less than 100 pounds.

Like the LMI Lambda, the Explorer is based on the NuBus architecture, which was developed at MIT and now is licensed to TI. The NuBus is a simple and flexible architecture that allows you to attach a variety of devices to the system. Unlike the multi-slot processors featured by LMI and Symbolics, the Explorer includes a single-slot LISP processor; that is, all the components of the processor are contained on a single printed circuit (PC) board. *Figure 9-8* illustrates the design of the Explorer's hardware system architecture.

Memory

The Explorer can have up to 16 Mb of RAM and over 1 Gb of disk space by linking eight drives.

The Explorer comes with two megabytes of RAM, expandable to a maximum of 16 megabytes. Although an Explorer with two megabytes of RAM may suffice as a *delivery* system, TI recommends that a *development* system contain at least four megabytes of RAM.

The "mass storage enclosure" of the Explorer has room for one or two 140-megabyte disk drives or for one disk drive and a 60-megabyte cartridge tape drive for "backing up" the disk (making a copy of the data on the disk to ensure that the data is not lost if the

[6] *Explorer Technical Summary* (Austin, TX: Texas Instruments, 1985).

Figure 9-8.
The Explorer Hardware
Architecture
(*Source:* Explorer Technical
Summary, *Copyright © 1985,*
Texas Instruments Incorporated)

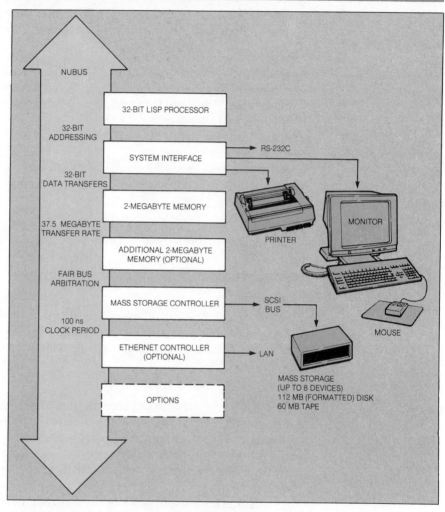

disk is damaged or erased). By linking eight drives (four enclosures with two drives each), you can configure an Explorer with a disk capacity of over one gigabyte. The Explorer uses the industry-standard small computer system interface (SCSI) to link mass storage enclosures.

Monitor

The Explorer has a high-resolution, bit-mapped display and the monitor can be adjusted on three axes.

The Explorer's monitor features a 17-inch (measured diagonally), bit-mapped "landscape" screen with a resolution of 1024 pixels by 808 pixels. (A *landscape* screen is wider than it is high; a screen that is higher than it is wide is known as a *portrait* screen.) The monitor is designed with a "footprint" of only about 15.5 inches by 12.5 inches, so as not to require much desk space. (An object's *footprint* is the amount of space required to set its base on a surface.) Adjustable on three axes (height, tilt, and swivel), the monitor can be set to the precise viewing angle with which you are most comfortable.

Keyboard

As shown in *Figure 9-3*, the Explorer's keyboard is an expanded version of the keyboard on the Texas Instruments Professional Computer and is adjustable to angles of up to 15 degrees. It contains over 100 keys, including:

- A standard typewriter "QWERTY" keyboard,
- An 18-key numeric pad,
- A five-key block of cursor-control keys, and
- Special LISP function keys.

Mouse

The Explorer uses an optical mouse that tracks motion as fast as 30 inches per second with a resolution of 200 pixels per inch. The mouse has three buttons that allow you to perform a variety of operations without having to return your hand to the keyboard (*Figure 9-4*).

Communication

An Explorer can be used as part of a local area network with the Ethernet protocol. You also can configure an Explorer for telecommunication for purposes such as electronic mail and "remote" access.

Software

As discussed previously in this chapter, one of the distinguishing features of a LISP machine is a rich software environment that expedites the process of program development. Many of the features of the software environment are provided in the form of *utilities*, which are special programs that you can utilize to perform a specific function.

Texas Instruments divides the programs in the Explorer's software environment into the following categories:

- User Interface,
- LISP Language,
- Program Development Tools,
- Software Options, and
- System Facilities.

User Interface

The *user interface* is the combination of hardware and software that gives you access to the features of the computer. The hardware components of the Explorer's user interface—bit-mapped display, keyboard, and optical mouse—already have been discussed. The software portion of the user interface has two components: a window system and help facilities.

Window System

The *window system* controls the creation of windows and allocates windows among various programs. You can create any number of windows for different programs and split the screen to display several windows at one time (*Figure 9-9*). Much like papers on a desk, windows can vary in size and shape, and may overlap other windows. You can incorporate the window system into your own programs and customize windows according to the requirements of your applications.

To interact with a particular program, you create and activate a window by using the keyboard or mouse in conjunction with menus displayed on the screen. The active window receives input from the keyboard; in other words, what you type on the keyboard is directed to the program associated with the active window.

The screen can be split into windows, each of which can be activated from the keyboard or with the mouse.

**Figure 9-9.
The Explorer Window System**
(Source: Explorer Technical Summary, *Copyright © 1985, Texas Instruments Incorporated)*

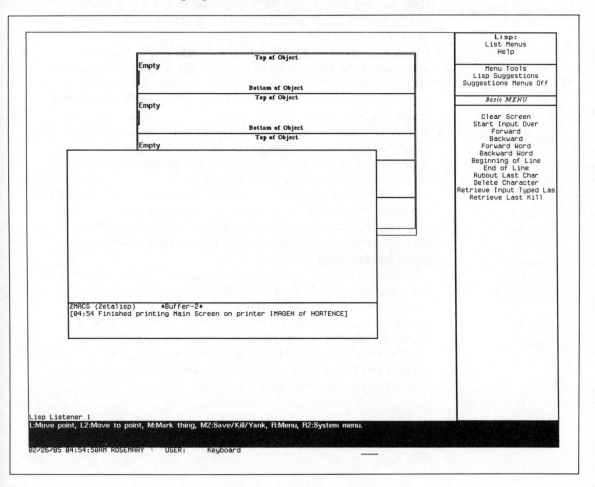

Certain items in a window are highlighted to indicate that they are *mouse-sensitive*. You can select a mouse-sensitive item by using the mouse to point to it and then clicking a mouse button. The screen contains a *mouse documentation line* that provides short descriptions of currently available mouse options.

These are the key features of the Explorer window system.

- Hierarchy of Windows—Just as the screen can be divided into windows, each window can be subdivided into *panes*. A group of related panes can be collected into a *frame*, which can be manipulated as a single object. Panes and frames are called the *inferiors* of a window; when you move a window, all of its inferiors move with it.

- Window Manipulation—The window system has many facilities for manipulating windows. You can create them, destroy them, move them around, and change their size and shape. A menu-based screen formatting program helps you perform these operations quickly.

- Graphics Support—The window system includes a number of operations for creating graphic displays. The Explorer also offers an optional Graphics Toolkit (discussed later in this chapter) that provides enhanced capabilities for creating and modifying graphic objects on the screen.

- Menus and Choice Facilities—A *menu* is a list of choices, each identified by a word or short phrase (such as the name of a command). Items on a menu are mouse-sensitive so that you can make your selection easily with the mouse.

Each major system utility that has a large number of commands includes a *Suggestions Menu* that lists available commands. When you use the mouse to point to an item on the Suggestions Menu, a short description of that item is displayed on the mouse documentation line.

Some menus are temporary, appearing only as they are needed. You can display the System Menu, for example, by clicking the right mouse button twice. The System Menu appears, overlaying whatever windows currently are displayed. After you make a selection from the System Menu, the menu disappears.

The window system also includes multiple-choice menus, which present you with a list of items accompanied by "yes/no" choice boxes that you can select with the mouse.

The features of the Explorer window system allow you to subdivide windows, manipulate windows, create graphic displays, and make selections from menus.

Help Facilities

The help facilities include utilities to complete partial commands, provide information on the system's status, help explain a utility, define terms, describe commands and functions, and present explanatory messages.

Most of the Explorer's utilities include special assistance features or commands to make them easier to use. For example, the system completes partially entered commands and maintains a record of the last 60 commands entered. Additionally, the Explorer offers the following help facilities.

- Who-Line—The *who-line* consists of the mouse documentation line and a line below it known as the *status line*, which provides system status information. The who-line is always visible; it cannot be overlaid by a window.
- HELP Key—Pressing the *HELP key* displays a menu of choices for the utility associated with the active window. One choice, "Basic Help," displays a general description of the utility and provides information to get you started. If you enter the name of a command or LISP function, the Explorer displays relevant information.
- Glossary Utility—The *glossary utility* provides definitions of terms specific to the Explorer and the LISP environment. If the definition of a term contains words or phrases that are also in the glossary, those words are highlighted; you can display their definitions by selecting them with the mouse. You also can add glossary files for your own applications.
- Online Documentation—The *online documentation* facilities provide information about command groups, individual commands, and LISP functions. Most commands and functions require only short descriptions, although longer documentation is provided for those that are more complex.
- Notification—When certain events occur, such as errors that are unrelated to the active window, the system notifies you by beeping and displaying an explanatory message in a *notification window*. You can use the mouse to remove the notification window; however, the notifications are saved so that you can review them later, if necessary.

LISP Language

The Explorer supports Common LISP and ZetaLISP, an extension of Common LISP which includes the flavor system and loop macro features.

The Explorer supports the use of Common LISP, a popular standardized version of "East Coast" LISP. Additionally, the Explorer supports an extension of the Common LISP environment called ZetaLISP, which also is supported by the LISP machines produced by LMI and Symbolics. The features of ZetaLISP include the following.

- Flavor System—The *flavor system* provides a powerful facility for *object-oriented* programming, an important technique first implemented by Xerox in Smalltalk. *Objects*, which represent items in the "real world," encompass data and the operations that can be performed on those data. A program communicates with an object by sending *messages* to it; the program does not need to be concerned with how the object actually is represented.

A *flavor* is an abstract object that describes an entire class of similar objects (*Figure 9-10*). Thus, a flavor forms a conceptual model of which each object is an *instance*. A flavor also has attached *methods* that define generic operations for any instance of that flavor. The Explorer includes a large number of predefined flavors that you can use in your own programs; the flavor system also can help you define your own flavors.

- Loop Macro—The *loop macro* is an extension to LISP that allows you to write iterative procedures in a format that looks more like stylized English than LISP code. A loop contains a body of code that can be executed several times and is composed of clauses introduced by keywords. A large number of keywords is available, allowing you to choose and combine clauses to define the iteration process.

Program Development Tools

The Explorer provides a comprehensive set of tools to expedite program development. The tools enable you to execute partially developed programs so that you can develop programs in pieces and rapidly move through the cycle of testing, debugging, and modifying your programs. The tools are integrated so that they interact with each other and provide a uniform software development environment.

Figure 9-10.
The Flavor System
(Source: Explorer Technical Summary, *Copyright © 1985, Texas Instruments Incorporated)*

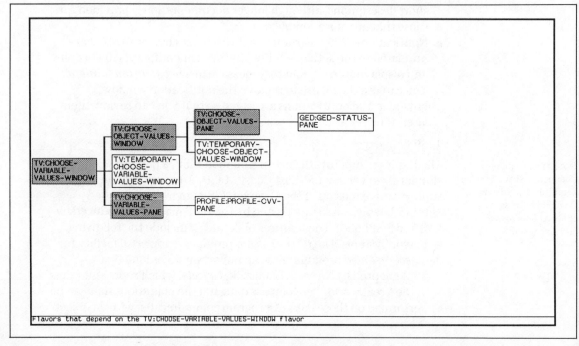

The Explorer provides program development tools which help you enter LISP programs, interact with the LISP interpreter, debug your programs, use the Suggestions Menus, change typefaces, and more.

The Explorer's program development tools consist of the following.

- ZMACS Editor—The *ZMACS editor*, based on MIT's EMACS editor, provides extensive support for writing LISP programs. ZMACS is window oriented; you can create any number of ZMACS windows to edit different files and switch among them rapidly. ZMACS also allows you to create *keyboard macros* that enable you to define a sequence of keystrokes and invoke the sequence with a single command.

  ZMACS is a *context-sensitive* editor. For example, if you use it to enter a Common LISP program, ZMACS processes the text you enter in accordance with the syntax rules of Common LISP; ZMACS matches parentheses, properly indents and aligns code, and evaluates or compiles functions. The ZMACS Suggestions Menu lists available commands and provides information about each command.

- LISP Listener—The *LISP Listener* is a window-oriented program that allows you to interact directly with the LISP interpreter. The Listener lets you enter a LISP expression, and then evaluates it and displays the results.

- LISP Compiler—The *LISP Compiler* converts LISP programs into machine language so that they execute faster and require less memory.

- Debugging Tools—The Explorer provides an interactive debugger, as well as other tools, to help you identify and correct errors in your programs. The debugger allows you to examine the environment in which an error occurs, take corrective action, and resume execution of the corrected program. A window-based debugger also is available, allowing you to view several different types of information at one time.

  Other debugging tools include:
  —A *break facility*, which halts execution of your program;
  —A *trace facility*, which allows you to trace the operation of specified functions;
  —A *step facility*, that lets you follow each step in the evaluation of a LISP expression;
  —An *advise facility*, that helps you modify a function temporarily to test potential modifications; and
  —*Error and condition handlers*, that allow you to specify the procedures to follow in the event of certain errors or conditions.

- Inspector—The *Inspector*, a window-oriented program that allows you to view and modify the components of LISP objects, is a useful tool for examining complex data structures. An Inspector window contains several panes serving various functions. For example, the *interaction pane* lets you enter LISP expressions to be evaluated and inspected; the *history pane* displays a list of all the objects that already have been inspected.

- Command Interface Toolkit—The *Command Interface Toolkit* consists of the *Universal Command Loop* (UCL) and a facility for customizing and creating new Suggestions Menus. The UCL includes a number of features that allow you to tailor Explorer commands to fit the requirements of specific applications. The *command editor*, for example, helps you create and modify command definitions (*Figure 9-11*).

Figure 9-11.
The Explorer Command Editor

(Source: Explorer Technical Summary, *Copyright © 1985, Texas Instruments Incorporated)*

```
                                                    Top
UNIVERSAL COMMANDS:
COMMAND NAME              ASSIGNED KEYSTROKE      DESCRIPTION
Build Command Macro       HYPER-CTRL-C           Creates a command which queues other commands for execution.
Build Keystroke Macro     HYPER-CTRL-M           Creates a command which forces a sequence of keys into the IO buffer.
Command Display           HYPER-CTRL-HELP        Displays the currently active commands in a scroll window.
Command Editor            HYPER-CTRL-STATUS      Allows editing of this program's commands in a scroll window.
Command History           HYPER-CTRL-P           Displays previous significant commands in a scroll window.
Command Name Search       HYPER-CTRL-N           Lists commands whose names contain a given substring.
Configure Type-In Modes   HYPER-CTRL-(           Allows modification of the modes used in interpretting and completing
Help                      HELP                   Pops up a menu of help-oriented commands.
Keystroke Search          HYPER-CTRL-K           Lists commands assigned to a given keystroke or keystroke sequence.
Load Commands             HYPER-CTRL-L           Load UCL commands saved earlier
Numeric Argument          CTRL-U                 Passes a numeric argument to next command(s)
Redo Command              HYPER-CTRL-R           Repeats previous command using same arguments.
Save Commands             HYPER-CTRL-S           Save all of the user's tailored commands out to disk.
System Menu               Mouse-RIGHT            Pops up the system menu for selection of programs, windows, etc.
Top Level Configurer      HYPER-CTRL-T           Modify the attributes of Command & Lisp type-in.

INPUT EDITOR COMMANDS:
COMMAND NAME              ASSIGNED KEYSTROKE      DESCRIPTION
Apropos Complete          SUPER-ESCAPE           Completes input as a substring, similar to the APROPOS function.
Auto Completion           SPACE                  Does ESCAPE (Recognition) completion on first symbol. Active only in U
Backward Character        CTRL-B                 Moves the cursor backward one character.
Backward Parentheses      META-CTRL-B            Moves the cursor backward one set of parentheses.
Backward Word             META-B                 Moves the cursor backward one word.
Basic Help                HELP                   Suggests variaous ways of getting help.
Beginning Of Buffer       META-<                 Moves the cursor to the beginning of the current input.
Beginning Of Line         CTRL-A                 Moves the cursor to the beginning of the current line.
Clear Input               CLEAR-INPUT            Clears the current input.
Complete                  ESCAPE                 Completes using Recognition style of completion.
Delete Character          CTRL-D                 Deletes the character under the cursor.
Delete Parentheses        META-CTRL-K            Deletes the Lisp form to the right of the cursor.
Delete Word               META-D                 Deletes the word to the right of the cursor.
Display Internal State    META-CTRL-HELP         Displays the internal state of the Input Editor.
End Of Buffer             META->                 Moves cursor to the end of current input.
End Of Line               CTRL-E                 Moves cursor to the end of current line.
Exchange Words            META-T                 Exchanges words on either side of cursor.
Forward Character         CTRL-F                 Moves the cursor forward one character.
Forward Parentheses       META-CTRL-F            Moves the cursor forward one set of parentheses.
Forward Word              META-F                 Moves the cursor forward one word.
Kill Line                 CTRL-K                 Kills input right of cursor on the current line.
Kill Region               CTRL-W                 Kills a region of input marked by user.
List Apropos Completions  SUPER-/                Lists possible Apropos-style completions on a symbol left of cursor.
List Commands             CTRL-HELP              Displays information on Input Editor commands in a scroll window.
List Completions          CTRL-/                 Lists possible ESCAPE (Recognition) style completions on a symbol left
List Input Ring           META-STATUS            Displays the input ring.
List Kill Ring            META-CTRL-STATUS       Displays the Zmacs kill ring.

                                          More Below
Command Display    (Press ⟨END⟩ to exit)
R:Command Menu   R2:System Menu

02/26/85 05:51:49AM ROSEMARY    USER:   Keyboard        + C8: IMAGEN; IMAGENP.XFASL#116  1002 21905
```

■ Large System Maintenance Tools—The Explorer provides two facilities to help you manage and maintain large programs.

— The *system definition facility* allows you to define the files that comprise a program as a *system*, thus simplifying the manipulation of those files.

— The *patch facility* lets you manage new versions of a system and issue small *patches* (changes) to update old versions.

■ Font Editor—A *font* is an assortment of type in a particular style and size. The Explorer supplies many predefined fonts. The *font editor* allows you to modify existing fonts or create new ones. A grid is displayed on which you can draw magnified characters, and a *sample pane* shows you how the characters appear in normal size.

Software Options

The software options available for the Explorer supplement its graphics capabilities, help you build an NLI for a program, support database operations, allow you to use PROLOG and Grasper, and let you format your documentation.

In addition to the standard programs that comprise the Explorer's software environment, a set of software options is available to provide extended functionality. TI currently offers the following software options for the Explorer.

■ Graphics Toolkit—The *Graphics Toolkit* enhances the Explorer's graphics capabilities with the following three tools that allow you to create, modify, and manipulate specific objects within a picture.

— The *graphics window system* lets you incorporate a number of objects into an application, including lines, arcs, circles, polygons, etc. Once drawn, the objects can be copied, moved, erased, enlarged, reduced, or combined. All programs that use the graphics window system can share pictures with each other.

— The *graphics editor* provides an interactive method of drawing pictures. It includes all the capabilities of the graphics window system, as well as a system of rulers and grids that can overlay the display to increase the accuracy of your drawings. You can use the graphics editor to create pictures for presentations, reports, or manuals.

— The *tree editor* graphically displays any tree-structured entity, such as the hierarchy of combined flavors. You can use the tree editor to format the display either vertically or horizontally and to pan or zoom in on the displayed structure.

■ Natural Language Menu System—The *Natural Language Menu System* (NLMenu) helps you build natural language interfaces for your programs. An NLMenu interface, which is similar to the NaturalLink™ interface described in Chapter 4, presents you with a set of windows and menus that contain words and phrases in English. You construct command sentences by using the mouse to select the appropriate words and phrases (*Figure 9-12*).

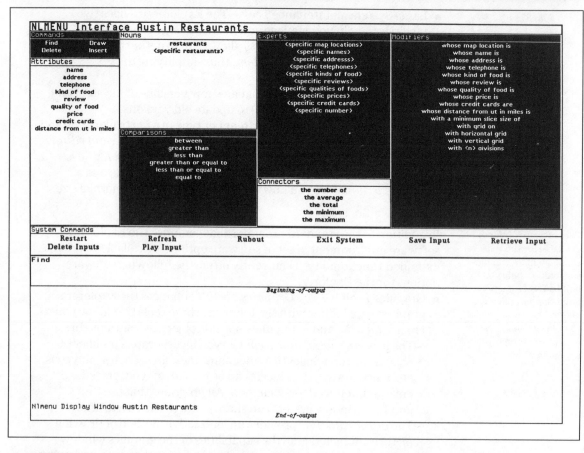

Figure 9-12.
The Natural Language
Menu System
(Source: Explorer Technical
Summary, *Copyright © 1985,*
Texas Instruments Incorporated)

■ Relational Table Management System—The *Relational Table*
Management System (RTMS) provides basic database operations by
allowing you to build, access, and manipulate any kind of
information in tabular format (*Figure 9-13*). RTMS is integrated into
the LISP environment so that you can invoke its functions from the
LISP Listener or from your own application.

■ Knowledge Engineering Tools—The Explorer currently offers two
knowledge engineering tools to help you develop AI programs.
—The *PROLOG Toolkit* includes two components that allow you to
integrate PROLOG code into your programs. The *PROLOG*
interpreter executes PROLOG programs and allows you to
develop programs that mix PROLOG with LISP. The *sample*
expert system tool provides a PROLOG inference engine and a
user interface that you can use to build simple rule-based expert
systems.

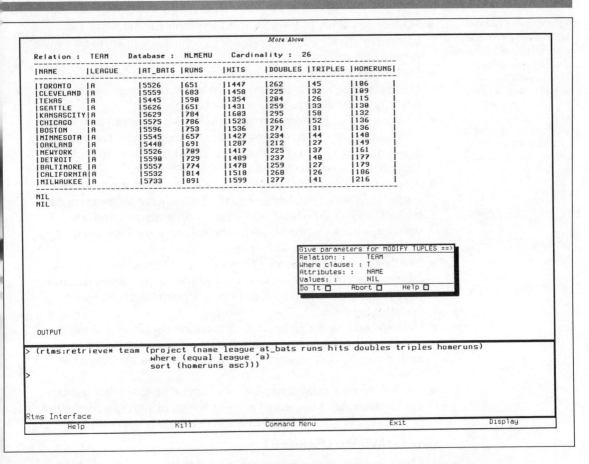

**Figure 9-13.
The Relational Table
Management System**
(*Source:* Explorer Technical
Summary, *Copyright* © 1985,
Texas Instruments Incorporated)

—*Grasper* is a knowledge representation language that you can use to describe knowledge that is represented graphically as a network (see Chapter 7). Grasper includes functions that allow you to create, delete, and evaluate the various elements of a network, including nodes, edges, and spaces (collections of objects).

■ Formatter—The *Formatter* allows you to create publication-quality documents such as reports and manuals. Used in conjunction with the ZMACS editor, the Formatter lets you concentrate on writing rather than on the details of formatting, page layout, and typography.

System Facilities

The Explorer provides many facilities for the efficient implementation of LISP programs, including the following.

■ Memory Management—The Explorer manages its memory so that it has a virtual memory of up to 128 megabytes.

The Explorer's system facilities improve the implementation of LISP programs by managing the system's memory, implementing many functions in machine language, scheduling the active operations, communicating with peripherals in a uniform manner, and more.

- Microcode—Many of the important Explorer functions are implemented directly in *microcode* (machine language) to maximize system performance.
- Performance Monitoring—You can monitor the performance of your programs with a "metering" system to determine which parts of the program require the greatest execution time.
- Processes—The Explorer provides facilities that allow you to create and control your own *processes* (series of operations). The *scheduler* utility manages the active processes, allowing them to execute concurrently and to communicate with each other.
- Stream I/O—The Explorer relies on *streams* to perform input and output (I/O) with peripheral devices. A stream is a sequence of data that allows you to communicate with peripherals in a uniform manner, without worrying about the nature of the individual peripheral.
- File System—The Explorer's *file system* provides a tree-oriented, multiple-level directory system for disk file maintenance, similar to the file system provided by MS-DOS, a popular microcomputer operating system.
- Backup and Restore—The Explorer provides facilities that allow you to *back up* (copy) information from a disk to a cartridge tape and subsequently to *restore* (retrieve) that information from the tape.
- Peek—The *Peek* utility is a window-oriented program that displays information about the status of various system activities, including processes, file system, windows, and networks (*Figure 9-14*).

WHAT HAVE WE LEARNED?

1. LISP machines are computers that are designed specifically for the development of AI software and generally are intended to be used by one programmer at a time.
2. Hardware features of LISP machines include a high-speed processor, a large memory, a bit-mapped display, a specialized keyboard, a mouse, and communication capabilities.
3. LISP machines feature sophisticated software development environments that include screen windowing techniques.
4. The LISP machines offered by LMI, Symbolics, and Texas Instruments are outgrowths of research performed at the MIT AI lab; the LISP machines offered by Xerox are based on different technology developed at Xerox PARC.
5. The software features of the Texas Instruments Explorer can be divided into categories that include its user interface, the LISP language, program development tools, software options, and system facilities.

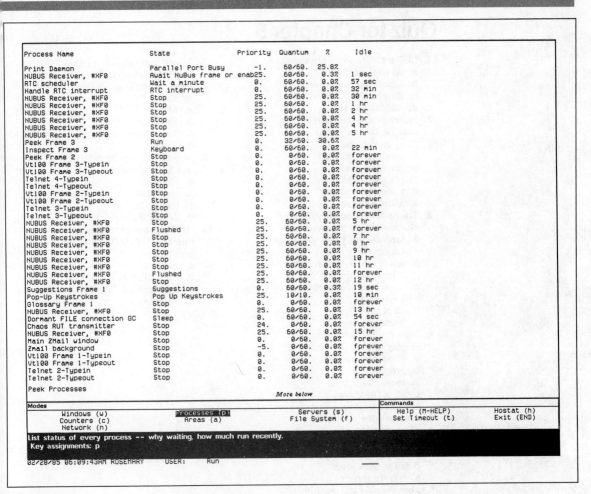

```
Process Name              State                 Priority  Quantum   %     Idle

Print Daemon              Parallel Port Busy      -1.      60/60.   25.8%
NUBUS Receiver, #XF0      Await NuBus frame or enab25.     60/60.   0.3%   1 sec
RTC scheduler             Wait a minute            0.      60/60.   0.0%   57 sec
Handle RTC interrupt      RTC interrupt            0.      60/60.   0.0%   32 min
NUBUS Receiver, #XF0      Stop                    25.      60/60.   0.0%   30 min
NUBUS Receiver, #XF0      Stop                    25.      60/60.   0.0%   1 hr
NUBUS Receiver, #XF0      Stop                    25.      60/60.   0.0%   2 hr
NUBUS Receiver, #XF0      Stop                    25.      60/60.   0.0%   4 hr
NUBUS Receiver, #XF0      Stop                    25.      60/60.   0.0%   4 hr
NUBUS Receiver, #XF0      Stop                    25.      60/60.   0.0%   5 hr
Peek Frame 3              Run                      0.      32/60.   30.6%
Inspect Frame 3           Keyboard                 0.      60/60.   0.0%   22 min
Peek Frame 2              Stop                     0.      0/60.    0.0%   forever
Vt100 Frame 3-Typein      Stop                     0.      0/60.    0.0%   forever
Vt100 Frame 3-Typeout     Stop                     0.      0/60.    0.0%   forever
Telnet 4-Typein           Stop                     0.      0/60.    0.0%   forever
Telnet 4-Typeout          Stop                     0.      0/60.    0.0%   forever
Vt100 Frame 2-Typein      Stop                     0.      0/60.    0.0%   forever
Vt100 Frame 2-Typeout     Stop                     0.      0/60.    0.0%   forever
Telnet 3-Typein           Stop                     0.      0/60.    0.0%   forever
Telnet 3-Typeout          Stop                     0.      0/60.    0.0%   forever
NUBUS Receiver, #XF0      Stop                    25.      60/60.   0.0%   5 hr
NUBUS Receiver, #XF0      Flushed                 25.      60/60.   0.0%   forever
NUBUS Receiver, #XF0      Stop                    25.      60/60.   0.0%   7 hr
NUBUS Receiver, #XF0      Stop                    25.      60/60.   0.0%   8 hr
NUBUS Receiver, #XF0      Stop                    25.      60/60.   0.0%   9 hr
NUBUS Receiver, #XF0      Stop                    25.      60/60.   0.0%   10 hr
NUBUS Receiver, #XF0      Stop                    25.      60/60.   0.0%   11 hr
NUBUS Receiver, #XF0      Flushed                 25.      60/60.   0.0%   forever
NUBUS Receiver, #XF0      Stop                    25.      60/60.   0.0%   12 hr
Suggestions Frame 1       Suggestions              0.      60/60.   0.3%   19 sec
Pop-Up Keystrokes         Pop Up Keystrokes       25.      10/10.   0.0%   10 min
Glossary Frame 1          Stop                     0.      0/60.    0.0%   forever
NUBUS Receiver, #XF0      Stop                    25.      60/60.   0.0%   13 hr
Dormant FILE connection GC Sleep                   0.      60/60.   0.0%   54 sec
Chaos RUT transmitter     Stop                    24.      0/60.    0.0%   forever
NUBUS Receiver, #XF0      Stop                    25.      60/60.   0.0%   15 hr
Main ZMail window         Stop                     0.      0/60.    0.0%   forever
ZMail background          Stop                    -5.      0/60.    0.0%   fprever
Vt100 Frame 1-Typein      Stop                     0.      0/60.    0.0%   forever
Vt100 Frame 1-Typeout     Stop                     0.      0/60.    0.0%   forever
Telnet 2-Typein           Stop                     0.      0/60.    0.0%   forever
Telnet 2-Typeout          Stop                     0.      0/60.    0.0%   forever

Peek Processes
                                                    More below
```

Modes			Commands	
Windows (w)	Processes (p)	Servers (s)	Help (M-HELP)	Hostat (h)
Counters (c)	Areas (a)	File System (f)	Set Timeout (t)	Exit (END)
Network (n)				

```
List status of every process -- why waiting, how much run recently.
Key assignments: p

02/28/85 06:09:43AM ROSEMARY    USER:    Run
```

Figure 9-14.
The Peek Utility
(*Source:* Explorer Technical
Summary, *Copyright © 1985,*
Texas Instruments Incorporated)

WHAT'S NEXT?

This book has discussed the history of AI, current AI technologies, and
software and hardware products specifically designed to expedite the
development of AI software. The next chapter explores three major
continuing AI efforts that are important to the future of artificial
intelligence.

Quiz for Chapter 9

1. LISP machines also are known as:
   a. AI workstations.
   b. super minicomputers.
   c. time-sharing terminals.
   d. all of the above.

2. Prior to the invention of time sharing, the prevalent method of computer access was:
   a. batch processing.
   b. remote access.
   c. telecommunication.
   d. none of the above.
   e. a and b above.

3. The hardware features of LISP machines generally include:
   a. large memory and a high-speed processor.
   b. letter-quality printers and 8-inch disk drives.
   c. a mouse and a specialized keyboard.
   d. all of the above.
   e. a and c above.

4. High-resolution, bit-mapped displays are useful for displaying:
   a. clearer characters.
   b. graphics.
   c. more characters.
   d. all of the above.
   e. b and c above.

5. A mouse device may be:
   a. electro-chemical.
   b. mechanical.
   c. optical.
   d. all of the above.
   e. b and c above.

6. The original LISP machines produced by both LMI and Symbolics were based on research performed at:
   a. CMU.
   b. MIT.
   c. Stanford University.
   d. Xerox PARC.

7. The LISP machine produced by LMI is called the _____, after a LISP procedure.
   a. CADR
   b. CONS
   c. Dandelion
   d. Lambda

8. Which company offers the LISP machine considered to be "the most powerful symbolic processor available"?
   a. LMI
   b. Symbolics
   c. Texas Instruments
   d. Xerox

9. Graphic interfaces were first used in a Xerox product called:
   a. Ethernet.
   b. InterLISP.
   c. Smalltalk.
   d. ZetaLISP.

10. NLMenu, a natural language interface for the TI Explorer, is similar to:
    a. Ethernet.
    b. NaturalLink.
    c. the Personal Consultant.
    d. PROLOG.

Continuing Efforts in Artificial Intelligence

ABOUT THIS CHAPTER

The previous chapters have discussed where artificial intelligence has been and where it is now. This chapter explores AI from a different perspective: where it is going. Although it is impossible to foretell the future of any field with complete accuracy, the sections in this book that have discussed the various AI technologies have included predictions of future products and trends. This chapter takes a broader and more general view, discussing continuing AI efforts that may have major effects on the United States and the world.

Specifically, this chapter explores three continuing large-scale efforts to develop technology that may have profound implications for the future of artificial intelligence. These three efforts are:

- The DARPA Strategic Computing Program—A massive American effort to develop military applications of artificial intelligence,
- The Fifth Generation Project—The Japanese research project that is attempting to overtake the United States as the world leader in high technology, and
- Microelectronics and Computer Technology Corporation (MCC)— What many regard as the American response to the challenge of the Fifth Generation Project.

This chapter begins with a discussion of advances in computer technology which directly affect artificial intelligence and which are integral parts of the three efforts discussed.

ADVANCED COMPUTER TECHNOLOGY

Advances in computer technology have made it possible to run more sophisticated AI programs. Continuing research in the areas of Very Large Scale Integration and parallel processing is striving to improve computer performance to handle even more complex AI programs.

Advances in artificial intelligence have always been limited by existing computer technology. AI programs generally require more computing resources than other programs; in fact, some AI theories have not been implemented as software because existing computers simply have not been powerful enough.

However, as computer technology has advanced, it has become possible to develop more sophisticated AI programs. It is not surprising, then, that the three major AI efforts discussed in this chapter are not limiting their research to AI software; they are all trying to develop more sophisticated computing technology as well.

Although the new technology may provide significant benefits for "traditional" computing, much of the research is designed to optimize computers for AI applications. This section discusses two areas of that research: Very Large Scale Integration and parallel processing.

Very Large Scale Integration (VLSI)

VLSI techniques, which combine several hundred thousand electronic components on a single semiconductor chip, and new computer architectures are major factors in the development of more powerful fifth generation computers.

The process of combining electronic components into a single compact device is known as *integration*, and the devices containing multiple electronic components are *integrated circuits* (IC's) or *chips*. Since the invention of the IC in the late 1950's by Jack Kilby of Texas Instruments, computer scientists have been trying to combine more and more components on a single IC. Because integration can increase processing speeds and decrease costs at the same time, advances in integration often are accompanied by the development of more powerful computers.

In the 1970's, the techniques of *Large Scale Integration* (LSI) allowed IC manufacturers to combine the functions of several thousand components on a single IC. This may seem somewhat miraculous since IC's may measure only about a quarter of an inch square; however, it pales in comparison to modern techniques of *Very Large Scale Integration* (VLSI), which allow several hundred thousand electronic components to be combined on a single chip (*Figure 10-1*).

Figure 10-1.
The TMS320 VLSI Chip

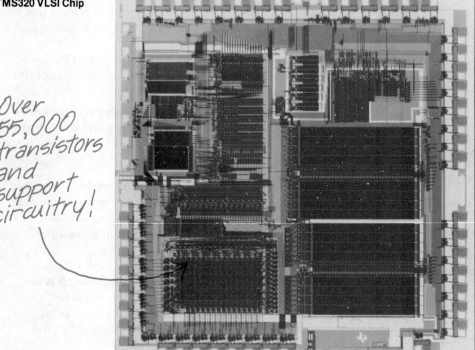

Over 55,000 transistors and support circuitry!

All three efforts discussed in this chapter are exploring advanced VLSI techniques that could form the basis of more powerful "fifth generation" computers. Advanced VLSI techniques may allow computers to feature the large memory and high processing speeds that are essential for many AI applications. For example, the Japanese Fifth Generation Project hopes to develop computers with memories as large as 1,000 gigabytes (1,000,000,000,000 characters) and with processing speeds of up to 1 billion logical inferences per second.

(*Logical inferences per second*, or *LIPS*, is a measure of the speed of computers used for AI applications. A logical inference usually consists of from 100 to 1,000 computer instructions; therefore, a computer operating at 1 billion LIPS could execute from 100 billion to 1,000 billion computer instructions each second. In the mid-1980's, by way of contrast, an exceptionally high-speed computer might operate at a mere 20 million instructions per second.)

Parallel Processing

In 1945, American mathematician John von Neumann wrote a paper entitled *Report on the EDVAC* (Electronic Discrete VAriable Computer) in which he outlined a logical structure of processing information with a computer. In the paper, von Neumann specified a theory of information processing that has permeated the development of computers ever since. In fact, modern computers sometimes are called "von Neumann machines" because the information-processing methods they use descended directly from his theories. One important element of the von Neumann machine that has stood the test of time is the concept of *sequential processing*.

In contrast to sequential processing where actions are performed one at a time, parallel processing allows several actions to be performed simultaneously.

Computers, which may seem to be doing many things at once, actually perform actions one at a time, in sequence. One of the goals of advanced computer research is to increase computing speeds, and one method of increasing speed is to abandon the sequential processing model of the von Neumann machine and have more than one process executing at a time. This technique, called *parallel processing* (*Figure 10-2*), is indeed the subject of intense investigation in the research efforts discussed in this chapter.

"Now that the economics of VLSI have made processors among the least expensive of the components in a computer," notes Brattle Research, "the idea that fantastic processing speeds can immediately be achieved by ganging together multiple processors in parallel is receiving a great deal of play."[1]

---

[1] Brattle Research Corporation, *Artificial Intelligence Computers and Software* (Cambridge, MA), p. 105.

**Figure 10-2.
Sequential Processing
vs. Parallel Processing**

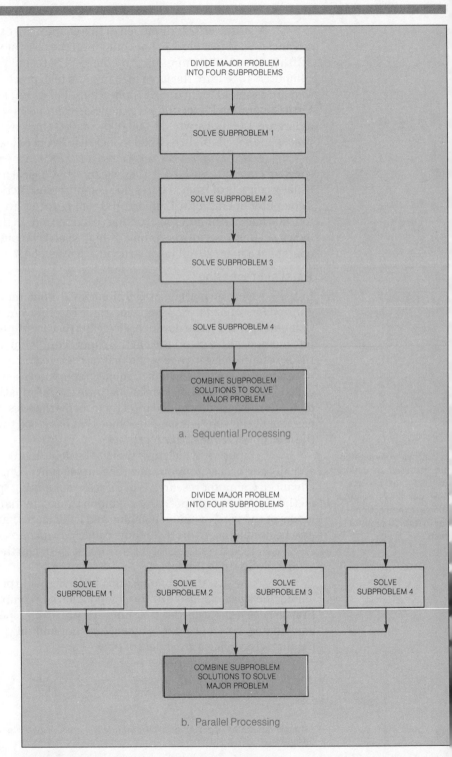

a. Sequential Processing

b. Parallel Processing

THE DARPA STRATEGIC COMPUTING PROGRAM

The DARPA Strategic Computing Program is supporting research projects in AI and other computing areas in order to develop three military applications.

In 1983, the Defense Advanced Research Projects Agency (DARPA) announced one of the most ambitious scientific research projects ever attempted: the Strategic Computing Program (SCP). The SCP, which began in 1984, is scheduled to last five years and cost $600 million.

The SCP actually contains a number of projects in a wide range of AI and other computing areas. As shown in *Figure 10-3*, DARPA plans to fund SCP projects in several diverse areas, such as:

- VLSI and other microelectronic technology;
- Multiprocessors, signal processors, and other avenues of computer architecture technology; and
- AI technologies such as expert systems, natural language, computer vision, speech recognition, and planning systems.

Figure 10-3.
The Structure and Goals of the DARPA Strategic Computing Program
(*Source:* Strategic Computing, *Defense Advanced Research Projects Agency, 28 October 1983*)

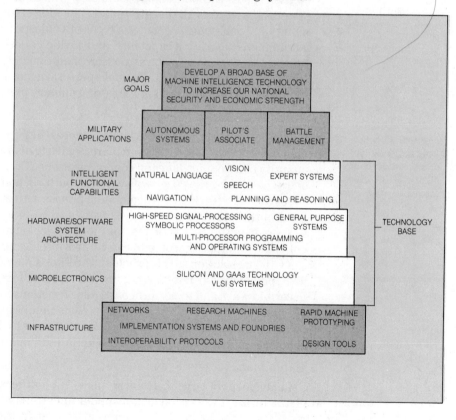

The ultimate goal of the SCP, in the words of the 70-page DARPA report that explains the project, "is to provide the United States with a broad line of machine intelligence technology and to demonstrate applications of the technology to critical problems in defense."[2] Specifically, DARPA plans for the SCP to result in the development of three military applications:

- Autonomous Systems,
- Pilot's Associate, and
- Battle Management System.

Autonomous Systems

Autonomous systems are vehicles and other systems that incorporate computer vision and expert system technologies so that they can run by themselves without human operation. "Examples of autonomous systems," according to the SCP report, "include certain 'smart' munitions, cruise missles, various types of vehicles possessing an autonomous navigation capability, and a wide variety of mobile and fixed robotic systems."[3] The attraction of autonomous systems to the military is obvious: the systems could perform a multitude of "intelligent" tasks without endangering military personnel.

Autonomous systems are vehicles that would be able to run by themselves to avoid endangering human lives in certain military situations.

Pilot's Associate

Because military aircraft have become increasingly complex, the SCP plan reports that "pilots in combat are regularly overwhelmed by the quantity of incoming data and communications. They can be equally overwhelmed by the dozens of switches, buttons, and knobs that cover their control handles demanding precise activation."[4] In many areas of the military, technology is growing too quickly for operators to keep up with; there soon may be more devices available on an aircraft, for example, than a pilot can control intelligently.

The Pilot's Associate would help a pilot operate our increasingly complex military aircraft, especially in combat.

The solution to this problem, the Pilot's Associate, is classified as a "personal associate" in that it will be trained to respond to a pilot in certain ways and to perform particular functions for that pilot. Using speech recognition and expert system technologies, the pilot will be able either to delegate portions of certain tasks to the Pilot's Associate or to instruct the device to initiate actions on its own.

Battle Management System

"Management of large scale enterprises," notes the SCP report "is characterized by decision making under uncertainty."[5] If the large scale enterprise in question happens to be a battle, the consequences

The Battle Management System would assist in decision making during battle.

---

[2] Defense Advanced Research Projects Agency, *Strategic Computing* (28 October 1983), p. ii.
[3] Ibid., p. 21.
[4] Ibid., p. 24.
[5] Ibid., p. 27.

of making an incorrect decision can be especially devastating. An intelligent Battle Management System would provide welcome assistance to military decision makers in battle situations.

The Battle Management System, as envisioned by DARPA, would use expert system, speech recognition, and natural language technologies to assist in all phases of the decision-making process. Commander Ronald Ohlander of DARPA discusses his view of battle management in *Figure 10-4*.

**Figure 10-4.
An Interview with
Commander Ron
Ohlander on "Battle
Management"**

Q: Can you tell me more of what you mean by *battle management*?

OHLANDER: *Battle management* is management of tactical warfare in the field—the scheduling of assets to support a particular mission, the assessment of threat situations, etc.

Imagine that you're in charge of achieving a military objective, and you have assets available at your disposal—but they're a limited resource. You have a threat that you have some information on, but you are also trying to gather more information about the other side. So you have sources that present a tremendous amount of information to you, at various times, about what's going on in the external world. Some of that information is *good* information; some of it's *bad* information. It conflicts in some cases, and it confirms in some cases.

At the same time, you have resources that are in various stages of ability to respond over a period of time. They're at various places, and they have various capabilities. Given a situation, you're asked to perform a mission of some sort. How do you allocate your limited resources in such a way that you can satisfy near-term objectives as well as long-term objectives and take advantage of weaknesses or strengths of what you think is going on in the external world?

Q: How would a battle management system be implemented?

OHLANDER: All battle management takes place from a control center of some sort. We are not yet ready to consider the distributed use of portable computers in the field. On a battlefield, you're talking about vans, control vans—some kind of vehicle on which you have a control platform.

Generally, you're trying to assign scarce resources to meet a particular objective. You never have enough of what you want. Human intuition—human judgment in decision making—certainly far surpasses the ability of any computer to make decisions in that arena now. The important thing the computer can do is to keep track of detail—how many assets you've got, how many objectives you are trying to attack—breakdowns of things that humans can't do very well at all.

Q: Would you call that an AI application?

OHLANDER: Well, to a certain degree it is. It is not just a matter of listing assets; there is *judgment* involved concerning recommendations for the best use of resources. Also, there is great potential for the evolutionary development of intelligent interfaces and increased reasoning capacity in the area of automated decision making aids.

**Figure 10-4.
An Interview with
Commander Ron
Ohlander on "Battle
Management"
(Continued)**

My view of a battle management system in the future is a true symbiotic relationship between man and machine, where the machine understands very well what the human is trying to do and what his shortcomings are, and at the same time recognizes its own. The human also knows the shortcomings of the machine, and what it can do well, etc.

Even if the machine can understand a good part about solving the problem, to be truly useful to the human being, it has to understand part of the problem-solving task—what comes next? What does he want to see? What is the best information I could give him? So it is not just a case of the machine going off and digesting so much input, chunking it over for a number of milliseconds or seconds, and spitting out an answer. It is a true interchange of information.

These problems are exceedingly difficult. Humans don't solve them that well. It requires a true interchange of information, where the human prompts for more information, and the machine anticipates what he wants and presents things in the most digestible format.

Ramifications of the Strategic Computing Plan

DARPA anticipates that the results of the Strategic Computing Program will help not only military leaders but also industrial and political leaders.

DARPA's vision for the success of the SCP goes well beyond military applications. "The timely, successful generation and application of intelligent computing technology," DARPA notes, "will have profound effects. If the technology is widely dispersed in applications throughout our society, Americans will have a significantly improved capability to handle complex tasks and to codify, mechanize, and propagate their knowledge. The new technology will improve the capability of our industrial, military and political leaders to tap the nation's pool of knowledge and effectively manage large enterprises, even in times of great stress and change."[6]

THE FIFTH GENERATION PROJECT

One of the goals of the Japanese Fifth Generation Project is to develop a fifth generation of computers for AI applications.

"Knowledge," according to Ed Feigenbaum and Pamela McCorduck, "is power."[7] They freely admit that they are not the original source of that adage; in their book, *The Fifth Generation*, they attribute the quotation to a treatise on *The Art of War* dating back to the fourth century B.C. However, Feigenbaum and McCorduck have applied the ancient wisdom to a less belligerent and more modern context: the power inherent in the knowledge provided by intelligent machines.

In particular, Feigenbaum and McCorduck refer to the economic power that the Japanese hope will accrue to them as a result of an ambitious project known by various names, the most popular of which is the *Fifth Generation Project*. The project, which commenced

[6] Ibid., p. ix.
[7] Edward A. Feigenbaum and Pamela McCorduck, *The Fifth Generation* (New York: Signet, 1984), p. 5.

in 1982, is a 10-year effort with a variety of goals, the central focus being the development of a "fifth generation" of computers designed specifically for artificial intelligence applications.

Currently, the Japanese excel at the implementation of technology, such as in producing cars, stereos, calculators, watches, and integrated circuits.

The United States traditionally has been the greatest source of technological innovation in the world. More recently, the Japanese have founded their own "tradition" in what has been called their "economic miracle" during the years since World War II: they have become the acknowledged masters at the *implementation* of technology. For example:

- The automobile first was mass-produced in the United States; but by applying American technology and management techniques in innovative ways, Japanese automobile manufacturers have impacted the American automobile industry dramatically and irrevocably.
- It is becoming increasingly difficult to purchase a high-quality stereo, television, or other electronic device that was not manufactured in Japan.
- Although hand-held calculators and digital watches both were invented in the United States, creative Japanese competition has driven nearly every American manufacturer out of those markets.
- The process of electronic miniaturization was created in the United States, first with transistors and then with integrated circuits (IC's). Japanese companies are now among the largest producers of IC's in the world and may be on the verge of dominating that market.

Instead of implementing what someone else discovers, the Japanese are planning to spend about $1 billion to develop AI technology themselves.

If these kinds of trends were to continue, you might expect the Japanese to wait until American manufacturers had commercialized AI successfully and had developed a wide range of AI products. Then, if past scenarios were to be adhered to, Japanese companies would develop clever, creative, and inexpensive products based on the mature American technology. But this time, the Japanese have served notice that they no longer are content to create innovative uses for American technology. This time, they intend to develop the technology themselves; this time, they plan to make their own discoveries.

The Japanese have marshalled an impressive array of resources to implement their far-reaching goals. For the first several years, the project has not required private funding; $450 million of financing has been provided by the powerful Ministry of International Trade and Industry (MITI). By the time it is complete, the Fifth Generation Project may require more than $1 billion in a typical Japanese combination of public and private financing.

A new organization, the Institute for New Generation Computer Technology (ICOT), has been established in Tokyo to bring the project to fruition. "Forty of the brightest young computer researchers in the country"[8] have been brought together at ICOT; these researchers are on loan from many of the same Japanese technology firms whose products currently dominate American markets, including NEC, Toshiba, Sharp, Mitsubishi, and Matsushita (the manufacturers of Panasonic products). Over 150 other researchers in various locations contribute to the project under contract to ICOT.

Fifth Generation Technology

The Fifth Generation Project plans to improve the storage and retrieval of information in a database; to provide inference capabilities in PROLOG; to incorporate various AI technologies to make computers easier to use; and to develop intelligent programming tools.

The ultimate aim of the Fifth Generation Project is, of course, the development of fifth generation computers. To achieve this goal, the Japanese have divided the project into the following four parts.

- Data Access—As we have discussed, AI programs typically require large amounts of data. The ability to *retrieve* information as needed is just as important as the ability to store the information in the first place. Although this data-retrieval problem exists in other areas of computer science, it is particularly acute in AI due to the volume of data. The Fifth Generation Project already has developed a prototype of a computer called the "Relational Database Machine" that is designed specifically to facilitate the storage and retrieval of information.

- Inference—As discussed in Chapter 3, an *inference engine* is an essential component of a knowledge-based system. The Fifth Generation Project is developing a prototype computer known as the "Personal Sequential Inference Machine" to provide inference capabilities in PROLOG, the logic-based AI language discussed in Chapter 7. "After that task is done," reports the New York Times, "the Inference Machine will be used by researchers as a tool to write programs for other parts of the project."[9]

- Ease of Use—The Fifth Generation Project includes research into several areas of AI that investigate ways of making computers easier to use, including computer vision, speech recognition, and natural language processing. In the second year of the project, it was reported that this part was faltering; however, several private Japanese companies now are tackling these problems on their own.

- Intelligent Programming—Intelligent programming tools, such as those discussed in Chapter 6, are being developed to expedite the programming efforts in all phases of the project.

[8] Ibid., p. 27.
[9] Andrew Pollack, "Japan Faltering Somewhat in Drive To Create 'Fifth Generation' Computer," *N. Y. Times News Service*, 14 October 1984.

Because the original goals of the project were stated in general and imprecise terms, evaluating its progress is difficult. Although there are those in the United States who cite the project's budgetary and other difficulties as evidence that it ultimately will fail, the Japanese remain confident. Even skeptics generally concede that the Fifth Generation Project is having a positive affect on AI research everywhere. "They have shaken up the rest of the computer science community around the world, and that's no small accomplishment," claims George Lindamood of Burroughs Corporation. "It will change the course of computer history."[10]

Knowledge Is Power

The Japanese want to be the first to market AI technology successfully because they believe it will give them numerous economic advantages, including making their products better than the competition's.

Why are the Japanese so intent on supplanting the United States and becoming the world leader in computer technology? What is it about intelligent machines that is leading them to devote so many resources to their development? Why is it so important to be first?

Quite simply, the Japanese believe that knowledge, supplied by a new generation of intelligent machines, is poised to become the basis of a new economic order. They believe that the world is evolving towards a "post-industrial" society in which the wealth of nations will be measured not in terms of gold or oil, but in terms of information. The nation that is first to commercialize AI technology successfully will gain an enormous economic advantage over other nations, the Japanese believe; not only will it give that nation an obvious advantage in the computer industry, it will have repercussions throughout a wide range of human affairs.

The United States currently dominates the processing of information by computers worldwide. Because information processing in the U.S. is nearly a $100 billion industry, it is a dominance that the U.S. scarcely can afford to lose. And yet, losing a preeminent position in the computer industry might be just the tip of the iceberg, merely the most obvious of the widespread economic advantages that the Japanese hope the Fifth Generation Project will provide for them. The successful development, implementation, and proliferation of AI technology could render *all* Japanese products, according to Feigenbaum and McCorduck, "so much better than the competition's, thanks to the degree of knowledge that will be brought to bear on their design and manufacture, that the Japanese expect to dominate markets in conventional products, too."[11]

Although many American AI researchers do not believe that the Fifth Generation Project will be a complete success, no one is prepared to discount its prospects with complete confidence. Even if the goals for the project are realized only in part, the Japanese will

[10] Ibid.
[11] Edward A. Feigenbaum and Pamela McCorduck, *The Fifth Generation* (New York: Signet, 1984), p. 19.

have developed technologies that will make their competition as formidable in a post-industrial society as it currently is in the industrial age. And the Japanese expect additional, unanticipated side effects of the project to enhance their position even further. "It is felt certain," they claim, "that fifth generation computers will trigger the realization of developments and phenomena heretofore undreamed of."[12]

MICROELECTRONICS AND COMPUTER TECHNOLOGY CORPORATION (MCC)

Microelectronics and Computer Technology Corporation consists of American high-technology companies who are supporting long-term computer technology research.

In early 1982, representatives of several major American high-technology companies met to discuss an unusual proposal by William Norris, founder and Chief Executive Officer of Control Data Corporation (CDC). Norris called the meeting to explore ways that the companies, normally competitors, could combine their resources to achieve significant advances in computer technology. Although there were some initial fears that such a cooperative effort might run afoul of anti-trust regulations, Norris felt that the threat to American technological leadership posed by programs like the Japanese Fifth Generation Project demanded a coordinated response.

The venture that grew out of that meeting, Microelectronics and Computer Technology Corporation (MCC), began formal operations in early 1983 under the direction of Admiral Bobby Inman, a former director of the National Security Agency. With Inman's prestige and expertise behind the organization, MCC has grown, as of this writing, to a consortium of the 21 firms listed in *Figure 10-5*. Equally important, Inman guided the MCC concept through the scrutiny of the U.S. Justice Department, which decided that it did not object to this unique business arrangement.

According to its charter, MCC eventually may have as many as 30 shareholders. The price of joining MCC has risen since its inception; at the beginning of 1985, the cost of admission doubled to $1 million. Unlike the Fifth Generation Project, MCC is totally a private sector initiative, receiving no financial support from the government. MCC operates with the funds provided by its shareholders and other private donations.

A member that participates in an MCC program supplies personnel for the project and shares in any resulting profits.

MCC members may elect to participate in any or all of the four programs discussed below. Members who participate in a program contribute scientists and engineers, and share in whatever technologies the program develops. MCC grants an exclusive technology license to participating members for three years after a technology is developed. After three years, the technology may be licensed to other companies, with the participating members sharing in the royalty income.

[12] *Proceedings of the International Conference on Fifth Generation Computer Systems* (New York: Elsevier-North Holland, 1982).

**Figure 10-5.
Shareholders in the
Microelectronics and
Computer Technology
Corporation (MCC)**

MCC

Advanced Micro Devices
Allied Corporation
Bell Communications Research (Bellcore)
BMC Industries, Inc.
The Boeing Company
Control Data Corporation
Digital Equipment Corporation
Eastman Kodak Company
Gould Inc.
Harris Corporation
Honeywell, Inc.
Lockheed Corporation
Martin Marietta Corporation
Mostek Corporation
Motorola, Inc.
National Semiconductor Corporation
NCR Corporation
RCA Corporation
Rockwell International Corporation
Sperry Corporation
3M

MCC Programs

*Presently, MCC is working
on four projects with the
common goal of improving
the operation of
computers.*

MCC currently is engaged in four long-term projects with a common
goal: to "provide the technology necessary to make computers faster,
more reliable, and capable of performing more complex tasks at a
higher level of quality and a much lower cost."[13] By concentrating on
long-term goals (six to ten years) rather than seeking an immediate
profit, MCC is free to follow a long-range strategy that might have
been difficult for its members to pursue individually; corporations
often are under intense stockholder pressure to generate short-term
profits, frequently at the expense of long-term goals.

The four programs undertaken by MCC fall into four major
areas:

- Packaging,
- Software Technology,
- VLSI/Computer-Aided Design, and
- Advanced Computer Architecture.

[13] *Microelectronics and Computer Technology Corporation* (MCC).

The following descriptions of the MCC programs are taken from MCC literature.[14]

Packaging

The packaging project is a six-year program to advance state-of-the-art semiconductor packaging and interconnect technology. Emphasis is on technologies compatible with automatic assembly at both the circuit and system level.

Software Technology

The MCC software technology effort is a seven-year program to develop new techniques, procedures, and tools that can be used to improve the productivity of the software development process by one to two orders of magnitude.

VLSI/Computer-Aided Design

MCC's program in the area of VLSI/computer-aided design is an eight-year project to improve computer-aided design technology and to develop an integrated set of tools that will have particular application to complex systems and the very complex VLSI chips from which they will be built.

Advanced Computer Architecture

MCC's advanced computer architecture project is researching ways to represent human knowledge, to improve the storage and retrieval of information in a database, to incorporate AI technologies into the design of computers, and to improve parallel processing.

The most complex and ambitious of the MCC programs, this 10-year effort focuses on the following projects:

- AI/Knowledge-Based Systems—Realize the computer's problem-solving potential by developing new ways to represent human knowledge and thought concepts, as well as new engineering models and tools to apply human expertise to a wide range of problems;
- Database System Management—Improve database design and storage methods and capacities to permit more flexible storage and faster retrieval of a broader range of more complex information;
- Human Factors Technology—Improve the relationship between man and computer by simplifying the use of computers through techniques such as improved voice or character recognition or use of natural languages; and
- Parallel Processing—Develop the languages and architectures to allow computers to perform tasks simultaneously instead of sequentially, with corresponding increases in processing speed.

---

[14] *Microelectronics and Computer Technology Corporation* (Austin, TX: MCC).

WHAT HAVE WE LEARNED?

1. Several continuing efforts in AI are investigating advanced computer technology in areas such as VLSI and parallel processing.
2. The DARPA Strategic Computing Program is focusing on the development of three military applications: autonomous systems, the Pilot's Associate, and a battle management system.
3. The Japanese Fifth Generation Project is attempting to gain economic power for Japan through the development of a fifth generation of computers, optimized for artificial intelligence applications.
4. Microelectronics and Computer Technology Corporation (MCC), headed by Admiral Bobby Inman, is a consortium of 21 American companies that is investigating semiconductor packaging, software technology, VLSI and computer-aided design, and advanced computer architecture.

Quiz for Chapter 10

1. The integrated circuit was invented by Jack Kilby of:
   a. MIT.
   b. Texas Instruments.
   c. Xerox.
   d. none of the above.

2. Using VLSI techniques, it is possible to combine over _____ components on a single chip.
   a. 1,000
   b. 50,000
   c. 100,000
   d. 5,000,000

3. The speed of computers used for AI applications is measured in _____ per second.
   a. cycles
   b. instructions
   c. logical inferences
   d. revolutions

4. Parallel processing research is attempting to improve on the traditional sequential processing techniques specified by:
   a. John McCarthy.
   b. Ronald Ohlander.
   c. Alan Turing.
   d. John von Neumann.

5. The Strategic Computing Program is a project of the:
   a. Defense Advanced Research Projects Agency.
   b. Jet Propulsion Laboratory.
   c. National Science Foundation.
   d. all of the above.
   e. none of the above.

6. The applications in the Strategic Computing Program include:
   a. autonomous systems.
   b. battle management.
   c. pilot's associate.
   d. all of the above.
   e. none of the above.

7. The new organization established to implement the Fifth Generation Project is called:
   a. ICOT.
   b. MCC.
   c. MITI.
   d. SCP.

8. The Fifth Generation Project is based on the premise that _____ will become the basis of a new economic order.
   a. food
   b. gold
   c. knowledge
   d. power

9. Who is the head of MCC?
   a. John McCarthy
   b. William Norris
   c. John von Neumann
   d. none of the above

10. MCC is investigating the improvement of the relationship between people and computers through a technology called:
   a. computer-aided design.
   b. human factors.
   c. parallel processing.
   d. none of the above.

Bibliography

"The Academics Cashing In at Carnegie Group." *Business Week*, 9 July 1984, p. 58.

Baker, James D. "DIPMETER ADVISOR: An Expert Log Analysis System at Schlumberger." In *The AI Business*, pp. 51-65. Edited by Patrick H. Winston and Karen A. Prendergast. Cambridge, MA: MIT Press, 1984.

Barr, Avron, and Feigenbaum, Edward A. *The Handbook of Artificial Intelligence*. vols. 1-2. Los Altos, CA: William Kaufman, 1981-82.

Barstow, David R., et al. "Languages and Tools for Knowledge Engineering." In *Building Expert Systems*, pp. 283-345. Edited by Frederick Hayes-Roth, Donald A. Waterman, and Douglas B. Lenat. Reading, MA: Addison-Wesley, 1984.

Beechhold, Henry F. "Expert Choice." *InfoWorld*, 28 January 1985, pp. 45-50.

Bobrow, Daniel G., and Hayes, Patrick J., eds. "Artificial Intelligence—Where Are We?" *Artificial Intelligence* 25 (March 1985): 375-415.

Brachman, Ronald J., et al. "What Are Expert Systems?" In *Building Expert Systems*, pp. 31-57. Edited by Frederick Hayes-Roth, Donald A. Waterman, and Douglas B. Lenat. Reading, MA: Addison-Wesley, 1984.

Brady, J. Michael. "Intelligent Robots: Connecting Perception to Action." In *The AI Business*, pp. 179-203. Edited by Patrick H. Winston and Karen A. Prendergast. Cambridge, MA: MIT Press, 1984.

Brattle Research Corporation. *Artificial Intelligence and Fifth Generation Computer Technologies*. Boston: Brattle Research Corporation.

Brattle Research Corporation. *Artificial Intelligence Computers and Software*. Cambridge, MA: Brattle Research Corporation.

Buchanan, Bruce G., and Shortliffe, Edward H., eds. *Rule-Based Expert Systems*. Reading, MA: Addison-Wesley, 1984.

Buchanan, Bruce G., et al. "Constructing an Expert System." In *Building Expert Systems*, pp. 127-167. Edited by Frederick Hayes-Roth, Donald A. Waterman, and Douglas B. Lenat. Reading, MA: Addison-Wesley, 1984.

Clarke, Arthur. *2001: A Space Odyssey*. NAL, 1980.

Cohen, Paul R., and Feigenbaum, Edward A. *The Handbook of Artificial Intelligence*. vol. 3. Los Altos, CA: William Kaufman, 1982.

Crabb, Don. "Expert Ease." *InfoWorld*, 28 January 1985, pp. 44-45.

Davis, Randall. "Amplifying Expertise with Expert Systems." In *The AI Business*, pp. 17-40. Edited by Patrick H. Winston and Karen A. Prendergast. Cambridge, MA: MIT Press, 1984.

Davis, Randall. "Interactive Transfer of Expertise." In *Rule-Based Expert Systems*, pp. 171-205. Edited by Bruce G. Buchanan and Edward H. Shortliffe. Reading, MA: Addison-Wesley, 1984.

Davis, Randall, and Buchanan, Bruce G. "Meta-Level Language." In *Rule-Based Expert Systems*, pp. 507-530. Edited by Bruce G. Buchanan and Edward H. Shortliffe. Reading, MA: Addison-Wesley, 1984.

Davis, Randall, et al. *The Hardware Troubleshooting Group*. Cambridge, MA: Artificial Intelligence Laboratory, Massachusetts Institute of Technology.

Decision Support Software. *Expert Choice Office Relocation Model*. McLean, VA: Decision Support Software, 1983.

Defense Advanced Research Projects Agency. *Strategic Computing*. 28 October 1983.

Dreyfus, Hubert. *What Computers Can't Do: The Limits of Artificial Intelligence*. New York: Harper & Row, 1972.

Encyclopedia Britannica, 1985 Yearbook of Science and the Future. S.v. "Artificial Intelligence: Toward Machines that Think," by Bruce G. Buchanan.

Feigenbaum, Edward A., and Feldman, Julian. *Computers and Thought*. New York: McGraw-Hill, 1963.

Feigenbaum, Edward A., and McCorduck, Pamela. *The Fifth Generation*. New York: Signet, 1984.

Fox, Mark S. *Artificial Intelligence in Manufacturing*. Pittsburgh: Intelligent Systems Laboratory, Robotics Institute, Carnegie-Mellon University, 1984.

Gevarter, William B. *Intelligent Machines*. Englewood Cliffs, NJ: Prentice-Hall, 1985.

Harmon, Paul, and King, David. *Expert Systems*. New York: Wiley Press, 1985.

Harris, Larry R. "Natural Language Front Ends." In *The AI Business*, pp. 149-161. Edited by Patrick H. Winston and Karen A. Prendergast. Cambridge, MA: MIT Press, 1984.

Hayes-Roth, Frederick; Waterman, Donald A.; and Lenat, Douglas B., eds. *Building Expert Systems*. Reading, MA: Addison-Wesley, 1983.

Heite, Ned. "Exsys." *InfoWorld*, 28 January 1985, pp. 43-44.

Hofstadter, Douglas R. *Gödel, Escher, Bach: An Eternal Golden Braid*. New York: Vintage, 1980.

Kay, Alan. "Inventing the Future." In *The AI Business*, pp. 103-119. Edited by Patrick H. Winston and Karen A. Prendergast. Cambridge, MA: MIT Press, 1984.

Kraft, Arnold. "XCON: An Expert Configuration System at Digital Equipment Corporation." In *The AI Business*, pp. 41-49. Edited by Patrick H. Winston and Karen A. Prendergast. Cambridge, MA: MIT Press, 1984.

LISP Machine Inc. *More Than Just a LISP Machine*. Los Angeles: LISP Machine Inc., 1984.

Mace, Scott. "Can Natural Language Sell?" *InfoWorld*, 12 November 1984, pp. 36-41.

MCC. *Microelectronics and Computer Technology Corporation*. Austin, TX: MCC.

MCC. *Microelectronics and Computer Technology Corporation*. MCC.

McCorduck, Pamela. *Machines Who Think*. New York: Freeman, 1979.

Minsky, Marvin. *Computation: Finite and Infinite Machines*. Englewood Cliffs, NJ: Prentice-Hall, 1967.

Newell, Allen. Foreword to *Rule-Based Expert Systems*, by Bruce G. Buchanan and Edward H. Shortliffe. Reading, MA: Addison-Wesley, 1984.

Pollack, Andrew. "Japan Faltering Somewhat in Drive To Create 'Fifth Generation' Computer." *N.Y. Times News Service*, 14 October 1984.

Pople, Harry E., Jr. "CADUCEUS: An Experimental Expert System for Medical Diagnosis." In *The AI Business*, pp. 67-80. Edited by Patrick H. Winston and Karen A. Prendergast. Cambridge, MA: MIT Press, 1984.

Proceedings of the International Conference on Fifth Generation Computer Systems. New York: Elsevier-North Holland, 1982.

Rich, Charles. "The Programmer's Apprentice." In *The AI Business*, pp. 121-132. Edited by Patrick H. Winston and Karen A. Prendergast. Cambridge, MA: MIT Press, 1984.

Rich, Elaine. *Artificial Intelligence*. New York: McGraw Hill, 1983.

Ritchie, David. *The Binary Brain*. Boston: Little, Brown, 1984.

Rose, Frank. "The Black Knight of AI." *Science 85*, March 1985, pp. 46-51.

Rose, Frank. *Into the Heart of the Mind*. New York: Harper & Row, 1984.

Schank, Roger. "Intelligent Advisory Systems." In *The AI Business*, pp. 133-148. Edited by Patrick H. Winston and Karen A. Prendergast. Cambridge, MA: MIT Press, 1984.

Schank, Roger C., and Childers, Peter G. *The Cognitive Computer*. Reading, MA: Addison-Wesley, 1984.

Shannon, Claude E. "Computers and Automata." *Proceedings of the IRE*, 1953.

Shelley, Mary. *Frankenstein*. Airmont, 1964.

Software A & E. *Knowledge Engineering System General Description Manual*. October 1984.

Stefik, Mark, et al. "The Architecture of Expert Systems." In *Building Expert Systems*, pp. 89-126. Edited by Frederick Hayes-Roth, Donald A. Waterman, and Douglas B. Lenat. Reading, MA: Addison-Wesley, 1983.

Symbolics. *Symbolics Inc*. Cambridge, MA: Symbolics.

Symbolics. *The Symbolics 3670*. Cambridge, MA: Symbolics, 1984.

Tennant, Harry. *Natural Language Processing*. Princeton: Petrocelli Books, 1981.

Texas Instruments Incorporated. *Explorer Technical Summary*. Austin, TX: Texas Instruments Incorporated, 1985.

Turing, Alan M. "Computing Machinery and Intelligence." *Mind* LIX.

van Melle, William. "The Structure of the MYCIN System." In *Rule-Based Expert Systems*, pp. 67-77. Edited by Bruce G. Buchanan and Edward H. Shortliffe. Reading, MA: Addison-Wesley, 1984.

Villers, Philippe. "Intelligent Robots: Moving toward Megassembly." In *The AI Business*, pp. 205-222. Edited by Patrick H. Winston and Karen A. Prendergast. Cambridge, MA: MIT Press, 1984.

Waterman, Donald A., and Hayes-Roth, Frederick. "An Investigation of Tools for Building Expert Systems." In *Building Expert Systems*, pp. 169-215. Edited by Frederick Hayes-Roth, Donald A. Waterman, and Douglas B. Lenat. Reading, MA: Addison-Wesley, 1984.

Williams, Chuck. "Software Tool Packages the Expertise Needed To Build Expert Systems." *Electronic Design*, 9 August 1984, pp. 153-167.

Winston, Patrick H. "Perspective." In *The AI Business*, pp. 1-13. Edited by Patrick H. Winston and Karen A. Prendergast. Cambridge, MA: MIT Press, 1984.

Winston, Patrick H., and Prendergast, Karen A. *The AI Business*. Cambridge, MA: MIT Press, 1984.

Winston, Patrick Henry, and Horn, Berthold Klaus Paul. *LISP*. Reading, MA: Addison-Wesley, 1984.

Xerox. *The Keys to Artificial Intelligence Are at Xerox*. Pasadena, CA: Xerox.

Trademarks

AI-BASE, Extended-Streams Interface, LMI, LMI Lambda, Lambda/E, RTime, and ZetaLISP-Plus are trademarks of LISP Machine Inc.

AMIGA is a trademark of Commodore International Limited.

ART is a trademark of Inference Corporation.

Arborist, Business-Pro, NuBus, NaturalLink, Personal Consultant, and Explorer are trademarks of Texas Instruments Incorporated.

C-3PO, R2-D2, and STAR WARS are registered trademarks of Lucasfilm Ltd.

CONSIGHT and KEYSIGHT are trademarks of General Motors Corporation.

Clout, Microrim, and R:BASE are trademarks of Microrim, Inc.

dBASE II is a trademark of Ashton-Tate.

DEC and VAX are trademarks of Digital Equipment Corporation.

Dipmeter Advisor is a trademark of Schlumberger, Inc.

Ethernet, InterLISP, Smalltalk, and Xerox are trademarks of Xerox Corporation.

Expert Choice is a registered trademark of Decision Support Software.

Expert Ease is a trademark of Human Edge Software Corporation.

FranzLISP is a trademark of the University of California at Berkeley.

GEM is a trademark of Digital Research Incorporated.

IBM, IBM PC, and IBM PC/XT are trademarks of International Business Machines Corporation.

KEE and Knowledge Engineering Environment are trademarks of IntelliCorp.

Lotus and Lotus 1-2-3 are trademarks of Lotus Development Corporation.

MacLISP, SCHEME, and EL are trademarks of MIT Artificial Intelligence Laboratory.

Macintosh is a trademark of Apple Computer, Inc.

M.1 and S.1 are trademarks of Teknowledge Inc.

MS and MS-DOS are trademarks of MicroSoft Corporation.

Multibus is a trademark of Intel Corporation.

RuleMaster is a trademark of Radian Corporation.

STAR TREK is a registered trademark of Paramount Pictures Corporation.

Symbolics, Symbolics 3600, Symbolics 3640, Symbolics 3670, and ZetaLISP are trademarks of Symbolics Inc.

TOMY is a trademark of TOMY Corporation.

UNIX is a trademark of Bell Laboratories, Inc.

WordStar is a trademark of MicroPro International Corporation.

Glossary

AI Workstation: A LISP machine.

Algorithm: A step-by-step procedure which has a specific beginning and end and is guaranteed to solve a specific problem.

Allophone: A unit of speech that represents a particular sound as it actually occurs in a word.

ASCII: American Standard Code for Information Interchange. This is a standard code used to represent letters, numbers, and special functions as a series of zeros and ones.

Assembly Language: A low-level language where each instruction is assembled into one machine-language instruction.

Atom: A number or symbol.

Automatic Programming: An area of AI research involved in creating AI software that can generate programs from a programmer's specifications.

Backward Chaining: A search technique which starts in a goal state and works toward an initial state.

Bit-Mapped Display: A display screen which allows a programmer to turn each individual pixel on or off.

Breadth-First Search: A search technique which evaluates every node at a given level of the search space before moving to the next level.

Cell: The structure used in a computer to represent a list. Each cell has two fields for storing data and pointing to other cells in the list.

Certainty Factor: A percentage supplied by an expert system that indicates the probability that the conclusion reached by the system is correct.

Cognitive Science: The field that investigates the details of the mechanics of human intelligence to determine the processes that produce intelligence in a given situation.

Common LISP: A standardized version of "East Coast" LISP.

Compiler: A program that converts an entire high-level language program into machine language.

Computer Vision: An area of AI research which is attempting to enable computers to understand visual images.

Connected Word Recognition: An approach to speech recognition that recognizes words spoken in normal context.

Continuous Speech Recognition: An approach to speech recognition that understands speech in typical conversations of normal durations.

Database: Information stored in a computer for subsequent retrieval.

Default Value: A value that is used if no other value is specified.

Degrees of Freedom (DOF): The "joints" in a robot arm.

Depth-First Search: A search technique which advances from the first level to a terminal node. If the terminal node is a goal state, the search is finished. If not, the process is repeated.

Development Tool: A program designed to assist programmers in the development of software. Intelligent tools incorporate AI techniques.

Domain: The problem area of an expert system.

Domain Expert: A person with expertise in the domain of the expert system being developed. The domain expert works closely with the knowledge engineer.

Edge Detection: A computer vision technique which helps the computer understand the visual images it receives by locating the edges of an object.

End Effector: Another name for a robot hand. It also is called a gripper.

Expert System: A computer program which contains both declarative knowledge (facts about objects, events, and situations) and procedural knowledge (information about courses of action) to emulate the reasoning processes of human experts in a particular domain. Two types of expert systems are rule-based and model-based. The components of an expert system are a knowledge base, an inference engine, and a user interface.

Explanation Facility: The component of an expert system that can explain the system's reasoning, such as how a conclusion was reached or why a particular question was asked.

First-Order Predicate Calculus: A system of formal logic that is based on predicate calculus with the addition of functions and other analytical features.

Forward Chaining: A search technique which starts in an initial state and works toward a goal state.

Frame-Based CAI: A computer-assisted instruction technique based on the method used in a programmed instruction text. The material presented to the student depends on how the questions asked are answered.

Frames: A way of representing knowledge that stores a list of an object's typical attributes with the object. Each attribute is stored in a separate slot.

Heuristic: A rule-of-thumb approach that provides a procedure for attempting to solve a problem. Heuristic approaches do not guarantee solutions to specific problems.

Hierarchical Plan: One category of AI techniques used for planning. A hierarchical plan starts at a general level of planning and moves down to a specific, detailed plan.

High-Level Language: A language in which the instructions more closely resemble English. One high-level language instruction often is converted into several machine-language instructions.

Inference Engine: The component of an expert system that controls its operation by selecting the rules to use, accessing and executing those rules, and determining when a solution has been found. This component is known also as the control structure or rule interpreter.

Integrated Circuit: An electronic circuit containing multiple electronic components fabricated at the same time in steps on a single slice or wafer of semiconductor material. When separated into individually packaged integrated circuits, they are known also as IC's or chips.

Intelligent Computer-Assisted Instruction (ICAI): An area of AI research with the goal of creating training programs that can analyze a student's learning pattern and modify their teaching techniques accordingly. The components of an ICAI program are problem-solving expertise, student model, and tutoring module.

Intelligent Robot: A robot which includes AI techniques to allow it to understand its environment and change its actions based on external situations. An intelligent robot is known also as a sensor-controlled robot.

IPL (Information Processing Language): An AI programming language and a forerunner of LISP.

Isolated Word Recognition: An approach to speech recognition that uses pattern-matching techniques to recognize isolated words.

Knowledge Base: The component of an expert system that contains the system's declarative and procedural knowledge.

Knowledge-Based System: Another name for "expert system."

Knowledge Engineer: An AI specialist responsible for the technical side of developing an expert system. The knowledge engineer works closely with the domain expert.

LISP: LISt Processor. An AI programming language that is especially popular in the United States.

LISP Machine: A single-user computer designed primarily for the development of AI programs. LISP machines also are known as AI workstations.

List: A sequence of elements enclosed in parentheses, where each element is either an atom or another list.

Local Area Network (LAN): A means of computer communication in which the computers are physically connected to share resources.

Logical Inferences Per Second (LIPS): A means of measuring the speed of computers used for AI applications.

Machine Language: The language in binary code that the computer understands.

Machine Translation: An area of AI research that is attempting to use computers to translate text from one language to another. These programs often use a combination of natural language understanding and generation.

Manipulator: Another name for a robot arm.

Menus: A list of the options available at a particular place in a computer program.

Meta-rule: A rule about a rule. Meta-rules are a type of production rule used in expert systems to specify the conditions under which certain rules should be followed instead of others.

Model-Based System: A type of expert system which is based on a model of the structure and behavior of the device it is designed to understand.

Model-Based Vision: A computer vision technique in which image templates or descriptions of features of objects are stored to help the computer identify an object.

Mouse: A small, sliding, handheld pointing device which controls the movement of a pointer on the computer screen. The two types of mouse devices are mechanical and optical.

Natural Language Generation: The part of natural language processing research which is attempting to have computers present information in English. Natural language generation programs must decide when to say something, what to say, and how to say it.

Natural Language Interface (NLI): A program that allows you to communicate with a computer in normal English. An NLI typically includes both natural language understanding and generation capabilities. These programs are known also as natural language front ends.

Natural Language Processing: An area of AI research that allows people to communicate with computers in a natural language, such as English. Natural language processing is divided into understanding and generation.

Natural Language Understanding: The part of natural language processing research which is investigating methods of allowing computers to understand instructions given in English.

Nonalgorithmic: A problem-solving approach that does not follow a step-by-step procedure.

Non-hierarchical Plan: One category of AI techniques used for planning. A non-hierarchical plan represents a plan on one level only.

Parallel Processing: The computer technique of performing several processing actions at the same time.

Pattern-Matching: An AI technique which recognizes relationships and patterns in objects, events, and processes.

Phoneme: A unit of speech that is the sound of an individual consonant or vowel.

Pixels: The individual dots on a computer screen. Letters, numbers, and symbols consist of pixels arranged in a matrix.

Planning and Decision Support: An area of AI research that is applying AI techniques to the planning and decision-making process to help managers who have decision-making responsibilities.

Predicate Calculus: A system of formal logic that is based on propositional calculus with the added capabilities of specifying relationships and making generalizations.

Problem-Solving Expertise: The component of an ICAI program that contains the information being presented to the student.

Production Rule: A rule in the form of an "if-then" or "condition-action" statement which is often used in expert systems. A production rule represents a heuristic.

PROLOG: PROgramming in LOGic. An AI programming language that is especially popular in Europe and Japan.

Propositional Calculus: A system of formal logic that provides a step-by-step inference system for determining whether a given proposition is true or false.

Pruning: A means of reducing the size of a search space which usually is accomplished with heuristic rules.

Random Access Memory (RAM): A memory into which data can be placed (written) and from which data can be retrieved (read).

Recursion: Defining an item in terms of itself.

Robotics: An area of AI research involved in developing intelligent robots.

Rule-Based System: A type of expert system where the procedural knowledge is integrated with the declarative knowledge in the form of production rules.

Scripts: A way of representing knowledge that stores the events that take place in familiar situations in a series of slots. A script is composed of a series of scenes which are composed of a series of events.

Search: The process of starting in some initial state and attempting to reach a goal state by evaluating possible alternative solutions.

Search Space: All of the possible states that could be evaluated during a search. The search space often is represented as an inverted tree, called a search tree.

Semantic Network: A means of representing facts as nodes in a graph and their relationships to other facts as the links or arcs.

Sequential Processing: The computer technique of performing actions one at a time in sequence.

Servomechanism: A device that can correct a robot's performance.

Simulation: An AI technique which uses a model of intelligent human behavior to determine if the computer will exhibit the same intelligent behavior as a human.

Speaker-Dependent Recognition: An approach to speech recognition which recognizes the speech of a particular person.

Speaker-Independent Recognition: An approach to speech recognition which recognizes the speech of any speaker.

Speech Recognition: An area of AI research with the ultimate goal of allowing computers to recognize and understand human speech, regardless of the speaker.

Speech Synthesis: The generation of speech by a computer.

Student Model: The component of an ICAI program that analyzes the student's performance to determine why the student is having difficulty.

Syllable: A unit of speech consisting of a vowel and the surrounding consonants that are pronounced together.

Telecommunication: A means of communication in which computers use telephone lines to transmit and receive information.

Time Sharing: An approach to using computers that allows many people to share the resources of a computer at the same time.

Turing Test: An "imitation game" devised by Alan Turing which is used to determine if a computer is thinking. An interrogator attempts to discover which of two respondents is a person and which is a computer by engaging in thoughtful conversation.

Tutoring Module: The component of an ICAI program that selects the strategies for presenting tutorial information to a student.

User Interface: The component of an expert system that allows bidirectional communication between the expert system and its user. Most user interfaces utilize natural language processing techniques.

Very Large Scale Integration (VLSI): The process of combining several hundred thousand electronic components on a single chip of semiconductor material.

Virtual Memory: A system of managing RAM and disk space so that a computer appears to have more memory that it really does.

Windowing: A means of dividing the computer screen into several areas so that a variety of information can be displayed simultaneously.

Index

Answers to Quizzes

Chapter 1	Chapter 2	Chapter 3	Chapter 5	Chapter 7	Chapter 9
1. e	1. b	1. b	1. d	1. a	1. a
2. d	2. d	2. d	2. c	2. c	2. a
3. b	3. a	3. a	3. e	3. d	3. e
4. a	4. a	4. d	4. d	4. a	4. d
5. d	5. c	5. d	5. d	5. d	5. e
6. c	6. c	6. c	6. c	6. b	6. b
7. d	7. a	7. d	7. c	7. c	7. d
8. b	8. a	8. e	8. b	8. a	8. b
9. a	9. b	9. e	9. a	9. a	9. c
10. d	10. c	10. c	10. b	10. c	10. b
11. c	11. a				
12. b	12. b				
13. a	13. c	**Chapter 4**	**Chapter 6**	**Chapter 8**	**Chapter 10**
14. d	14. a	1. b	1. a	1. d	1. b
15. c	15. b	2. d	2. c	2. a	2. c
16. d	16. c	3. e	3. d	3. b	3. c
17. a	17. b	4. d	4. b	4. b	4. d
18. c	18. b	5. a	5. a	5. e	5. a
19. c	19. d	6. d	6. c	6. c	6. d
20. d	20. a	7. d	7. d	7. d	7. a
		8. e	8. a	8. a	8. c
		9. c	9. d	9. d	9. d
		10. d	10. a	10. a	10. b

Understanding Series™ Books

The Understanding Series books form a library written for anyone who wants to learn quickly and easily about today's technology, its impact on our world, and its application in our lives.

ISBN NO.	UNDERSTANDING SERIES TITLE	TI STOCK NO.	RETAIL PRICE
D-89512-183-2	Understanding Advanced Solid State Electronics	LCB8605	14.95
D-89512-188-3	Understanding Artificial Intelligence	LCB8651	14.95
D-89512-164-6	Understanding Automation Systems—2nd Edition	LCB8472	14.95
D-89512-167-0	Understanding Automotive Electronics—2nd Edition	LCB8475	14.95
D-89512-016-X	Understanding Calculator Math	LCB3321	9.95
D-89512-166-2	Understanding Communications Systems—2nd Edition	LCB8474	14.95
D-89512-182-4	Understanding Computer Science Applications	LCB8604	14.95
D-89512-161-1	Understanding Computer Science—2nd Edition	LCB8452	14.95
D-89512-158-1	Understanding Data Communications	LCB8483	14.95
D-89512-163-8	Understanding Digital Electronics—2nd Edition	LCB8471	14.95
D-89512-165-4	Understanding Digital Troubleshooting—2nd Edition	LCB8473	14.95
D-89512-051-8	Understanding Electronic Control of Energy Systems	LCB6642	9.95
D-89512-105-0	Understanding Electronic Security Systems	LCB7201	9.95
D-89512-160-3	Understanding Microprocessors—2nd Edition	LCB8451	14.95
D-89512-049-6	Understanding Optronics	LCB5472	9.95
D-89512-162-X	Understanding Solid State Electronics—4th Edition	LCB8453	14.95
D-89512-159-X	Understanding Telephone Electronics—2nd Edition	LCB8482	14.95